Crime Scene Management
and Evidence Recovery

Crime Scene Management and Evidence Recovery

Deborah Beaufort-Moore

OXFORD
UNIVERSITY PRESS

OXFORD
UNIVERSITY PRESS

Great Clarendon Street, Oxford OX2 6DP

Oxford University Press is a department of the University of Oxford.
It furthers the University's objective of excellence in research, scholarship,
and education by publishing worldwide in

Oxford New York

Auckland   Cape Town   Dar es Salaam   Hong Kong   Karachi
Kuala Lumpur   Madrid   Melbourne   Mexico City   Nairobi
New Delhi   Shanghai   Taipei   Toronto

With offices in

Argentina   Austria   Brazil   Chile   Czech Republic   France   Greece
Guatemala   Hungary   Italy   Japan   South Korea   Poland   Portugal
Singapore   Switzerland   Thailand   Turkey   Ukraine   Vietnam

Oxford is a registered trade mark of Oxford University Press
in the UK and in certain other countries

Published in the United States
by Oxford University Press Inc., New York

© Deborah Beaufort-Moore 2009

The moral rights of the author have been asserted

Crown copyright material is reproduced under Class Licence Number
C01P0000148 with the permission of OPSI and the
Queen's Printer for Scotland

Database right Oxford University Press (maker)

Reprinted 2011

All rights reserved. No part of this publication may be reproduced,
stored in a retrieval system, or transmitted, in any form or by any means,
without the prior permission in writing of Oxford University Press,
or as expressly permitted by law, or under terms agreed with the appropriate
reprographics rights organization. Enquiries concerning reproduction
outside the scope of the above should be sent to the Rights Department,
Oxford University Press, at the address above

You must not circulate this book in any other binding or cover
And you must impose this same condition on any acquirer

ISBN 978-0-19-956045-5

Printed and bound in Great Britain by
CPI Antony Rowe, Chippenham and Eastbourne

Preface

The term, police officer within this book is used to encompass the roles of PCSO and other designated police support staff employed by police authorities to undertake aspects of policing roles, where applicable.

The original idea for this book was developed with the role of the operational police officer or support staff investigator in mind. There are many books on forensic science that offer guidance to Crime Scene Investigators (CSIs) or those studying or working in forensic science disciplines. However, many of these do not consider in depth the role of the first responding officer regarding the preservation and recovery of potential forensic evidence.

The role of the first responding officer is absolutely crucial in the success or otherwise of a forensic examination. Police officers are generally the first people in the investigative process to arrive at the scene of an incident, and the actions taken at this time can have a huge impact on the outcome of the investigation.

The CSI or forensic scientists are entirely dependant on the first responding officers to ensure the potential forensic evidence is maximized. This book has been written for police officers and support staff investigators, with the aim of offering guidance on how to preserve and recover material for forensic examination and to ensure the evidential potential is maximized.

Ideally any item required for forensic analysis should be recovered by a CSI, however this will not always be the case as the CSI may not be available. Officers will be required to recover items for forensic examination in such circumstances, whether this is from the location, or from suspects in custody or victims and witnesses.

This book has been written to offer investigators practical guidance on the preservation and recovery of forensic material. In addition to practical examples for the recovery, packaging and storage of forensic material, there are chapters which provide a basic overview of the different types of forensic evidence that are commonly encountered, the evidential potentials and the limitations of the different analysis of such material. These have been included in order for officers to develop a basic understanding of the potential evidence and intelligence offered by forensic analysis and why certain actions are required.

The information in this book is not intended (nor appropriate) for investigators to undertake the role of a CSI, but to provide an awareness of the potentials available for the forensic examination of crime scenes and the techniques available to a CSI for the recovery of potential forensic evidence. It is important for investigators to be aware of what is available to them in order to consider the best course of action to recover evidence.

The role of the CSI is to support the police investigator in the investigation of crimes, by gathering all the relevant material at a crime scene. Where an investigator feels a particular process would be beneficial to their enquiry, to corroborate or refute allegations, they should not hesitate to request that the CSI undertake these processes. The CSI may not have all the available information, and such communication is vital to ensure a thorough scene examination is achieved.

Forensic science has provided investigators with great benefits regarding the evidence potentially available to identify persons and link crime scenes, however a key disadvantage to the technological advances is that it can lead to investigators becoming overly reliant on forensic evidence. Whilst forensic science undoubtedly offers huge benefits, investigators must not neglect other aspects of the criminal investigation.

There can be numerous defences regarding the presence of forensic material and it is imperative that an investigator is aware of potential defences and ensures a thorough and robust investigation is undertaken in order to put any forensic evidence into context. Forensic analysis alone will not solve crimes.

Deborah Beaufort-Moore
September 2008

Acknowledgements

Sincere thanks must go to the following who have offered support, guidance and advice during the construction of this book: Nicholas Hunt, Ian Saunders, Pete Waugh, Paul Granger, Ray Josey, Dave Sharp, Paul Drever, Debbie Homer and Caroline Vost of Wiltshire Police.

A very special thanks must also go to my partner, Steve, and son, Alexander for the support shown during this project.

Grateful thanks also to the anonymous reviewers (you know who you are) whose wisdom, comments and guidance during the writing process have been gratefully received, as has the support and guidance offered by Lindsey Davis and Peter Daniell of Oxford University Press.

Contents

Table of Legislation   xiii
List of Figures and Tables   xv
Glossary   xvii

1   Roles and Responsibilities in Crime Scene Investigations   1

1.1	Introduction	2
1.2	Roles and Responsibilities within Scientific Support	4
1.3	Other Key Roles in the Investigation of Serious or Complex Cases	10
1.4	Health and Safety at Crime Scenes	14
1.5	Chapter Summary	16

2   Crime Scene Preservation and Management   19

2.1	Introduction	20
2.2	Roles of First Officer	26
2.3	The Five Building Blocks Principle	27
2.4	Chapter Summary	37

3   Exhibit Handling   41

3.1	Introduction	42
3.2	Principles of Exhibit Handling	42
3.3	Basic Principles for Packaging of Exhibits	48
3.4	Packaging Materials	51
3.5	Exhibit Labels	56
3.6	Chapter Summary	59

4   Forensic Evidence Recovery from Persons   65

4.1	Introduction	66
4.2	Forensic Material on Clothing	66
4.3	Recovery of Non-Intimate Samples from Persons in Custody	72
4.4	Firearm and Explosive Residue	78
4.5	Smartwater Recovery	80
4.6	Chapter Summary	82

Contents

5	**Fingerprints**	**85**
5.1	Introduction	86
5.2	Types of Fingerprint Evidence at Crime Scenes	86
5.3	The Role of the CSI in the Recovery of Fingerprint Evidence	88
5.4	Chemical Development Techniques for Fingerprint Recovery	89
5.5	The Role of the Fingerprint Identification Officer	93
5.6	National Fingerprint Database—Ident 1	94
5.7	Taking Fingerprints	97
5.8	Chapter Summary	102

6	**DNA—Deoxyribonucleic Acid**	**107**
6.1	Introduction	108
6.2	What is DNA?	109
6.3	The National DNA Database (NDNAD)	115
6.4	Sources of DNA	119
6.5	Recovery and Preservation of DNA Material	122
6.6	DNA Samples from Persons	123
6.7	Chapter Summary	128

7	**Blood Pattern Analysis (BPA)**	**133**
7.1	Introduction	134
7.2	Principles of Bloodstain Pattern Analysis	134
7.3	Transfer Bloodstains	141
7.4	Preserving Items for BPA	143
7.5	Health and Safety Considerations	144
7.6	Chapter Summary	144

8	**Sudden Deaths**	**149**
8.1	Introduction	150
8.2	Post-Mortem Changes	150
8.3	Decomposition	155
8.4	Cause of Death Indicators	158
8.5	Drowning	161
8.6	Role of First Officers at Scenes of Sudden Death	163
8.7	Chapter Summary	167

9	**Firearms and Ballistic Evidence**	**171**
9.1	Introduction	172
9.2	Firearm Definition	173
9.3	Types of Firearm and Ammunition	173
9.4	Ballistic Examinations	178
9.5	Scenes of Shooting Incidents	179
9.6	Forensic Examination of Firearms and Ballistic Material	180

9.7	Examination to Establish Cause	183
9.8	Taser	184
9.9	Chapter Summary	185

10 Footwear, Tyre and Tool Marks — 189

10.1	Introduction	190
10.2	Footwear	190
10.3	Tyre Marks	195
10.4	Tool Marks	196
10.5	Chapter Summary	197

11 Glass, Paint, and Soils — 201

11.1	Introduction	202
11.2	Glass	202
11.3	Paint	210
11.4	Soils	212
11.5	Chapter Summary	213

12 Hair and Fibres — 217

12.1	Introduction	218
12.2	Hairs	219
12.3	Fibres	222
12.4	Transfer and Retention of Hairs and Fibres	224
12.5	Chapter Summary	225

13 Drugs of Abuse — 229

13.1	Introduction	230
13.2	Types of Drugs	230
13.3	Illicit Laboratories	236
13.4	Forensic Potentials from Drugs Packaging	237
13.5	Bulk and Trace Analysis of Drugs	238
13.6	Chapter Summary	239

14 Document Examination — 243

14.1	Introduction	244
14.2	Handwriting Analysis	244
14.3	Forged Handwriting	246
14.4	Indented Impressions	248
14.5	Other Document Examinations Available	249
14.6	Recovery and Preservation of Documents	251
14.7	Chapter Summary	252

Bibliography 257
Index 259

Table of Legislation

UK Statutes

Crime and Disorder Act 1998
   s 65 101
Criminal Justice Act 2003 .... 104, 124, 127, 130
   s 9(2) 101
Criminal Justice and Police Act 2001 97
   s 82 97
Criminal Justice and Public Order Act 1994 .... 101, 128
Criminal Procedure and Investigations Act 1996
   Pt II 26
Firearms Act 1968 173
   s 1 .... 173, 185
   s 5 .... 173, 184, 186
Human Rights Act 1988 .... 36, 82
Misuse of Drugs Act 1971 230
Police and Criminal Evidence Act 1984 .... 44, 63, 68, 73, 123, 124, 125
   s 1 44
   s 8 .... 36, 44
   s 17 36
   s 18 .... 36, 44
   s 19 .... 36, 44, 61, 62
   s 19(2) 44, 61
   s 19(3)(b) 44, 61
   ss 54, 55 44
   s 61 .... 101, 104
   s 61(2), (6) 101
   s 61A(3) 68, 192
   s 62 .... 73, 83
   s 62(9) 73
   s 63 .... 73, 83, 127, 130
   s 63(1)–(4), (6) 127
   s 65 127
   s 65(1) 101, 103
Police Reform Act 2002 .... 44, 61, 101, 127
Terrorism Act 2000
   s 33 36

Police and Criminal Evidence Act 1984 Codes of Practice

Code B (Code of practice for searches of premises by police officers and the seizure of property found by police officers on persons or premises) 36, 44
Code C (Code of practice for the detention, treatment and questioning of persons by police officers)
   para 8.5 71
Code D (Code of practice for the identification of persons by police officers)
   s 4
      para 4.1–4.4 101
      para 4.18 68
   s 6 .... 73, 127
      para 6.6 124
      para 6.7 128
      Note 6B 124

European Legislation

European Convention on Human Rights 1950 62
   Art 3 82
   Art 8 .... 36, 44
   Art 8(1), (2) 36, 44
First Protocol
   Art 1 82

List of Figures and Tables

Figures

1.1	A typical management structure within scientific support departments	3
1.2	A typical scientific support management structure at a serious incident	5
2.1	Potential forensic links	24
2.2	Example of an assault scene	33
3.1	Packaging technique for damp/wet items	50
3.2	Example of packaging materials	51
3.3	Sealing of brown paper evidence sacks	52
3.4	Unique identifying barcode and reference number on tamper-evident bags	53
3.5	Securing items into a box	54
3.6	'Swan necked' sealing technique to preserve suspected accelerant	56
3.7	The chain of continuity generated from one initial exhibit	60
4.1	Recovering footwear from persons	69
4.2	Example of the appropriate sequence for seizure of clothing	71
4.3	Swabbing techniques	72
4.4	Fingernail sampling kit	74
4.5	Fingernail clipping	75
4.6	Fingernail swabs	76
4.7	Hair sampling kit	77
5.1	Summary of crime scene fingerprint identification procedure	96
5.2	Good and poor fingerprint impressions	99
5.3	Taking a rolled fingerprint impression	99
5.4	Plain impressions	99
5.5	Good and poor palm prints	100
6.1	Diagrammatic representation of the structure a cell	109
6.2	Laboratory submissions routes and potential forensic links	113
6.3	Summary of routine NDNAD process	117
7.1	Typical passive bloodstains	135
7.2	Blood spot with scalloped edges	136
7.3	Direction of travel as indicated by the tail of bloodstain	136
7.4	Angle of impact of projected blood drop and resulting stain	137
7.5	Blood patterns created from medium velocity impact	138
7.6	Typical linear pattern of cast-off stains	138
8.1	Lividity development	153

9.1	Cross section of rifled barrel	174
9.2	Typical round construction	175
9.3	Cartridge base markings	175
9.4	Typical shotgun cartridge components	176
9.5	Internal structure of a typical shotgun cartridge	177
9.6	Impact evidence from fired rounds	182
11.1	Side view of breaking glass	203
11.2	Fracture pattern to determine sequence of blows	204
11.3	Chonchoidal lines on broken edge of glass	204
11.4	Backward fragmentation of breaking glass	206
11.5	Decreasing evidential value of glass fragments	207
14.1	Example of ESDA lift	250

Tables

4.1	Summary of intimate and non-intimate samples	73
6.1	Summary of the possible initial analysis results	113
6.2	Match report results	118
6.3	Summary of sample types and DNA recovery potential	123
6.4	Summary of status codes on the PNC	124
6.5	Taking of new samples	125
7.1	Chemical development techniques for recovery of marks in blood	143
13.1	Sampling guidelines for cannabis cultivation scenes	233

Glossary

Accelerant A flammable material usually in liquid form that is used to promote the ignition and/or spread of fire.

Adipocere The post-mortem process whereby body fats become waxy due to the presence of moisture.

Blood Pattern Analysis (BPA) The analysis of blood stains that may determine impact types, and points of impact to aid in reconstruction of events.

Common Approach Path (CAP) A route established from the cordon to the main scene, to be used by all entering/leaving the scene.

Continuity (of evidence) The audit trail which details the movements of an exhibit from the point of recovery to presentation in court.

Cordon A physical barrier to restrict access to a crime scene.

Crime Scene Co-ordinator (CSC) The person with overall responsibility for managing the scientific support functions in serious incidents.

Crime Scene Investigator (CSI) A person trained to identify, record and gather forensic material to support the officers in the investigation of incidents. The title of CSI is not used by all police forces, other titles such as CSE (Crime Scene Examiner), SOCO (Scenes of Crime Officer) for example may be used to denote the same role.

Crime Scene Manager (CSM) A CSI who will have responsibility for the processing of a particular crime scene.

Diatoms Aquatic micro-organisms found in water. They can display individual characteristics that can enable the source of water they originated from to be determined.

ESDA Electrostatic document apparatus used to recover indented impressions on paper.

ESLA Electrostatic lifting apparatus used to recover footwear marks in dust.

Exhibit Any item or material recovered from a crime scene to be used as evidence in an investigation.

Family Liaison Officer (FLO) A person who acts as a point of contact between a victim or victim's family and the police investigation.

Firearm Discharge Residue (FDR) The residues of the propellant and primer produced as a cloud particles following the discharge of a firearm.

Forensic Service Provider The supplier of forensic analytical techniques.

HOLMES The Home Office Linked Major Enquiry System, a computer system for the storage and cross-referencing of information from the investigation of serious incidents.

Ident 1 The national system used to compare fingerprints. Formerly known as NAFIS.

Glossary

Integrity (of evidence) The principle which must be demonstrated to show that the evidence is as it was when recovered and that no unaccountable interference has occurred to it from the crime scene, throughout any examination to the ultimate destination of the court room. The honesty and accountability of evidence.

Latent Not visible to the naked eye.

Livescan A system which enables the electronic scanning of fingerprints.

Liver mortis The post-mortem process whereby blood settles into the lowermost areas of a body to present as discolouration.

Locard's 'Principle of Exchange' The principle on which forensic examination is based, which states that there will be a two-way transfer of material when there is contact.

Low Copy Number (LCN) A very sensitive technique for recovering DNA from minute samples.

Match probability The likelihood of two randomly selected individuals having an identical DNA profile.

Mitochondrial DNA (MtDNA) Present in cells, it is passed down via the maternal line.

Mummification A post-mortem process that occurs in warm, dry conditions.

NABIS National Automated Ballistics Intelligence System. A national database holding information on recovered firearms and ballistic material.

NAFIS National Automated Fingerprint Identification System. A national database of fingerprints recovered from crime scenes and persons.

NDNAD National DNA database holding DNA profiles from crime scenes and persons.

Nuclear DNA The DNA material present in the nucleus of cells.

Officer in Charge (OIC) The police officer in charge of the overall investigation of volume crime incidents.

Petechiae Pin-prick haemorrhages that can appear in the eyes and skin.

Post-mortem The period following death.

Post-mortem Examination An examination to determine cause of death.

Post-mortem Interval (PMI) The period of time elapsed between death and the discovery of a body.

Presumptive test Tests that can be undertaken to ascertain the presence of certain substances. Positive test results require further analysis for confirmation.

Ricochet The deviation from the original trajectory of a missile, following impact with a surface.

Rigor mortis The post-mortem stiffening of the body.

Senior Investigating Officer (SIO) A senior officer with overall responsibility for the investigation of serious and complex cases.

Ten prints A set of fingerprints taken from persons in order to be checked against crime scene marks.

1

Roles and Responsibilities in Crime Scene Investigations

1.1	Introduction	2
1.2	Roles and Responsibilities within Scientific Support	4
1.3	Other Key Roles in the Investigation of Serious or Complex Cases	10
1.4	Health and Safety at Crime Scenes	14
1.5	Chapter Summary	16

Chapter 1: Roles and Responsibilities in Crime Scene Investigations

1.1 **Introduction**

The investigation of crimes will generally include some aspect of forensic examination. However, the level of resources utilized will be dependant on the nature of the incident under investigation. Many police forces will have a scientific support department that offers a range of forensic crime scene examination capabilities. Within these departments there are a number of key roles, which will be outlined within this chapter.

Each of the units within scientific support departments (or equivalent) has a specific role to support the investigating officers in the investigation of incidents. The overall responsibility for an investigation however, will be that of a police officer. The investigating officer has overall responsibility for the investigation of an incident as it is they who will be presenting the case to a court.

Where an officer feels that a particular aspect of forensic examination could be beneficial to the investigation, they should not hesitate to make such requests to a Crime Scene Investigator (CSI). It can often be the case that a CSI will not be aware of all the information regarding the incident. In order to maximize the potential forensic recovery, officers should give a full and comprehensive account of the incident, outlining the points to prove to the CSI. It is also important to update the CSI on any new information that comes to light as this may have implications for the scene examination and any subsequent forensic analysis.

There may be valid reasons why a certain process will not be undertaken and a CSI should explain their rationales as to their examination decisions. Every person involved in the investigation is accountable for their actions (or otherwise) and the decisions made should be recorded.

Following the initial police attendance at a crime scene, the involvement of different personnel undertaking specific roles will be dependant on the circumstances of the incident. (The role and responsibilities of the first responding officers are outlined in Chapter 2.)

For volume crime incidents, the responsibility for carrying out the overall investigation will fall to a police officer or designated support staff investigator, who may be the designated officer in charge (OIC) of the overall investigation.

For more serious or complex cases a detective may be designated as the OIC. In cases of murder, manslaughter or infanticide, or complex serious/major incidents, a senior investigating officer (SIO) will take overall responsibility for all aspects of the investigation including strategic and budgetary responsibilities.

Forensic examination of crime scenes will generally be at the direction of the OIC or SIO, depending on the incident and in line with national and individual force policies. Initially, the examination of crime scenes for potential forensic material will typically be undertaken by the appropriate units within the scientific support department in force. Depending on the nature of the case, specialist personnel such as forensic scientists may be invited to attend the scenes.

The key roles that are typically undertaken in serious/complex investigations are covered within this chapter, providing a basic overview of the roles and responsibilities when dealing with such incidents.

1.1.1 Scientific support in the police service

The increased use of forensic evidence in criminal investigations has led to the growth and development of scientific support departments within the police service. The composition of scientific support departments may vary between forces in the structure, role titles and responsibilities. This chapter will offer a general indication of the typical departmental structure found in the UK, although role titles and departmental structures may differ slightly.

In 1988 a Home Office directive to chief constables and police authorities identified aspects of policing duties that could be undertaken by support staff. Scientific support functions for crime scene examination was an aspect of the investigative process that was identified as being appropriate for non-police officers to undertake. In some forces, the scientific support roles such as CSIs are undertaken entirely by support staff, others have support staff working alongside warranted police officer CSIs.

1.1.2 Scientific support department structure

An overall departmental head, scientific support manager or equivalent, will have the overall responsibility for the scientific support department, which will generally contain a Crime Scene Investigation Unit, a Fingerprint Bureau, a photographic/video unit and a chemical development laboratory. Each of these units may have a dedicated departmental head who reports to the scientific support manager.

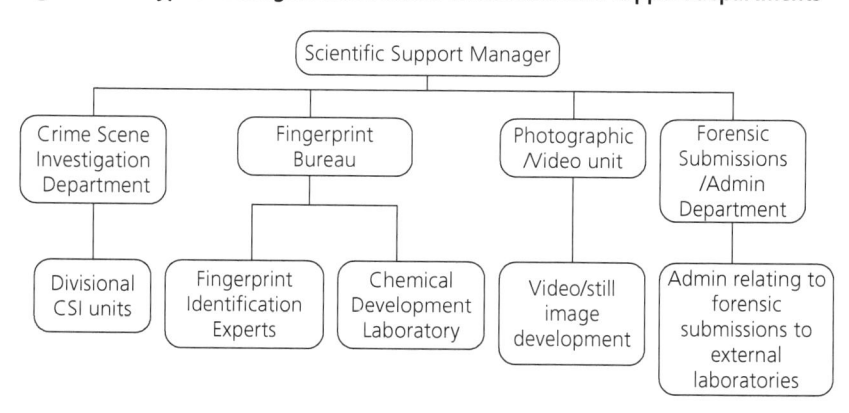

Figure 1.1 A typical management structure within scientific support departments

```
                        Scientific Support Manager
    ┌───────────────────┬───────────────────┬───────────────────┐
Crime Scene         Fingerprint         Photographic        Forensic
Investigation         Bureau            /Video unit        Submissions
 Department                                                  /Admin
                                                           Department
    │               ┌───────┴───────┐          │               │
Divisional      Fingerprint      Chemical   Video/still   Admin relating to
 CSI units     Identification   Development    image         forensic
                  Experts       Laboratory  development   submissions to
                                                             external
                                                           laboratories
```

1.2 Roles and Responsibilities within Scientific Support

1.2.1 Crime scene investigation

The role title may differ depending on the force and can include titles such as scenes of crime officers (SOCO), crime scene examiners (CSE) and volume crime scene examiners (VCSE). For clarity, the title of CSI will be used throughout this book to denote this role.

A number of key responsibilities for the CSI role were identified by the Association of Chief Police Officers (ACPO) and the Forensic Science Service in 1996. A joint report 'Using forensic science effectively' was published which outlined the key responsibilities of CSIs as consisting of:

- Photographic and/or video recording of crime scenes, victims and property;
- Locating and recovering potential physical evidence;
- Locating and recovery of finger and palm marks at crime scenes;
- Packaging and storage of potential physical evidence to prevent contamination;
- Recording and sharing of intelligence on modus operandi (MO);
- Offering advice on scientific matters;
- Preparation of statements and giving evidence in court.

The main function of CSIs is to record, gather and preserve all available potential physical evidence to support the investigating officer in their enquiry. In addition to the physical evidence, CSIs should bring to the attention of an investigating officer any intelligence aspects of the crime scene that are observed during the examination of the scene. The 'National Crime Scene Investigation Manual (2007)' (ACPO/NPIA) states that: 'The CSI should take all reasonable steps to collect fingerprints, forensic and/or photographic evidence from the scene, as appropriate. In all cases as evidence is collected, it must be correctly packaged, sealed and identified, using either a label or indelible marker.'

CSIs can also be an invaluable asset in the gathering of intelligence. They are in a position to identify links between crime scenes such as a series of burglaries that have the same MO and/or the presence of similar footwear or glove marks for example.

CSIs will attend court to give evidence on their role in an investigation where required. It is important to be mindful that a CSI can give statements of fact rather than opinion. They can state what they did and how, but CSIs are not deemed to be 'expert witnesses' in the sense of being able to give an interpretation of what the evidence may mean.

The types of scenes a CSI will attend are to some extent, dependant on force policies. Although all serious and major investigations will be attended, where volume crime scenes are concerned, the attendance criteria of the force will dictate the CSI response.

1.2 Roles and Responsibilities within Scientific Support

1.2.2 Key roles within CSI

Crime scene manager (CSM)

Depending on the nature of the incident, a crime scene manager (CSM) may be allocated to oversee the examination of a particular scene. The CSM is generally an experienced CSI who has undertaken training in the role of scene manager. In essence the CSM is responsible for the CSIs examining a particular scene where several potential scenes may be identified. They will undertake the necessary risk assessments and ensure the welfare of the examining team in addition to the prioritization and co-ordination of the examination strategy of the scene, in consultation with the investigating officer and crime scene co-ordinator where appropriate.

Crime scene co-ordinator (CSC)

A crime scene co-ordinator (CSC) will be required where there are multiple scenes and for serious complex cases. A CSC will advise the SIO on the appropriate scientific matters and generate forensic strategies in consultation with the SIO which will detail the priorities and processes required from the examination of the scene. It is the role of the CSC, where multiple scenes exist, to ensure staffing resources are met to avoid any contamination or transfer of material by CSIs attending more than one scene.

Figure 1.2 A typical scientific support management structure at a serious incident

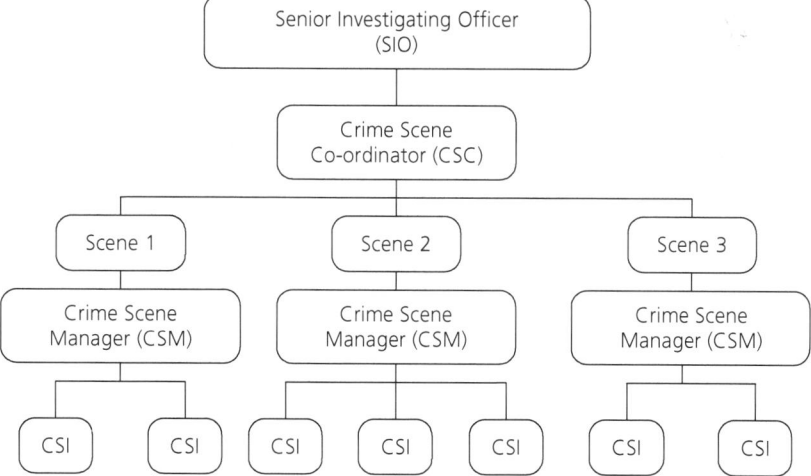

```
                    Senior Investigating Officer
                            (SIO)
                              |
                       Crime Scene
                    Co-ordinator (CSC)
          _____|_____
         |                    |                    |
      Scene 1              Scene 2              Scene 3
         |                    |                    |
    Crime Scene          Crime Scene          Crime Scene
   Manager (CSM)        Manager (CSM)        Manager (CSM)
      |     |         |     |     |            |     |
     CSI   CSI       CSI   CSI   CSI          CSI   CSI
```

The crime scene is a key part of the investigation and as such is ultimately the responsibility of the investigating officer who is in charge of the overall investigation. The crime scene examiners are trained to identify, record and gather potential evidence in order to corroborate or refute allegations that may arise during the investigation and to offer advice and guidance to the investigating officers regarding forensic issues.

It is important to consider that due to the civilianization of the role, the CSI may not have the investigative experience and background of a police officer. It can often also be the case that a CSI will not be party to all the information generated in an investigation. In order to maximize the potential of a crime scene examination it is important to discuss the particular case with the examining CSIs to ensure that the examination is as thorough as possible.

It can be difficult for CSIs to make an accurate assessment of the forensic potentials at a crime scene if they are not aware of the circumstances that are being investigated. It is important to update the scene examiners where further circumstances come to light which can impact on the scene examination.

Caution must be exercised in deciding the relevance or otherwise of potential evidential material to an investigation. The role of an investigator is to gather *all the available appropriate material*.

It can be easy to dismiss something as irrelevant only to find out later from a suspect or witness account that it was in fact very relevant to the investigation. Be mindful that the first opportunity to gather potential evidence can often be the last opportunity. In the early stages of an investigation, it is impossible to know what may or may not be relevant, so all material must be gathered unless it clearly has no bearing on the incident in question.

An example of where the potential to gather evidential material may be missed is where a defence of legitimate or public access is possible. The term 'legitimate access' is often used to describe circumstances where potential forensic evidence can be expected to be recovered due to lawful reasons. For example, fingerprints on items at a burglary where the householder suspects a previous occupant as being the offender can often lead the investigator to feel there is no benefit in having the scene forensically examined.

In such circumstances, it is important to gather any potential evidence that can support or refute this assertion, keep an open mind, rule nothing in and rule nothing out. The home owner may be wrong in their belief that they know the offender; conversely they may be correct in their belief. An investigator cannot know what the outcome will be at the time of the scene examination.

It is the role of an investigator to examine *all the available evidence* and allow the court to draw their conclusions on the validity or otherwise of any material gathered.

Case study—Legitimate access

A report was received of a male taking photographs of females in the adjoining cubicles at a public swimming baths. A decision was made not to forensically examine the scene as the cubicle was accessible to the public, and the suspect could claim 'legitimate access' therefore any potential evidence found would not 'prove the case'.

1.2 Roles and Responsibilities within Scientific Support

Whilst this is essentially true, it does not in any way reduce the need for a forensic examination. The suspect may deny being at the location in interview, the forensic evidence may show otherwise.

Consider that the suspect's fingerprints may have been recovered from the cubicle, but from the top edge between the two cubicles in question. That would lead to deeper questioning, as legitimate access would not usually involve such contact. The location of such evidence here is important in corroborating or refuting the allegations.

Where the potential defence of legitimate or public access is anticipated from a suspect, investigators should aim to gather as much available evidential material as possible. It is ultimately the decision of the court as to what weight they feel can be placed on such potential evidence.

Legitimate or public access situations warrant a more thorough examination rather than being a reason not to undertake examination of a scene.

The material gathered may not identify a suspect, nor 'prove' or 'disprove' the offence in this case, but can be used as intelligence and perhaps be linked to other cases or scenes.

Without a thorough forensic examination it is not possible to know what will be recovered from such scenes.

An investigating officer should not be afraid to question the CSI regarding the scene examination in order to clarify what has been done and the rationales employed. If an investigator does not fully understand the processes and the possible value of any potential material gathered, others may not be able to do so either.

1.2.3 The Fingerprint Bureau

The comparison and identification of fingerprints is undertaken by fingerprint experts whose key role is the searching for, and comparison of finger and palm prints from a crime scene with those of persons on the national database 'Ident 1', formerly NAFIS (National Automated Fingerprint Identification System), in the identification of deceased persons where identity is unknown or uncertain, and in the comparison of fingerprints for elimination purposes, where a householder, for example, has given their fingerprints to be compared with those recovered from a burglary at their home.

The bureau staff also deal with the inputting of the 'tenprint' marks taken from detained persons onto the database (see Chapter 5 for details of fingerprint recovery and identification). In some forces, fingerprint experts may attend crime scenes to assess the quality of marks found and direct the CSI to recover the marks identified.

The fingerprint identification officers will give evidence in court and are deemed as holding 'expert witness' status, in that they can offer statements of opinion and interpretation of the fingerprint evidence where applicable.

1.2.4 The chemical development laboratory

Force laboratories differ in their titles, partly due to the fact that they can offer a range of applications for evidential recovery in addition to the traditional chemical development of fingerprints. Many in-force laboratories undertake techniques to recover finger/palm and footwear marks utilizing chemical processes to develop marks on items that are not able to be recovered by a CSI at the scene.

However, many in-force laboratories are not restricted to the development of such marks and may offer a range of forensic techniques such as document examination, searching items for biological material and fibres utilizing forensic light sources, the location and recovery of potential blood, firearm residue and controlled drugs. Many forces also have the capacity for laboratory technicians to attend crime scenes to utilize the specialist techniques available.

1.2.5 The video and/or photographic department

The photographic and video units can give additional specialist support to the CSI for the video recording of the crime scene. The photographic department is generally responsible for the development of photographs of scenes and the production of photographic albums for court and evidential purposes and may, if applicable, undertake and provide aerial photographs of scenes.

The video unit will generally undertake the editing and enhancement of video footage from CCTV, audio enhancements, the conversions of various media formats (old tapes/computer discs for instance), produce photographic stills from video footage and record crime scenes with video. The collation and editing of material from crime scenes to produce presentations and briefings which can be shown in court may also be undertaken.

1.2.6 Forensic submissions department

Material of potential forensic evidential value gathered from the crime scene(s) will usually be submitted to an external forensic laboratory for examination by forensic scientists. There are a number of forensic science providers offering a range of analytical processes including, for example, analysis of biological fluids for DNA profiling and comparison, the analysis of glass, paint, fibres, soils and drugs. The particular service provider used will differ according to force policies and the nature of the analysis required, as may the submissions procedure.

There are generally two methods for submission to a forensic laboratory. One submissions process will deal with crime scene material for the recovery of a potential DNA profile which can then be loaded onto, and searched against, the national DNA database (NDNAD). This method is generally for *identification* purposes and typically involves the completion of a simple one-page forensic submissions form (MGFSPGF111 or equivalent).

The second submissions route is for the analysis and comparison of glass on clothing with glass samples from the crime scenes for example. The submission forms for this require much more detail regarding the examination required. The form (MGFSP or equivalent) may be referred to as a HOLAB, a reference to when the Home Office Laboratory was the main provider of such analysis to the police service. Chapter 6 deals with forensic submissions in further detail.

The forensic submissions department in-force will typically ensure that the relevant documentation is completed accurately and will authorize the submission of the material to the appropriate service provider. The key considerations that are made as to whether material will be submitted for forensic analysis include the value of the potential evidence to the investigation, the likelihood of obtaining a useable result, and budgetary considerations.

If material is incapable of having an impact on the case, it is unlikely it will be submitted for analysis.

When completing the documentation for a laboratory submission, be clear and concise as to the required outcomes for example:

> To compare a pair of bolt croppers found on person 'A' with the cut padlocks recovered from crime scenes X, Y and Z to establish whether they were the same instrument used in these cases.

Ensure that there are sufficient details regarding the case; be mindful that the forensic submissions team and subsequently, the forensic scientist, will not have any prior knowledge or information on your case other than what is supplied on the documentation. If this is vague and does not put the request for analysis into context, the material may not be authorized for submission.

1.2.7 The role of the forensic scientist

Forensic science is the application of scientific analytical principles for the purposes of providing potential evidence in criminal investigations. The role of the forensic scientist is to examine and analyse any material submitted to them from the crime scene in an impartial and robust manner.

Forensic scientists are qualified and experienced in a particular scientific discipline. The reporting officer (RO) is the person who has the overall responsibility for a particular analytical discipline and will be the person to submit reports and provide any evidence in court.

Forensic scientists are deemed as having 'expert witness' status and can offer statements of opinion and interpretation of the evidence.

There may be the requirement for more than one reporting scientist to examine a particular item, for example where there is DNA and fibre evidence that contributes to a case. The specialist nature of the differing disciplines within forensic science means that the scientists will tend to develop their expertise in one particular area. They may have a good knowledge of other forensic disciplines but would not typically report or give evidence in court on such.

The forensic analysis of material is generally undertaken by external forensic service providers. The analysis can take a number of forms, depending on the case requirements and the material submitted. For instance, a scientist may be able to establish links between materials on a suspect with material from a crime scene, confirm the identity of a person, substance or item, identify and interpret a sequence of events and compare material gathered from different sources. The chapters on the different evidence types contain information on the appropriate scientific applications that may be utilized.

Forensic scientists can also offer expert advice and guidance at crime scenes and may be able to offer additional forensic recovery techniques that are not available in-force. The forensic service providers are generally happy to discuss any queries an investigator may have and will offer advice and guidance where required.

Following any forensic examination, the scientist will provide a report of their findings and give expert testimony on their findings in court where applicable.

Many providers will refuse to examine items that are improperly packaged where the continuity and integrity of the material may be compromised (see Chapter 3 for packaging guidance).

1.3 Other Key Roles in the Investigation of Serious or Complex Cases

1.3.1 The exhibits officer

An exhibits officer is responsible for the collation of all material gathered in an investigation. The exhibits officer is a single point of contact for the SIO regarding any material gathered and will provide the SIO with accurate reports on the status of any material that has been submitted for forensic analysis.

It is a key role of the exhibits officer to accurately document the movements of material and ensure that the continuity and integrity of all the material is maintained. During the course of the investigation any material gathered must be recorded and, where applicable stored by the exhibits officer.

1.3.2 Family liaison officers (FLO)

FLOs are generally deployed in cases involving fatalities but can also be utilized in cases where there has been no fatality, for victims of hate crime for example. The FLO is the point of contact between the victim and/or the victim's family (where the victim is deceased) and the police investigation.

It is the role of the FLO to ensure that the information required for the investigation is obtained with as little impact on the victim or the victim's family as possible, and to provide them with information on the progress of the case and offer explanations into the investigative procedures.

The information given to victims and/or victims' families regarding the investigation must be authorized by the SIO in order that the investigation is not compromised.

The FLO will be instrumental in ensuring support mechanisms are put in place as appropriate, such as referral to Victim Support and other organizations as required.

1.3.3 **The coroner**

The role of the coroner is to establish the medical cause of death in order to record this on a death certificate. In addition a coroner will establish the manner of death, for example whether death occurred through natural causes, accident or suicide.

Where a doctor has attended and is satisfied that the death of an individual is due to natural causes with no suspicious circumstances, they can issue a death certificate and give authorization for the body to be released to the family for funeral arrangements. However, where cremation is planned a second medical examination is required prior to the issue of a death certificate.

The doctor may consult with the coroners' officer (see below) to discuss a case in order to seek guidance and ascertain whether the particular case should be officially referred to the coroner.

There are certain cases that, although deemed to be 'natural causes', must always be reported to the coroner. These include the following circumstances:

- Where death occurs in legal custody, even where such death may occur in a hospital during the serving of a custodial sentence;
- Where food poisoning is suspected;
- Where an individual has undergone a surgical procedure in the three months preceding death;
- Where the deceased has not been seen by a doctor in the two weeks preceding death;
- Where industrial diseases are suspected;
- Where the individual is known to be an alcoholic.

In all cases where the death is regarded as unnatural, unexpected or suspicious in any aspect, the doctor cannot issue a death certificate. The death will be reported directly to the coroner for investigation. The coroner typically receives notification of such deaths from doctors, hospitals and the police.

If the coroner decides that the death is due to natural causes, the police investigation will not continue. If the coroner deems that the death requires further investigation, they may request a pathologist carries out a post-mortem examination. Where the post-mortem demonstrates that the death was due to natural causes, the coroner is not legally required to hold an inquest and the body can be released for a funeral.

An inquest will be held where the coroner is not satisfied that the death was due to natural causes. The inquest is held to establish the facts surrounding the death, which include the identification of the deceased, the medical cause of death and when, where and how the death occurred. It is not for a coroner's inquest to apportion blame or culpability, which is the remit of the criminal court procedures. Where a body has been released for burial and the police feel that the case requires further investigation the coroner can order an exhumation of the body for further examination.

1.3.4 The coroners' officer

This role can be fulfilled by a police officer or support staff and provides a point of contact between the coroner, pathologist, the police investigators, family liaison officer (FLO) and the family of the deceased, the defence teams and any other interested party, for example the Health & Safety Executive.

The coroners' officer will undertake the organization and collation of material surrounding the identification of the deceased and the circumstances surrounding the death, and will gather as much information and potential evidence as required to support the coroner in the investigation of case.

1.3.5 The pathologist

The pathologist will undertake an examination of the body, known as the post-mortem (PM). This will typically involve an examination of the exterior of the body and where necessary an internal examination, depending on the circumstances of the case. The post-mortem examination can be split into two categories: the clinical and the medico-legal post-mortem.

POINT TO NOTE—CLINICAL AND MEDICO-LEGAL POST-MORTEMS

The clinical post-mortem will typically involve the examination of a body where the deceased has been treated for an illness prior to death and the cause of death is believed to be as a result of the illness. The clinical post-mortem is undertaken to verify the diagnosis of the illness and can only be undertaken with the consent of the next of kin.

The medico-legal post-mortem is undertaken where death has occurred unexpectedly and/or the circumstances surrounding the death are regarded as suspicious or unlawful. Such an examination can only be undertaken by pathologists who have undergone extensive forensic training and are registered with the Home Office.

1.3 Other Key Roles in the Investigation of Serious or Complex Cases

Home Office post-mortem examinations are generally attended by CSIs who will photographically record the examination and recover any material such as clothing and forensic samples.

In some cases a forensic scientist or appropriate specialist may be present on the invitation of an SIO depending on the nature of the case. The Home Office pathologists may also attend crime scenes to examine the body in situ if requested by the SIO.

Identification of the body should be made by two independent people where possible prior to a post-mortem, but this may not be possible due to the condition of the body, or where such persons may be involved in the death. In such cases other techniques such as fingerprints or DNA analysis may be required (see Chapter 8 on sudden death).

The pathologist will examine the body externally first, making notes of any observations. Any clothing will be carefully removed from the body and examined for any potential evidential features, such as cuts from a knife for example. The pathologist will generally take forensic samples from under the fingernails and any swabs required, assisted by a CSI. Once the external examination is completed, the body is opened up in order to examine the internal organs. Samples of body fluids such as blood and urine are taken along with, where appropriate, stomach and intestinal contents, and samples of organs such as the liver, heart and lungs may be recovered depending on the circumstances.

Such examinations do not require the consent of the next of kin and need to be dealt with sensitively, explaining that the reason for the examination is in order to find out what happened and to bring the offenders to justice.

Be aware that some cultures have very stringent rules regarding the burial or cremation processes and it is important to be mindful of such and—where possible—accommodate the needs of the family if appropriate.

It can also be necessary for a number of post-mortem examinations to be undertaken on behalf of the defence team, as each defendant can direct an independent post-mortem to be carried out with the permission of the coroner. The undertaking of independent post-mortem examinations should not unduly delay the release of the body as this can cause further distress to the family.

Where a person has died whilst hospitalized following an assault for example and a post-mortem examination is potentially required, organ donation must not be allowed to occur without the consent of the coroner and where applicable, the defence team where a person has been charged.

The SIO, coroner and pathologist will consider all the implications any organ donation would have on the post-mortem examination before reaching a decision on such matters.

1.4 **Health and Safety at Crime Scenes**

One aspect of crime scene examination that is the responsibility of all police personnel is to ensure the health and safety of all persons present at the scene and those who will be handling any materials subsequently recovered.

In addition to the general hazards which will be covered by operational generic risk assessment of injuries being sustained from slips, trips, and falls, the crime scene can contain specific hazards which will require a dynamic risk assessment to be undertaken. Crime scenes can include a variety of hazards, including those arising from biological fluids or tissue, chemicals, toxins and bites from insects.

The hazards potentially present at crime scenes are numerous, the following list contains some potential hazards that may be present, but is by no means exhaustive.

1.4.1 **Blood borne infections**

The hepatitis B virus is present in body fluids such as blood, saliva, semen and vaginal fluid. It can be passed from infected body fluids via an open wound, or needle stick injury where an infected needle punctures the skin. A vaccine is available for those at risk of becoming exposed to potentially infected body fluids—contact the Occupational Health Unit (OHU) in-force for guidance regarding obtaining a vaccination.

Hepatitis C is also a blood borne viral infection, although it can, very rarely, be transmitted through other body fluids. It is a commonly encountered disease amongst intravenous drug users. It is transmitted when infected blood enters the blood stream, such as needle stick injuries where a syringe containing infected blood punctures the skin

HIV is a virus spread through bodily fluids such as blood, semen, and vaginal fluids. The virus can also be spread through sharing needles. It can be passed from infected body fluids via an open wound, or needle stick injury where an infected needle punctures the skin.

The risk of infection from body fluids can be high and protective clothing must be worn when handling material contaminated with body fluids or tissue. Be mindful that dried blood can be as hazardous as wet blood with regard to the transmission of infections. As blood dries small particles can become airborne and subsequently be inhaled or ingested.

All officers who are required to respond to such incidents should ensure that their hepatitis B and tetanus inoculations are up to date.

Wounds such as cuts or animal bites can become infected with bacteria, especially if the wound is deep or if it gets contaminated with soil or manure, but even small wounds can allow enough bacteria to get into your body to cause tetanus.

All personnel who are exposed to the risk of sustaining cuts from items that are dirty with soil or manure must ensure that their tetanus inoculation is up to

1.4 Health and Safety at Crime Scenes

date. Occupational health units in-force can offer advice and guidance regarding inoculations.

1.4.2 Chemical burns

Hydrofluoric acid is extremely corrosive and can cause chemical burns to the skin.

Burned out vehicles present the risk of contact with hydrofluoric acid as the material used for many gasket rings and seals, when heated to around 400°C, will decompose on contact with water to form a charred or black sticky mass.

Touching such areas with bare skin must be avoided at all costs. If it is required to check the vehicle for identifying marks or serial numbers this should be done wearing safety goggles and sturdy impervious gloves, ensuring that bare skin is not exposed.

If contact with bare skin occurs, the area should be rinsed in clean water and Calcium Gluconate solution or gel should be applied to the area as soon as possible (the solution or gel may be available from the CSI). Medical treatment must be sought following any contact with hydrofluoric acid and line managers informed. Gloves or clothing that may contain hydrofluoric acid must be destroyed in line with force policies regarding contaminated items.

1.4.3 Weil's disease

This can be transmitted via the urine of rats, cattle, foxes and other wild animals. The urine may be present in soil or water. The disease can enter the body via exposed cuts or through the nose, mouth and other mucus membranes such as the eye.

Although Weil's disease is relatively rare, be mindful of the potential for the risk of this and other infections when searching areas that may be contaminated by the urine of animals.

1.4.4 Lyme's disease

This can be contracted from ticks which are generally found on sheep, deer, hedgehogs and other wild animals. When searching areas of woodland, grassland or similar overgrown areas where ticks could be present, protective oversuits and gloves should be worn, which prevent ticks from gaining access to bare skin.

1.4.5 Legionnaire's disease

This is caused by the inhalation of water droplets that contain high levels of the Legionella bacteria. The bacteria are extremely hardy and can develop and survive in streams, lakes, moist soil, and mud. The bacteria can also be found on the inner surface of moisture bearing pipes that contain a layer of slime.

The bacteria normally tends not to cause infections in the natural environment, but can develop to harmful numbers in man-made water systems such as in air-conditioning and cooling systems, spas and other warm-water baths, water reservoirs in humidifiers or indoor irrigation systems.

Be aware of the risk of infection when dealing with hydroponic systems such as those used in cannabis cultivation. As the bacterium is infectious by inhalation of water droplets, a mask covering the nose and mouth is required in addition to gloves.

1.5 Chapter Summary

The responsibility for the overall investigation into an incident will lie with a police officer who may employ the different specialisms available for the forensic examination of a crime scene, depending on the nature of the incident.

The CSI unit is generally the most visible within this process as they will attend crime scenes to gather material that may bear potential forensic evidence. CSIs are trained to identify and recover appropriate material and submit items to the appropriate specialist unit in consultation with the OIC where necessary. For volume crime incidents the CSI will generally make the appropriate submissions in line with force policy to the applicable specialist unit, for example the fingerprint bureau, chemical development laboratory or forensic service provider.

For more serious incidents, a crime scene manager or crime scene co-ordinator will liaise with the OIC (who will generally be a detective) or SIO in order to establish a strategy for forensic submissions, depending on the circumstances of the case and an exhibits officer may be employed to collate the material generated in the investigation.

> **KNOWLEDGE CHECK—ROLES AND RESPONSIBILITIES IN THE INVESTIGATION OF CRIME SCENES**
>
> 1. What is the role of the CSI crime scene manager?
>
>   A CSM is responsible for the CSIs examining a particular scene, particularly where several potential scenes are identified. They will undertake the necessary risk assessments and ensure the welfare of the examining team, prioritize and co-ordinate the examination strategy of the scene, in consultation with the investigating officer and crime scene co-ordinator where appropriate.
>
> 2. Name the units that typically make up the scientific support department.
>
>   CSI, fingerprint bureau, photographic/video unit, forensic submissions unit, chemical development laboratory.

1.5 Chapter Summary

> 3. State the purpose of a coroner's inquest.
>
> A coroner's inquest is a public enquiry which seeks to establish the medical cause and the manner of death (for example, suicide, accidental or natural causes). It is not the remit of the coroner's inquest to establish any blame or culpability.
>
> 4. What is the role of a Home Office pathologist?
>
> To undertake a forensic medical examination of the deceased body in order to record and recover any potential evidential material in cases of unexplained or suspicious or unlawful deaths.
>
> 5. What circumstances surround who can issue a certificate of death?
>
> A doctor can issue a certificate of death and give authority to release the body to the family where there are no suspicious or unexplained circumstances, and the doctor believes death is as a result of natural causes.
>
> Where cremation is planned a second medical examination is required prior to the issue of a death certificate.
>
> A certificate of death cannot be issued without referral to the coroner where death occurs in legal custody, even where such death may occur in a hospital during the serving of a custodial sentence.
>
> Other circumstances which must be referred to the coroner include where:
>
> 1. food poisoning is suspected,
> 2. an individual has undergone a surgical procedure in the three months preceding death,
> 3. the deceased has not been seen by a doctor in the two weeks preceding death,
> 4. industrial diseases are suspected,
> 5. or if the individual is known to be alcoholic.
>
> In all cases where the death is regarded as unnatural, unexpected or suspicious in any aspect, the doctor cannot issue a death certificate.

Where fatalities occur, the Criminal Investigations Department, (CID) the coroner, a coroners' officer, possibly a family liaison officer (FLO) and pathologist may become involved.

The role of the CSI and specialist units is essentially to support the police investigator in the investigation of an incident and it is beneficial for officers to be familiar with the specialist roles and responsibilities that are available in order to maximise the potential evidence.

Chapter 1: Roles and Responsibilities in Crime Scene Investigations

Summary of the National Occupational Standards (NOS) for the Student Officer Learning Assessment Portfolio (SOLAP) relating to this chapter

The table below indicates where it may be possible to demonstrate the achievement of certain performance criteria.

NOS unit	Unit descriptor	Performance Criteria, Range, and Knowledge	Activity
2C1	Gather information and plan a response	**2C1.1** pc 1, 2, 3, 6 **Range** 1c, 2c **2C1.2** pc 1, 2, 5, 7, 8, 10, 11 **Range** 2a–2g inclusive, 3a, c, d, e **Knowledge** 4, 6, 7, 8, 9, 12	Assessment of the nature of a scene. Liaison or communication with supervisor, control room, CSI, SIO, coroners' officer (where applicable).
2G2	Conduct investigations	**2G2.1** pc 1, 2, 3, 4, 6, 8, 12, 13 **Range** 1e, 2a–c, 3b, 5c, 7a **Knowledge** 9, 23	The identification of the nature of the incident and the appropriate resources available.

Recommended Further Reading

ACPO Family Liaison Strategy Manual (2003) National Crime and Operations Faculty/ACPO Crime Committee.

ACPO Investigation of Volume Crime Manual <http://www.acpo.police.uk/asp/policies/Data/volume_crime_manual.doc>.

Murder Investigation Manual (2006) Association of Chief Police Officers (ACPO)/National Centre for Policing Excellence (NCPE).

National Crime Scene Investigation Manual (2007) ACPO/Centrex.

Post Mortem Examinations and the Early Release of Bodies Home Office Circular No. 30/1999.

Safety at Scenes of Crime Handbook (2004) The Forensic Science Service (FSS).

Using Forensic Science Effectively (1996) ACPO/FSS.

2

Crime Scene Preservation and Management

2.1	Introduction	20
2.2	Roles of First Officer	26
2.3	The Five Building Blocks Principle	27
2.4	Chapter Summary	37

Chapter 2: Crime Scene Preservation and Management

2.1 **Introduction**

Forensic evidence is increasingly being used in criminal investigations. The rapid technological advances within forensic science mean that the police service has to be aware of the implications of the issues of contamination and cross transfer of evidence and take steps to minimize such. Failure to do so can render any potential evidence inadmissible in a court of law. The success of the CSI or forensic examiner to recover potential material that can be used as evidence in court is dependant to a large extent on the actions of the initial responders.

Police officers are usually the first to arrive at the scene of a crime following a reported incident and have a number of responsibilities to undertake—some of which may conflict with the need to preserve the crime scene. It may not always be possible to keep a crime scene in a sterile condition; however the actions of the first officers can have a huge impact on the subsequent investigation. When dealing with crime scenes or potential evidential material, it is imperative to demonstrate that the two key principles of continuity and integrity of the material has been maintained.

> **POINT TO NOTE—TERMS**
>
> The term, police officer as used within this book encompasses the roles of PCSO and other designated police support staff employed by police authorities, where applicable to their role.

This chapter will outline the actions and procedures which should be employed to preserve the crime scene, to minimize the destruction or loss of material and to maximize the forensic evidential potential by demonstrating that the continuity and integrity of all material has been maintained at every stage in the investigation. The importance of the responsibility required of first responding officers cannot be understated in any successful forensic examination.

As crime scenes vary this can only be generalized guidance and you should always seek advice of a CSI if in doubt. The role of the first responding officers is to preserve and protect the scene to maximize the evidential recovery opportunities for the CSI.

2.1.1 **What is a crime scene?**

A crime scene is generally regarded as being the location where an offence occurred, however there will always be 'satellite' scenes. These are the other related aspects of the incident, such as offenders, victims, and possibly witnesses who may have had contact with the suspect or victim, any vehicles used, other related premises, and deposition sites where weapons, bodies or other relevant items may have been deposited.

Each is a separate and distinct 'crime scene' in its own right and should be approached with a view to preserving any available forensic material.

Consider that each offence always has a minimum of two 'scenes'. For example, a dwelling burglary where the home owner was not present has essentially a minimum of two scenes, the offender and the location. The number of scenes would increase where vehicles are used or the home owner was present and had contact with the offender. Locard's 'Principle of Exchange' illustrates the two-way transfer principle; every contact will leave a trace, making it possible to link scenes together.

Regarding offenders, victims, witnesses (where appropriate) and associated locations (vehicles or premises for example) each as a separate and distinct 'scene' means that the issues of transfer and contamination are brought to the fore. Investigating officers must be aware of such issues and take steps to reduce the risks. The simplest way to do this is to be mindful of which officer deals with which scene.

An officer who deals with the crime scene should avoid dealing with a suspect or victim or any other associated 'scene'.

Scenario 1—Potential forensic links

A homeowner returns home to find a person attempting to gain entry via a broken window. The victim tries to detain the person, a brief struggle ensues and the offender runs off. The homeowner runs after the offender and sees a vehicle making off at speed down the road. The homeowner reports that a window was smashed by the offender and that no entry was believed to have been gained. A plastic holdall and a metal bar have been left at the scene by the offender.

How many 'scenes' are there?

There are potentially four – the location, the homeowner, the offender and the vehicle. There may also be material that can be forensically linked to other crime scenes.

What potential evidence may be available at this scene?

The metal bar and bag may have fingerprints and/or DNA material available as they were brought to the scene by the offender. There will be footwear marks present which could be used if of sufficient quality. Tyre marks may be present which could be useful if of sufficient quality, to compare with suspect vehicle tyres. Glass fragments from the window can be compared with any glass on a suspect's clothing. Fibre evidence may be available on the window from the suspect. Fibres from the suspect may be on the victim's clothing and vice versa, due to the struggle.

The CSI should ideally attend and examine the scene and recover the bag, the metal bar, and a footwear mark beneath the window, glass samples, fibres and glove marks from the window frame.

Figure 2.1 illustrates the potential evidence available and the links that may potentially be made forensically, with a summary explanation of the evidential links in the checklist below.

Checklist – Summary of forensic links

Fibres

- Between victim and suspect. Fibres from the victim may be on the offender and vice versa due to the struggle.
- Fibres from the victim may also be found in the suspect's vehicle.
- The victim's clothing should be seized where there has been bodily contact with an offender.

Plastic holdall

- Between scene and suspect, may also link to other scenes due to material including fibres or glass recovered in or on the bag.
- Possibility of fingerprints being chemically developed on bag.
- Potential for DNA recovery on handles.
- May link to suspect's vehicle through fibres or similar from the vehicle being on the bag.
- Impressions left in a surface by a tool can be photographed and a cast made of the impressed mark. If a tool is used to break a window, there may be glass present on the tool.
- Consider whether the bag may have been stolen from previous incidents or a similar bag being described by witnesses at other scenes.

Metal bar

- Between suspect, scene, other scenes and possibly suspect vehicle.
- Fingerprints and DNA recovery may be possible depending on the condition of the bar.

Footwear mark

- Can be linked to the footwear that made the mark.
- Footwear marks will be present at every crime scene, the mark can be recorded and recovered to compare with suspect's footwear. It may be possible for the make and model of the footwear to be identified.

Tyre mark

- Tyre marks can be compared to the tyres that made the mark. It may be possible for the make and model of the tyre to be identified. A partial tyre mark with no distinct pattern will not enable investigators to identify the make and model of the tyre.

Glove marks

- May provide links between other scenes, the suspect and the suspect's vehicle.
- Glove marks can provide evidence of links between different scenes.
- The glove marks may also be in the suspect's vehicle, premises or indeed on the suspect's person.
- The gloves may contain glass from the scenes.

Glass

- Links may be made between the suspect, the location and the suspect's vehicle.
- Glass fragments may be recovered on the suspect or suspect's clothing and in the suspect's vehicle. Links with glass recovered from other scenes may also be established.

Chapter 2: Crime Scene Preservation and Management

Figure 2.1 Potential forensic links

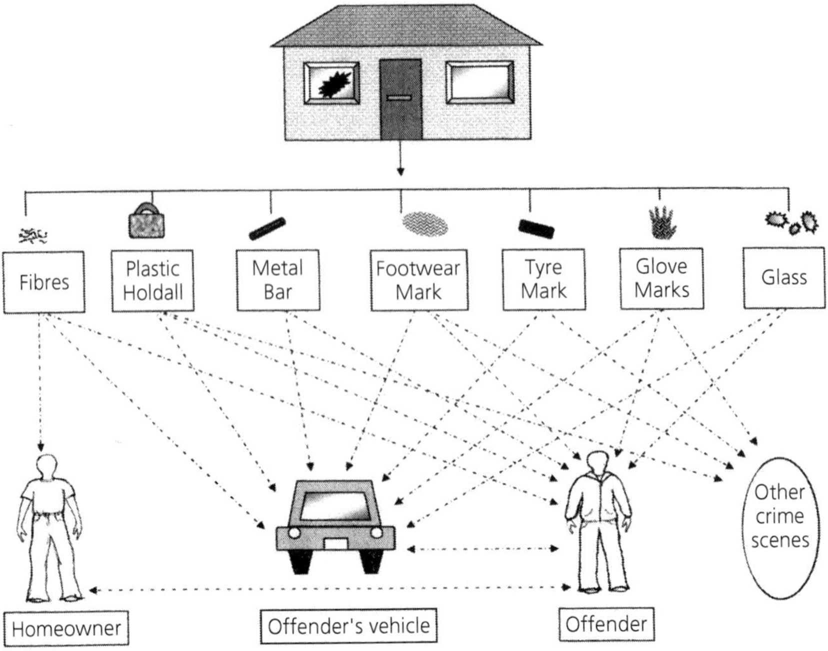

It is important to remember that potential forensic evidence can be present in microscopic amounts, which are not readily visible. Such material is therefore vulnerable to loss, damage, destruction, contamination and cross-transfer if preservation of the scene is not undertaken.

Cross-transfer of material such as glass, fibres and body fluids can occur in police vehicles. For example, fibres from a victim transported in a police vehicle can transfer to the vehicle seat.

If a suspect is later arrested and transported in the same vehicle, it can be argued that any fibre evidence linking the victim and suspect was gained through both parties sitting on the same seat. For this reason, recording the vehicle details in a pocket notebook is advisable.

In cases where evidence of contact is required, when transporting persons, placing a disposable paper sheet on the seat and backrests acts as a barrier to reduce the transfer of material, this sheet can then be retained and exhibited.

2.1.2 Purpose of crime scene preservation

It is vital that crime scenes are preserved in order to maximize the potential for gathering any material which can corroborate or refute allegations or versions of events. Much of the material gathered in the initial stages of the investigation may not be used in court, but this does not mean it should not be gathered.

Definition—Material

Material is defined in accordance with the Criminal Procedure and Investigations Act Code of Practice under Part II of the Act:

Material is material of any kind, including information and objects, which is obtained in the course of a criminal investigation and which may be relevant to the investigation; Material may be relevant to an investigation if it appears to an investigator, or to the officer in charge of an investigation, or to the disclosure officer, that it has some bearing on the offence under investigation or any person being investigated, or on the surrounding circumstances of the case, unless it is incapable of having any impact on the case.

Material can be used as evidence, intelligence or information or a combination of these.

It is very difficult to know what will be of use and what will not in the early stages of an investigation; therefore all material should be collected. The first opportunity to gather the material is often the last and it is much better to collect something that is not used, than to leave something behind that could be important.

Irrespective of the time elapsed since the incident and the attendance of investigators, failure to protect and preserve the scene at the earliest opportunity can lead to potential evidence being lost or destroyed.

At the outset of any investigation, information on the incident is usually limited, so it is vital to be open minded. The Core Investigative Doctrine (2005) sets out the approach that all investigators should adopt when dealing with any incident;

Assume nothing
Believe nothing
Challenge everything

In addition, the 'C' could include 'clarify, consider and check' everything. Investigators should never accept at face value what is presented to them and should always consider other possible explanations for the presence or absence of material. Officers should never hesitate to question the CSI or forensic scientists about any material they recover. If officers do not understand the material, it may be difficult to explain it to others.

It is not uncommon for the CSI at the scene to have a limited knowledge of the event under investigation, so communication with the forensic examiners at the scene is vital to ensure the scene potential is maximized

Continuity and integrity of evidence

The two key principles to adhere to when dealing with crime scenes and potential evidence are those of 'Continuity' and 'Integrity'. If these two principles cannot be demonstrated at each stage in the investigative process, three problems can arise:

Chapter 2: Crime Scene Preservation and Management

- The forensic scientist may refuse to examine/ analyse any item
- Any evidence gathered may be rendered inadmissible in court
- Loss or destruction of the material may occur

Definition—Continuity

A continuous record of the movements of the material from the crime scene, through the investigative or analytical process and to the ultimate destination in the court room.

Definition—Integrity

The handling, packaging and storage of material must demonstrate that no interference (contamination or cross-transfer or destruction or loss) could have occurred either accidentally or deliberately.

The purpose of preserving a crime scene is in order to maximize the potential recovery of material by the CSI, which can potentially provide evidence to identify and link offenders, victims and locations. In order for the recovered material to be admissible as evidence, it is vital that the integrity of the scene can be demonstrated and that no unaccountable interference or contamination could have occurred, either accidentally or deliberately.

The principles of crime scene preservation are essentially the same for a dwelling burglary or a murder: to protect the potential evidence. The scale and procedures employed will differ greatly according to the specific offence. For example, a volume crime incident such as criminal damage to a vehicle will not warrant the closing of roads and the instigation of a scene log, but the principles of preserving the evidence remain as valid for volume crime as for serious incidents.

2.2 Roles of First Officer

The actions taken by the first officers at the scene can have a huge impact on the investigation. Destruction, contamination and transfer of material are most likely at the time of the initial response. When an officer is tasked to an incident, there may be several demands competing for attention such as violent confrontations, public disorder, injuries, distressed victims or witnesses.

These must be dealt with first in order to instigate the five initial considerations as directed by the Murder Investigation Manual (2006). Described as the 'Five Building Blocks' for any investigation, these principles give a framework to the actions to be taken at a crime scene. The actions of the first officers should encompass the following where applicable:

- To Preserve Life.
- To Preserve Scenes.

- To Secure Evidence.
- To Identify Victim(s).
- To Identify Witness(es).

There are several considerations to be made with regard to the five building block principles which can sometimes be in conflict with the needs of the forensic recovery of material. Whilst the simplest rule is to stay out of crime scenes and touch nothing, this is not always appropriate.

There may be occasions where you have no choice but to enter a crime scene prior to the forensic examination in order to fulfil your role, such as to preserve life. When this function has been fulfilled however, officers must then concentrate on securing and preserving the scene until the CSI arrives.

Any actions undertaken at a crime scene must be recorded, rationalized and undertaken with as much care as possible in order to minimize any loss, destruction or contamination or transfer of evidence. It is important to be open and honest about your actions within a crime scene as these can be taken into account by the CSI.

Failure to report your actions within a crime scene accurately can lead to unnecessary and costly analysis being undertaken, not to mention the damage that will be done if something you do not declare initially is revealed in court.

Be mindful that the media at scenes may record your actions, as highlighted with the Omagh bombing appeal where it was reported that officers stated they wore protective suits at the scene, however media images showed that they did not. The implications of such exposure are huge, casting doubt on the honesty, integrity and professionalism of the investigators and the police service.

2.3 The Five Building Blocks Principle

The five building blocks principle is an excellent framework for approaching an investigation. With regard to the crime scene preservation, the framework can be applied with the following considerations.

2.3.1 To preserve life

The preservation of life is a fundamental responsibility of police officers; however this can sometimes be in conflict with the principles of scene preservation. Preservation of life will *always* take precedence over forensic issues. There are steps that can be taken to reduce the impact of the officers' and paramedics' initial actions to administer first aid or check for vital signs of life. In such situations:

- Record what has been done. If items have been moved, note the original position and final position.
- Make sketch plans and concise notes showing the layout of the scene.

Chapter 2: Crime Scene Preservation and Management

- Establish a single route into and out of the scene, known as common approach paths, which should be recorded on a sketch plan.
- Be prepared to hand over your footwear and clothing to the CSI.
- Inform the investigating officer and the CSI of your actions.
- Any materials used by medical teams should remain in situ, at the location and on the person in the case of fatalities.
- Ensure contact details of any medical crew attending are obtained.
- Request the medical crew retain any clothing that they may cut from the victim during transport to and/or at hospital if applicable.
- If injuries are life threatening, request that a pre-transfusion blood sample is taken.
- Ask the medical team for their prognosis on the condition of the victim so that you can update the investigating officer.
- Officers that have dealt with the victim within the scene have the potential to transfer material to other aspects of the scene. Avoid direct contact with the CSI or other officers who may be required to arrest suspects or examine related locations.
- Officers should record the fleet number of the vehicle travelled in after the event.

Case study—Initial observations

An officer arrived at an address to undertake a welfare check. This proved to be the scene of a murder. The officer secured the premises and waited outside the address for support to arrive. The officer noted a dry area the size of a vehicle on the road by the kerb outside the address. It had been raining heavily for some time, ceasing approximately 30 minutes before the officer arrived. By the time other officers arrived it had started to rain again and the dry area was disappearing.

The observation of this officer indicated the possible presence of a vehicle during a specific timeframe, enabling investigators to factor this in during questioning of neighbours. It transpired that the vehicle belonged to the victim and had been stolen by the offender within the 30 minutes prior to the officer's arrival. This kind of information was incredibly useful to the investigation.

2.3.2 Preserve scenes

Potential forensic evidence can be microscopic and not visible to the naked eye. Destruction, loss, transference and contamination of such material are very real risks. In order to maximize the recovery of potential material, the scene needs to be preserved.

The level of the response required to preserve the scene will be dependant on the nature of the incident. For example, offences of minor criminal damage will not warrant the closing of roads to set up a cordon.

In order to properly preserve crime scenes for forensic examination it is important to first identify the scenes. In some cases the scene may be fairly obvious, for example, a burglary scene may be the premises and the immediate vicinity such as garden area. In some cases the extent of the scene may not be obvious, look for entry and exit routes that may have been used by the offenders or victims and consider the possibility of other linked scenes, such as vehicles used.

> **Scenario 1—Cordons**
>
> A female victim awoke to find a male in her bedroom searching through her belongings. The offender made threats to shoot the female with the firearm he was holding if she screamed. The offender then left the premises. The first officers secured the bedroom where the alleged offence occurred by closing the door and stopping anyone going into the room.
>
> The problem here is that consideration was not given to the entry and exit points of the offender, who must have entered via the ground floor front door and traversed through the kitchen, and up the stairs (there was neither rear door access nor other viable routes to the bedroom).
>
> The potential for the loss and destruction of any potential evidence in this situation is huge as further officers arrived and walked around the ground floor.
>
> **What potential evidence may have been available from the entry and exit points?**
>
> Footwear marks, fingerprints, tool marks (if door was forced) fibres or hair at point of entry and on stairway, other particulates (soil or paint flakes) and DNA-bearing material
>
> **Where would you put the cordon in this instance?**
>
> A more appropriate cordon would be to cordon off the premises at the front gate and allow access only to scene examiners initially.

Once a potential scene has been identified it needs to be secured where forensic examination of the scene is required. Securing a scene means preventing access to the area by anyone other than authorized personnel (CSI, Home Office pathologist and those invited by the CSI or SIO).

Indoor scenes are relatively easy to secure by the closing of doors and restricting entry into the premises, initially by the presence of officers at entrance and exit points.

Restricting access at outdoor scenes can be achieved by the use of physical barriers or cordons. Methods for cordoning an area include the use of Police cordon tape, vehicles to block entrances, officers (police or designated support officers) positioned at key areas of potential entry can be utilized to set a cordon. Natural boundaries such as hedges and fences can form part of cordon, bearing in mind the potential for offenders to have discarded items such as weapons or stolen property over such boundaries.

The general rule for cordons is 'bigger is better'. It is less problematic to later reduce a crime scene cordon than it is to increase it. However, a cordon that is not controlled to ensure access is restricted is of little use. Cordons should be manageable, and whilst bigger is better, it is not always appropriate or practical on initial arrival.

For serious cases, two cordons may be set. A smaller inner cordon to protect the immediate area of the incident usually sited around the body or attack site. The size of an inner cordon ideally should enable room for forensic examiners to undertake examinations. A larger cordon, where applicable, should be set with wider parameters to allow a search of areas that may contain potential evidence and to stop public access to the area. This can often include closing off potential routes into and out of the area of the incident as offender(s) may discard items when they leave the scene for example.

If the main area of interest is for example a first floor room in a detached house, the house itself would constitute the inner cordon with the garden perimeter (at least) being the outer cordon. The CSI or CSM would be responsible for the activities inside the inner cordon and officers will be responsible for controlling the outer cordon.

Where circumstances dictate, once an initial cordon has been established by the first officers at a scene, the possible extent of the scene should be identified and colleagues directed to areas to set a wider outer cordon. It is not necessary for all officers to attend the main inner scene. Areas where additional resources, such as CSIs and other relevant personnel can meet, referred to as a rendezvous point (RV) should be identified as soon as possible.

The RV point should essentially have easy access for police and other relevant vehicles, enable access to the crime scene and, where possible, be away from public gaze. In circumstances such as terrorist incidents, the RV point should be searched to ensure there are no secondary devices or hazards.

....

Case study—Cordons

Two patrol officers were tasked to respond to reports of a fight between youths in a local park. On arrival the officers were faced with a group of about 20 people. A male lay injured on the floor. Most of the group made off on arrival of the police but a few remained and were very agitated. As one officer undertook first aid on the male on the ground, the second officer attempted to move the agitated group away.

The initial cordon, maintained by the physical presence of the officers, was therefore only about two square metres in size.

The male's condition was declared life threatening by paramedics. When further officers arrived, approximately ten minutes later, the cordoned area was immediately increased.

The weapon used was recovered within the boundaries of the second cordon.
....

2.3 The Five Building Blocks Principle

The initial cordon in such circumstances will be smaller than appropriate initially, but as soon as additional resources arrive the cordon should be extended.

Scene logs

A scene log should be instigated at the earliest opportunity where the incident is serious. All who enter the scene of serious incidents should be wearing protective clothing (scene suit; gloves; boot covers as a minimum).

Persons should not leave the outer boundaries of the scene wearing the protective clothing and then subsequently re-enter without changing their protective clothing. This is especially important in serious cases where the media may record such activities which could then lead to suggestions of contamination and transfer.

> **POINT TO NOTE—SCENE LOGS**
>
> Scene logs can be pre-printed booklets or written on a piece of notepaper or in your pocket notebook (PNB). Pre-printed scene log forms differ across forces, but are the ideal way in which to record the activity at the scene. Whatever the manner of recording (printed forms, pocket notebook, notepad, etc), it is vital that a scene log is instigated as soon as a cordon is set in place.
>
> The scene log becomes the exhibit of the person who instigates it, with those subsequently taking possession of it signing the exhibit label continuity. The log is an official document and subject to disclosure to the defence teams. Minimum details to be included in a scene log are:
>
> - The details of all those entering or leaving the scene
> - The time of arrival and departure of such personnel
> - The purpose or role at the scene
> - Telephone contact details
> - The person's signature.
>
> It is advisable to request some form of identification of those entering the scene if you do not know the person. Accuracy is of paramount importance—ensure the correct spelling of names to avoid later confusion.

It may be beneficial to also record details or descriptions of persons showing inappropriate levels of interest. Do not give any details out regarding the incident to anyone other than those known to be part of the investigation team. Persons asking a lot of questions could potentially be the offenders, media reporters or related in some way to the victim.

Common approach paths (CAP)

A common approach path should be established at the earliest opportunity. The common approach path should be the route into and out of the crime scene for all those subsequently attending the scene.

On initial arrival at a scene where the preservation of life is required, it is likely that the most direct route to the victims will have been taken by officers and medical teams in order to administer first aid or check for signs of life. Where possible, this route should be used to exit the area, unless it becomes clear that the offenders have used that route (for example, you note footwear marks or other potential evidence).

It is vital that the details of those initially attending are recorded and CSIs are informed of the route taken into and out of the scene. This can be achieved by a sketch plan, detailing the routes taken and positions of items of interest. Any sketch plan should be exhibited.

Ideally a common approach path should be established on a route least likely to have been used by offenders or victims. A common approach path needs to be wide enough to enable CSIs to carry in equipment and for the removal of any bodies where applicable. In cases of a serious nature, where there is only one route in, movement on this route must be restricted to the actions required for the preservation of life.

> *Tip:* At outdoor scenes use hardstanding or compacted path areas as much as possible to establish a common approach path as such surfaces are easier to search than grassland.

At serious incidents, the initial responding officers will soon have support available to them which can enable a review and possible relocation of cordons and common approach paths.

At a dwelling burglary however, the initial responding officer or CSI may be the only ones to visit the scene. Here, it is just as important to establish a common approach path, avoiding the route used by offenders. If it is reported that offenders entered and exited by the front door, officers should go to the back door (if available).

Case study—Common approach paths

An elderly person was subjected to a distraction burglary whereby offenders had gained entry through the front door. It was reported that there was one male who went into the kitchen with the victim on the pretence of checking the water.

The first officer attending went to the rear door of the property to speak to the victim, who wanted to walk around showing the officer what had been done. The officer declined to do this and suggested they go next door to neighbours to talk. When the CSI arrived, because the scene had been kept intact, a lot of footwear evidence was recovered which indicated three offenders and also indicated which rooms they had entered, which was more than the elderly victim was initially aware of.

2.3 The Five Building Blocks Principle

The actions of this officer ensured that potential evidence was maximized and intelligence gained on the number of offenders.

2.3.3 Secure evidence

The securing of a scene is perhaps the most important action to be taken in order to establish the chain of continuity and the integrity of any material subsequently recovered.

The securing of the scene can ensure the contamination, transfer, destruction or loss of potential evidence is minimized. It is important to be aware of factors that can result in loss or destruction of potential evidence.

Ideally, any material should always be left in situ for recording and recovery by a CSI. However, if there is a risk that the material will be lost or damaged steps should be taken to protect it. Any steps taken to protect potential evidence must be undertaken carefully and only when absolutely necessary.

> **Scenario 2—Preserving the potential evidence**
>
> This is the scene of an assault (Figure 2.2) that has taken place in the street. During the assault the window got smashed when the attacker hit it with their elbow, the attacker then used a piece of broken glass from the window to stab the victim. The victim has been taken to hospital. It has just started to rain.
>
> How may the potential evidence be preserved for the CSI examination?
>
> **Figure 2.2 Example of an assault scene**
>
> *[Illustration of a brick wall with two windows and a door. The left window is smashed. Labels: "Possible blood" pointing to the broken window and to a spot on the ground; "Piece of broken glass containing possible blood" pointing to the doorstep area.]*
>
> - Set up a cordon to stop anyone walking or driving through the scene.
> - The possible blood needs to be protected from the rain. The stains and glass (which may contain the attacker's fingerprints) on the floor can be covered with something that does not come into contact with the stain, a police

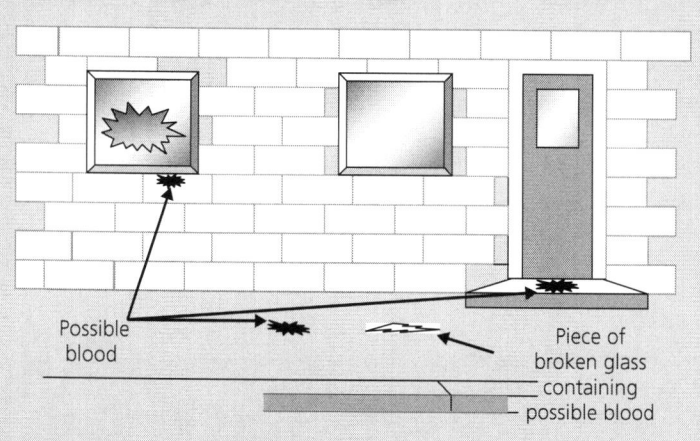

'stop' sign, a plastic bollard or a box lid, for example may be used. These are not ideal but in the absence of anything else it is better than losing the potential evidence.
- A clean plastic sheet or dustbin liner can be taped onto the wall to cover the window and preserve any evidence. The edges of the plastic should be secured onto the wall and not onto the window frame as there may be potential evidence such as fibres, hairs, possible blood and fingerprints around the frame and on the window. Be mindful that there may also be fibre or possible blood evidence on the wall, so ensure any tape used to secure the plastic sheet is away from likely areas of contact.
- The victim's clothing needs to be recovered. An officer, who ideally has not attended the scene, should attend the hospital with appropriate packaging material for the purpose of seizing the victim's clothing at the earliest opportunity.
- Be aware of the risk of damaging any evidence on the floor whilst securing the window area.
- Only undertake such preservation techniques if absolutely necessary, only if the potential evidence will be lost, damaged or destroyed if left exposed.
- Ensure you document your actions and inform the CSI and OIC of what has been done.

The weather can be problematic at outdoor scenes; evidence may be blown away or soaked with rain. Where items cannot reasonably be covered to protect them then they should be seized and exhibited if possible, noting the original position. If covering items to protect them, ensure the cover does not come into contact with the item and avoid using items of clothing or hats to cover items due to the risk if contaminating the item with DNA.

There may be rare occasions where the scenes need to be searched prior to the forensic examination. A risk assessment needs to be undertaken to consider the benefits of a search against the risks of contamination or destruction of material.

Factors that may warrant the search of the scene prior to a forensic examination as outlined by the Core Investigative Doctrine are:

- The need to preserve life.
- An immediate threat to life.
- Immediate pursuit of a suspect.
- The likelihood of destruction, damage or disposal of material caused by weather or outside interference with the material.
- The likelihood that recovering the material will lead to a rapid arrest of a suspect.

The potential risk of contaminating the scene is increased with such searches and unless circumstances dictate, the general rule is that the forensic examination *must take priority* unless one or more of the critical factors exists.

Any search must be properly risk assessed, rationalized, documented and undertaken with due regard to minimizing any potential damage, contamination or transfer of material. Where possible, the advice of a CSI should be sought on the most appropriate methods to employ.

Where it is clear that the incident is serious and there is no threat to life or risk of interference or damage to potential evidence, the first officer attending should secure the scene, inform a supervisor and await the arrival of additional resources.

> **POINT TO NOTE—LEGISLATION REGARDING CORDONS AT CRIME SCENES**
>
> Generally speaking, cordoning off a crime scene is not problematic. However consideration should be given to *DPP v Clive Winston Morrison* (2003) which highlights that the only authority in English law for the setting up of a cordon to restrict access is the Terrorism Act 2000, s 33 which is not generally applicable in most cases requiring a crime scene search.
>
> In summary, police attended a mall where reports of a fight between two groups of males had been reported. Within the mall, items believed to be weapons were observed. The area was cordoned off as a crime scene pending examination by CSIs. A person attempted to proceed through the cordon and was stopped. This person challenged the right of the police to stop him entering the cordoned off area. The cordoned off area was privately owned, no consent had been sought from the landowner and no warrant had been obtained.
>
> It was held in this case that although police officers do not have an unfettered right to restrict access on private land, they could rightly assume consent to act in setting up a cordon in such circumstances.
>
> Searches of premises can be undertaken on warrant, consider whether s 8, s 17, s 18 or s 19 and Code B of PACE may be applicable.
>
> The provisions of the Human Rights Act 1998 and Article 8 of the ECHR, must also be considered.
>
> Article 8(1) provides that:
>
> Everyone has the right to respect for his private life and family life, his home and his correspondence.
>
> Article 8(2) directs that:
>
> There shall be no interference by a public authority with the exercise of this right except such as is in accordance with the law and is necessary in a democratic society in the interest of national security, public safety or the economic wellbeing of the country, for the prevention of disorder or crime, for the protection of health or morals, or for the protection of the rights and freedoms of others.
>
> Providing the police do not go beyond what is reasonable and necessary to preserve evidence of the crime, the owners's consent can be assured for routine scenes of crime searches without warrant. Should consent be withdrawn, consideration to obtaining a warrant applicable to the needs of the investigation will be required.

Chapter 2: Crime Scene Preservation and Management

2.3.4 **Identify victims**

Consider the victim as a crime scene where the circumstances of the offence so dictate. In cases of serious or fatal injuries being caused to a victim, it can be beneficial to ascertain their identity as soon as possible as this can lead to the early identification of possible suspects or lines of enquiry.

The identification of an unknown victim can be undertaken initially by checking for any identification such as bank cards, etc. The search for such items must only be undertaken by a CSI due to the potential risk of damage to forensic material if suspicious circumstances exist. There are other methods to establish and confirm identity forensically such as fingerprints, DNA and dentition but these can take time to undertake. (See Chapter 8 on sudden death for forensic identification methods of deceased persons.)

Officers who deal with the victims should not subsequently deal with any potential suspects during the same shift, in order to avoid the potential for contamination and cross transfer of evidence.

....

Case note—Contamination and cross-transfer

Two officers attend an alleged fight occurring in the street. On arrival, the two officers administer first aid to a victim who is lying on the floor having been allegedly stabbed a number of times. It is then pointed out to the officers that members of the public are holding on to the alleged offender who is struggling violently, just around the corner. One officer leaves the victim to arrest the suspect.

What potential problems can occur as a result of this action?

Material from the victim can be transferred onto the alleged offender via the police officer.

What actions should the officer now take?

Inform the supervisor or CSI of this factor; arrange transport in a separate vehicle from their colleague who has dealt with the victim; document any visible material (blood, for example) that may be upon their person; exhibit their clothing for forensic examination at the earliest opportunity; do not deal with seizing any clothing or samples from the alleged offender.

There was no other appropriate course of action available to this officer at the time. Contamination and transfer of potential evidential material could not have been avoided in this situation. By recognizing this and taking appropriate steps, the impact of this on the case can be reduced.

The recording of the potential contamination or transfer issues and the seizing of the officer's clothing can enable the forensic scientist to assess whether any fibres or blood staining on the alleged offender may have been as a result of contact with the officer.

....

The consideration of any victims or witnesses (where appropriate) as crime scenes in their own right ensures that the potential forensic evidence can be maximized (see Chapter 4 for the recovery of forensic evidence from persons).

2.3.5 **Identify suspects**

The main feature of an investigation is to identify the offenders. It is possible to forensically link offenders to scenes and other associated persons based on Locard's 'Principle of Exchange'. There are generally at least two elements of a crime: the offenders and the location of the incident. This increases where victims are involved.

The suspects may be identified by forensic evidence such as DNA or fingerprints or by linking other evidence such as fibres, footwear marks, or glass for example, but the forensic evidence alone is rarely enough to present before a court, it must form part of a thorough investigation. The consideration of any suspects as crime scenes in their own right ensures that the potential forensic evidence can be maximized (see Chapter 4 for the recovery of forensic evidence from persons).

2.4 **Chapter Summary**

The purpose of protecting a crime scene is to maximize the potential evidence available for recovery by CSIs.

It is the role of an investigator to gather as much material as possible, as soon as possible, in order to corroborate or refute allegations and identify offenders.

The initial actions of the first officer can have an impact on both the quantity and quality of the material potentially available for the investigation.

The two key factors that investigators need to consider are how to establish the integrity and continuity of all material that may be present at a crime scene. This is vital if the material gathered is to be accepted at the ultimate destination, before the court.

The cordoning and control of crime scenes can go a long way to demonstrating the integrity and continuity of such material. The actions of the first officers can have a huge impact on any subsequent forensic examination and admissibility of any forensic evidence.

The responsibility of the role of securing and preserving the scene cannot be overstated. The control of cordons and the establishment and maintenance of scene logs is a vital role in ensuring a successful forensic examination.

> **KNOWLEDGE CHECK—CRIME SCENE MANAGEMENT**
>
> 1. What are the five building block principles?
>   Preserve life, Preserve scenes, Secure evidence, Identify victims, and Identify suspects.

2. State the ways scenes can be preserved to secure and protect potential evidence. Establish cordons to restrict access, Common approach paths, Instigate a scene log, Record details of initial observations made on arrival.

3. What is meant by the terms 'continuity' and 'integrity' in the context of crime scene management?
Continuity—A continuous record of the movements of the material from the crime scene, through the investigative or analytical process and to the ultimate destination in the court.
Integrity—The handling, packaging and storage of material must demonstrate that no interference (contamination or cross-transfer or destruction or loss) could have occurred either accidentally or deliberately.

4. What are the details required on a scene log?
Date and location of the offence; name and contact details of all entering the scene with the times of entry and exit; record the purpose of their attendance and obtain their signature (in case of a later dispute as to their presence).

5. Is the scene log an exhibit?
It is the exhibit of the person who starts it. Those who take it on should record on the log the time and date they take responsibility for it.

6. What is 'material'?
Material includes information and objects obtained in the course of a criminal investigation and which may be relevant to the investigation. Material may be relevant to an investigation if it appears to an investigation team that it has some bearing on the offence under investigation or any person being investigated, or on the surrounding circumstances of the case. Material can be used as evidence, intelligence or information, or a combination of these.

Summary of the National Occupational Standards (NOS) for the Student Officer Learning Assessment Portfolio (SOLAP) relating to this chapter

The table below indicates where it may be possible to demonstrate the achievement of certain performance criteria.

NOS unit	Unit descriptor	Performance Criteria, Range, and Knowledge	Activity
1A1	Use police actions in a fair and justified way	**1A1.1** pc 1, 2, 3, 4, 6 **Range** All **1A1.2** pc 1, 2, 3, 4, 5, 6, 7 **Range** 1a–1b, 2a–2b **1A1.3** pc 1, 2, 3, 4, 5, 6, 7, 8, 9 **Range** 1a–b, 2a–d, 3a–b **Knowledge** 1, 2, 3, 4, 5, 6, 7, 8, 9, 10, 11, 15, 16, 17, 18	Set up a crime scene cordon. Search premises and seizure of material.

2.4 Chapter Summary

NOS unit	Unit descriptor	Performance Criteria, Range, and Knowledge	Activity
2C1	Provide an initial police response to incidents	**2C1.1** pc 1, 2, 3, 4, 5, 6 **Range** All **2C1.2** pc 1, 2, 3, 4, 5, 6, 7, 8, 9, 10, 11 **Range** All **Knowledge** 1, 2, 3, 4, 5, 7, 8, 12, 13, 14, 15, 16	Initial actions at scene—identify nature of incident/identify scene parameters, attend injuries, update medical teams, CSI/SIOs, undertake and record risk assessment decisions.
2G2	Conduct investigations	**2G2.1** pc 1, 2, 3, 4, 5, 6, 7, 8, 9, 10, 11, 12, 13, 15, 16 **Range** 1e, 2a–c, 3b–c, 4a–c, 5c, 7d **Knowledge** 1, 2, 3, 10, 14, 15, 16, 17, 20, 23	Initial actions at scene—identify nature of incident/identify scene parameters, protect potential evidence, identify witnesses/victims, obtain medical assistance/FLO or victim support, CSI/SIOs, undertake and record risk assessment decisions.
2G4	Finalize investigations	**2G4.1** pc 8, 9, 12 **Range** 1c, 3b **Knowledge** 1, 2, 8	Ensure items of potential evidential value are recorded, properly packaged and stored to maintain integrity and continuity.
4G2	Reduce the risks to health and safety in your workplace	**4G2.1** pc 2, 3, 4, **Range** 1a, b, c, e **4G2.2** pc 1, 2, 4, 5, 8 **Range** 1a, **Knowledge** 1, 2, 3, 4, 5, 6, 7, 8, 9, 10, 13, 15	Identify biological and other hazards at a crime scene, alerting others (medical teams/CSI to the risk). Take steps to reduce the risks.

> **Recommended Further Reading**
>
> *PACE—A Practical Guide to the Police and Criminal Evidence Act* (2006) Ozin P, Norton H, and Spivey P.
> *The Core Investigative Doctrine 2005* (2005) ACPO/National Policing Improvement Agency (NPIA).
> *The Murder Investigation Manual* (2006) ACPO/NPIA.
> *The Police and Criminal Evidence Act 1984* (2007) Zander, M.

3

Exhibit Handling

3.1	Introduction	42
3.2	Principles of Exhibit Handling	42
3.3	Basic Principles for Packaging of Exhibits	48
3.4	Packaging Materials	51
3.5	Exhibit Labels	56
3.6	Chapter Summary	59

Chapter 3: Exhibit Handling

3.1 Introduction

Items that are required for forensic examination should be left, where possible, in their original position for recovery by a CSI, who is trained to identify any forensic potential and recover items appropriately to maximize the evidential value.

However, if the circumstances are such that the item may be lost, destroyed or damaged if left in its original position, it must be preserved immediately. If this involves recovering and exhibiting an item, its original location must be recorded and the CSI informed. The movement of items requiring forensic examination must be done with care and consideration to the potential forensic material available.

There will be occasions where officers may have to recover items for forensic examination as CSIs will not be available. This chapter covers techniques for the recovery of items in a manner that will ensure that any potential evidential recovery is maximized, health and safety is protected and the continuity and integrity of the exhibit can be demonstrated.

3.2 Principles of Exhibit Handling

When material is seized for use as potential evidence it is imperative to ensure that the two key principles of continuity and integrity are applied at the outset. The continuity and integrity of any material seized for evidential purposes must be demonstrated in order to show the items provenance and to prevent damage, loss or degradation of potential evidence and for the material to be admissible in court. The principles of the continuity and integrity of material begin on the arrival of the first officers dealing with a scene of a crime.

> **KEY POINT—CONTINUITY**
>
> This is the term used to describe the continuous audit trail which records the movements of the material from its initial recovery, through any forensic examination processes, and to its ultimate destination of the court room. Continuity of material can be easily demonstrated by accurately recording the description of the material, its exact location when recovered, the details of the person recovering the item and those subsequently handling the material and where the material has been stored.

> **KEY POINT—INTEGRITY**
>
> It is vital to demonstrate that any material recovered can be shown to have suffered no unaccountable interference or contamination, whether caused accidentally or deliberately, from the initial point of seizure, through forensic examination processes to the courtroom.

3.2 Principles of Exhibit Handling

> The correct packaging of material will minimize the opportunities for contamination and cross-transfer of potential evidence and ensure that an officer can be sure that the material initially recovered is in fact the same as the material presented in court.

When any physical material is recovered during an investigation, it becomes an exhibit. The handling, packaging and storage of exhibits must ensure that the items are not subject to any further damage and that potential for the recovery of forensic material is maximized. The continuity and integrity of exhibits must be proved beyond reasonable doubt in a court of law and the value of the principles of continuity and integrity is only ever really appreciated when an exhibit is lost, damaged, destroyed or the evidence devalued through the neglect of these principles.

This chapter covers the basic procedures to be applied for the handling, packaging and storage of the differing types of material that are typically encountered in the investigation of crimes. Adherence to these procedures will maximize the forensic potential and ensure that the continuity and integrity of items can be demonstrated. Details of the differing potential evidence types are discussed in this book, with the particular packaging considerations required for certain evidence types explained within the appropriate chapter.

3.2.1 What is an exhibit?

An exhibit is any physical item that is recovered by the police in the investigation of a crime or incident to which they have been tasked. The process of demonstrating the continuity and integrity of the exhibit begins at the first observation of an item that will subsequently become an exhibit. The minimum information required to begin the chain of continuity is an accurate description of the item and the date, time and location from which the item is recovered, along with the details of the officer seizing the item. This information should initially be recorded on the exhibit label and in the officer's pocket notebook (PNB).

All items seized should then be recorded on a centralized property recording system and details entered into investigation reports. It is important that the exhibit details recorded in the PNB and any subsequent investigation reports or statements are exactly the same as those on the exhibit label. A statement will be required for court purposes from the initial officer recovering the item and all those who have had subsequent access to it during the course of an investigation.

POINT TO NOTE—RECEIPT

In some cases it is prudent to supply the lawful owner with a receipt detailing the items seized, where appropriate. Any forensic material subsequently recovered from an item, such as a DNA profile or fingerprint will constitute an exhibit in its own right and be exhibited and recorded by the person who has recovered any such material.

3.2.2 **Legislation**

The provisions of the Police and Criminal Evidence Act 1984 (PACE) provide a general power to seize items.

Seizure of articles: PACE, s 19; Code B

Prior to the implementation of PACE, under common law the police, when undertaking a search under warrant, could seize any items that were reasonably believed to be covered by the warrant. Where a search was undertaken without a warrant, common law enabled the seizure of items in certain circumstances, such as where the item implicated the owner or occupier of the premises in the offence for which the search was undertaken or some other criminal offence, where other persons were implicated in the offence for which the search was undertaken or where a person, innocent of any involvement in the offence, refused to hand over material and the refusal was deemed unreasonable. PACE has given some clarity to the law regarding seizure of items.

PACE, s 19(2) provides that where a police officer is undertaking a search which is being undertaken lawfully under statutory powers, or by consent, they may seize anything on the premises providing that it is reasonably believed that it relates to the offence being investigated, or any other offence, and that seizure is necessary to prevent concealment, loss, alteration or destruction of the potential evidence (s 19(3)(b)). Property cannot be seized purely for intelligence purposes under this power. It is important that whilst a search may be undertaken with consent, such consent if subsequently withdrawn would mean officers are no longer 'lawfully' on the premises and as such may not seize items. This power under PACE also applies to designated support staff (CSI or support staff investigators, for example) under the Police Reform Act 2002.

PACE also provides more specific powers to search for property, including under s 1 (stop/search), s 8 (under warrant for indictable offences), and s 18 (search without warrant for indictable offence(s), s 32 (search after arrest for other offences), s 54, s 55 (arrested and detained in custody).

The provisions of the Human Rights Act 1998 and Article 8 of the ECHR, must also be considered.

Article 8(1) provides that:
Everyone has the right to respect for his private life and family life, his home and his correspondence.

Article 8(2) directs that:
There shall be no interference by a public authority with the exercise of this right except such as is in accordance with the law and is necessary in a democratic society in the interest of national security, public safety or the economic wellbeing of the country, for the prevention of disorder or crime, for the protection of health or morals, or for the protection of the rights and freedoms of others.

3.2.3 **Preservation of forensic material**

Locards 'Principle of Exchange' is essentially the foundation on which forensic examination is based. The principle illustrates that every contact will leave a trace and highlights that a two-way transfer of material can occur in the commission of an act. The transfer of such material can subsequently be used to establish links between objects or persons, for example a footwear mark at a crime scene can be linked to the shoe that made the mark, glass fragments on a suspect's clothing can link to a broken window at a burglary scene. Most potential forensic evidence however is microscopic; there may be very small amounts of material present that cannot be readily detected by officers handling such items.

The types of material available for transfer between suspects, locations and/or victims is infinite, with the most common potential evidence types including DNA from biological materials, fibres, hairs, glass, soil, paint, pollen, drugs. Such types of material can be present in microscopic amounts often referred to as trace or particulate evidence. The microscopic nature of such material can render it easily transferable and therefore extremely susceptible to cross-transfer and contamination.

Where evidence of contact is required it is vital that there can be no allegation or suggestion that any evidence found on one item is as a result of cross-transfer from another item. The continuity and integrity of such material can be demonstrated by adopting the appropriate handling, packaging, storage and recording procedures.

Definition—Cross-transfer and contamination

Cross-transfer—This is the term used to describe the manner in which material from one location can be inadvertently transferred to another. The most common situation for cross-transfer to occur is in police vehicles where a victim has been transported and then subsequently a suspect is transported in the same vehicle.

Material such as fibres, for example, may transfer onto the vehicle seat from a victim. A suspect could then pick up those fibres on their clothing when they later sit in the vehicle. In such circumstances any fibre evidence could be rendered useless.

This problem can also occur when an officer deals with a victim of crime and then subsequently deals with the suspect. Where evidence of contact is required, it is vital to ensure that it can be demonstrated that any such evidence has not occurred as a result of cross-transfer.

Contamination occurs when something is added to the sample, accidentally or deliberately. This can occur for example, by an officer sneezing over material that potentially bears DNA; the officer's DNA can then contaminate the stain. As forensic analytical techniques become more sensitive and able to detect increasingly smaller amounts of material, contamination is a very real issue.

Cross-transfer and contamination can be avoided by ensuring that officers deal with only one particular aspect of the investigation—an officer who deals with the victim for example should not then deal with a suspect on the same day. Records of the vehicles used by each officer should be made in the PNB, especially when transporting victims or suspects.

Gloves

The wearing of gloves when handling items of potential forensic value is essential, both to protect the evidence and protect officers—items may bear material that is hazardous or causes risks to the health and safety of those that handle them. Wearing gloves however, does not make the wearer immune to the possibilities of contamination and cross-transfer of evidence. Gloves should always be changed when handling different/separate items that potentially contain body fluids, drugs, firearm or explosive residues, due to the high transferability of such material and the sensitivity of the forensic analytical processes that may be required.

In such circumstances it is advisable to retain and exhibit the gloves worn for the recovery of the material in question. There are specific procedures for handling items potentially bearing residues of drugs, firearm/explosives and bodily fluids which are detailed in the appropriate chapters on particular evidence types.

Conditions of storage

Where an item is seized for the recovery of potential forensic material, it is important to ensure that it is kept in a condition which will maximize the potential for any forensic material to be recovered.

Where an officer has seized an item for any purpose, they have a duty to ensure that the item is kept in a good condition. Where such items will not require forensic examination or analysis and have been recovered for safe keeping or identification purposes, it must be borne in mind that such material may be returned to the lawful owner at some time. It should therefore be returned in the condition in which it was recovered.

Case study—A consequence of improper property storage

Items of clothing and personal effects were seized from a deceased person who was unidentified for some time. It was later found that no suspicious circumstances surrounded the death and the next of kin requested that the property from the deceased be returned to them. Due to improper packaging and storage, the items had developed a substantial amount of black mould upon them.

The police were liable to pay compensation for the damage caused to the property. In addition to the financial cost to the Police service, there is the damage caused to the reputation of the service as a professional organization.

3.2 Principles of Exhibit Handling

In the event that any forensic examination would have been required, the condition of the items could potentially mean that certain forensic analysis techniques would not be viable.

3.2.4 Health and safety considerations for exhibit handling

Items recovered from crime scenes may present risks to health and safety. There may be associated risks of infection from items containing bodily fluids and the risk of injury from items such as broken glass and knives for example. It is vital that officers take precautions to avoid the risk of injury or infection during the initial handling of potentially hazardous items and that any associated hazards are communicated clearly to all those who will subsequently handle the exhibit.

The wearing of disposable latex gloves to handle exhibits is the minimum requirement when handling exhibits, as protection from possible infections and to protect any potential forensic evidence. Disposable dust masks should be worn to protect from the inhalation of airborne materials at illicit drug laboratories and where dried blood/body fluids are present. Dried bodily fluids such as blood can become airborne as small particles when disturbed, these airborne particles can then subsequently be inhaled.

Bodily fluids can potentially transmit infectious diseases including HIV, hepatitis B and tetanus. Items bearing such bodily fluids must be labelled as 'Biohazard' in a manner that makes it clear to everyone who will subsequently handle the exhibit that there is a risk of infection from biological material. Where it is known that the donor of the body fluid has an infectious disease such as HIV or hepatitis B it is vital this information is documented and made available to those who will be undertaking any forensic analysis on the items.

'Health hazard' labelling should be used in circumstances where a risk to health exists but is not in the form of bodily fluid, for example, powdered drug residues that can be inhaled. Items that contain solvent and liquid accelerants such as petrol must be labelled as 'flammable' and stored in a cool, well-ventilated area. Exhibits that contain broken glass, knives and similar objects that can cause injury should be packaged in such a manner so as to prevent injury occurring to those that subsequently handle the items.

> **KEY POINT—FIREARMS**
>
> Firearms must not be handled until they have been cleared or made safe by an authorized firearms officer (AFO) or equivalent.
> See Chapter 9 for details of firearm forensic potentials.

In-force operational risk assessments (ORA) and occupational health departments will have details of the different risks and the appropriate actions required for the handling and storage of hazardous items.

Exhibits must be packaged in a manner that will protect the evidence and protect the health and safety of all those who will subsequently handle them.

3.3 Basic Principles for Packaging of Exhibits

There are certain principles that will always apply to the packaging of certain types of exhibits to ensure that potential forensic evidence is maximized.

Exhibits must always be packaged and sealed at the time of seizure to ensure that the continuity and integrity of the item can be demonstrated. Once securely packaged and sealed at the scene, the exhibit must not be subsequently opened to be shown in an interview with a suspect, for example.

Suggestions that any forensic material subsequently recovered from the exhibit has come from the suspect during the interview procedure can render any evidence of contact as inconclusive and possibly inadmissible in court. Where an exhibit needs to be opened, for photographing or sub-exhibiting purposes, this must be done in clean secure area to avoid any cross-transfer or contamination. Covering the bench or table with a clean paper sheet is recommended, gloves should be worn to remove or examine the item and a record of what has been done, by whom and where, should be made in the PNB. It may be advisable also to exhibit the paper sheets if material such as fibres, glass or body fluids could potentially have been transferred onto the paper.

Where an officer has taken the trouble to seize an item for evidential purposes, it is inexcusable to then jeopordize the potential evidence by the incorrect handling, packaging and storage of the exhibit. If items of potential forensic evidence are to have any value at all, it is imperative that they are handled with due care and consideration to the forensic potentials and the issues of cross-transfer and contamination. Officers should avoid giving support to a defence case by enabling the suggestion that the evidence lacks integrity and value.

3.3.1 Packaging of dry items

The type of potential evidence recovery required will determine the type of packaging method used. Generally, brown paper evidence sacks or plastic bags can be used for dry items, however the following considerations need to be made if the following types of forensic analysis are required.

Indented writing or footwear

Where paper has been walked over by an offender there may be indented impression of footwear on the paper. Similarly, pieces of paper may bear indented impressions of handwriting. To preserve indented impressions on paper any such item must be placed into a rigid package, either a box or between sheets of card, which is then sealed into a paper or plastic evidence bag. *Do not lean* on the item to write exhibit labels, as the indentations from this can show up when the item is processed. Chapter 14 details the analysis techniques available for the forensic examination of documents.

Fingerprints

Brown paper sacks or envelopes, cardboard boxes or plastic bags are suitable for items that may contain fingerprints. Consideration should be given to the fact that fingerprints can be removed or damaged by friction, so any movement of the item within the packaging should be restricted. Chapter 5 details the techniques available for the recovery of fingerprints.

Footwear or leather items

If dry, such items should always be packaged in paper evidence sacks or cardboard boxes. If sealed into plastic packaging, mould can develop on the items which will degrade any potential DNA material and disrupt or destroy the potential for any other evidence such as fingerprints or fibres.

Where possible, place footwear in a paper 'window' sack with the sole visible through the transparent panel. This enables the sole pattern to be viewed without having to unseal a bag.

If the item is wet, package as per the guidance given below. With footwear, package one shoe per bag, do not place both shoes in the same bag. (See Chapter 4 for details of recovering items of clothing from persons and Chapter 9 for the forensic analysis techniques available for the examination of footwear.)

3.3.2 Wet or damp items

Items that are recovered in a damp or wet condition should ideally be air dried as soon as possible in a designated secure and forensically clean area. One exception to this is where analysis for suspected accelerant is required. (See section 3.4.5 below.) Drying cabinets or rooms are generally available within the CSI department for this purpose but may not be accessible at all times. The drying cabinets used should undergo decontamination cleaning prior to and following each use to ensure that no transfer or contamination is possible. If there is to be a delay in accessing a drying cabinet or room, wet or damp items require freezing as soon as possible. Be mindful that items should not be air dried in a cabinet that contains items from different scenes to avoid potential cross-transfer and/or contamination.

Paper evidence sacks are porous and it has been noted on occasions that moisture from damp or wet items has been absorbed by the paper to be visible on the outer surface of the bag. By placing the item in an unsealed plastic bag, any seepage can be avoided, preserving the integrity and avoiding cross-contamination and any potential risks to health and safety.

Figure 3.1 Packaging technique for damp/wet items

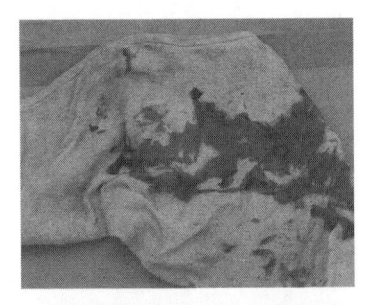

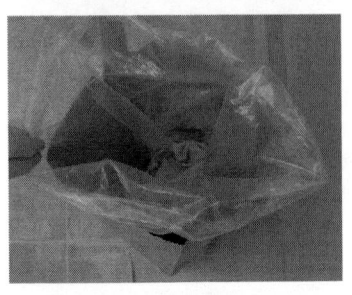

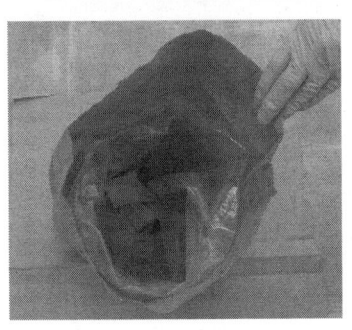

Example—A shirt stained with wet possible blood. Be mindful that where the positioning of potential blood or other wet staining will be required for the forensic examination, the item needs to be kept flat and not crumpled up to avoid transference of the stain to other areas of the item. Seek the advice of a CSI if in doubt. (Chapter 7 on blood pattern analysis outlines the basic principles of such pattern evidence in the examination of body fluids.)

Place the item into a clean plastic bag.

DO NOT SEAL THE PLASTIC BAG

Placed the unsealed plastic bag into a paper evidence sack. Securely seal the paper evidence sack as detailed in Figure 3.3.

Summary:

- Items that are wet or damp require air drying in a designated secure area or freezing as soon as possible.
- All original packaging must be retained and submitted with the item following air drying.
- The packaging for items that contain bodily fluids must be clearly marked as 'biohazard', either by using biohazard tape or by writing 'biohazard' on the exterior of the packaging so that it is clearly visible.

If stored in a freezer, the item should be air dried prior to submission for forensic analysis. Once dried the item should be repackaged either with the original packaging or with fresh packaging material. If using fresh packaging material, the original packaging materials must be dried, retained and submitted for any analysis along with the item, as it may contain vital potential evidence.

There are some variations in packaging requirements depending on the type of forensic analysis required—see the appropriate chapter dealing with a particular evidence type for specific guidance.

3.4 Packaging Materials

When an item containing potential forensic evidence is exhibited, consideration must be given as to the type of evidence that may be available and appropriate steps taken to ensure that:

- material is preserved in a manner that will maximize the potential for evidence recovery;
- the continuity and integrity of the exhibit is established and subsequently maintained.

In serious cases, most of the items required for forensic examination will be recovered by the CSIs who are trained to identify the forensic potential of items and who will have a range of purpose specific packaging available to them. There are occasions however, where it is necessary for a police officer or support staff investigator to recover items of potential forensic value. CSIs will offer advice and guidance on particular evidential recovery and packaging techniques if required.

Figure 3.2 Example of packaging materials

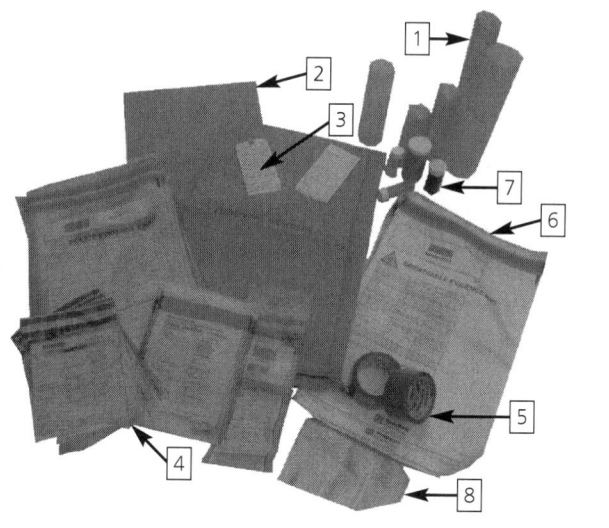

Key

1 Knife tubes

2 Paper evidence sacks

3 Exhibit labels

4 Tamper evident bags

5 Parcel tape

6 Breathable tamper evident bags

7 Poly pots

8 Plastic bags

There are various packaging materials available for the recovery of exhibits, and the type of packaging utilized should ensure that the item cannot suffer any damage, alteration, loss or destruction and that the health and safety of all those who may handle the exhibit is protected. The following materials are those that are commonly used for exhibit packaging.

Chapter 3: Exhibit Handling

3.4.1 Paper evidence sacks

Brown paper evidence sacks can be used for the packaging of all dry leather items, footwear (one shoe per bag) and other dry items. The technique as shown in Figure 3.3 for the sealing of the brown paper evidence sacks will ensure that the integrity of the exhibit can be demonstrated.

Figure 3.3 Sealing of brown paper evidence sacks

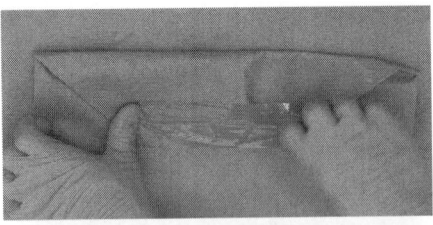

Fold over the top corners of the evidence sacks; fold over again to make a flap and tape this down, covering all the folded edges.

Fold the top edge over again and secure with tape ensuring the edges are covered.

Tape over the stitched seal at the bottom of the bag—this prevents loss of microscopic particulate evidence and increases the integrity of the exhibit.

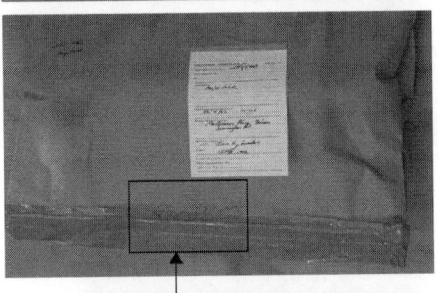

Sign and date over all the taped seals on all edges. An alternative to this is to use a signed and dated adhesive label placed over the seals.
A clear adhesive tape is then used to tape over the label and seal the bag, ensuring the signed label is visible.

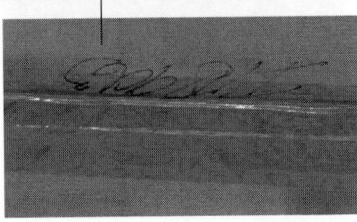

Securely attach the exhibit label or equivalent. Store in a cool dry secure store if exhibit is dry or in a freezer if exhibit is wet/damp or contains body fluids.

A 'breathable' tamper-evident evidence bag is an excellent alternative to the brown paper evidence sacks if available. These are tamper-evident bags that are paper based on one side with a transparent plastic panel on the other side, enabling the safe viewing of the exhibit. These bags also have a unique bar code imprinted upon them which is an ideal way to preserve the integrity and continuity of an exhibit.

3.4.2 **Tamper-evident bags**

These bags are plastic and have adhesive strip seal. They can be used for dry items and are particularly good for packaging items of value or cash or drugs or DNA bearing material as each bag has its own unique barcode and reference number (see Figure 3.4), making them particularly useful for continuity and integrity purposes. Record the reference number of the bag in your PNB and on the investigation logs.

The exhibit label is pre-printed on the bags and should be completed in a permanent marker or ballpoint pen, gel inks can easily be removed from the label.

Figure 3.4 Unique identifying barcode and reference number on tamper-evident bags

3.4.3 **Boxes**

Boxes are useful for packaging items that would suffer damage if not protected by a rigid container, such as indented writing or footwear impressions on paper or pieces of glass, for example. To secure items into a box to avoid movement, punch holes in the bottom of the box and secure the item with string or plastic

Chapter 3: Exhibit Handling

cable ties, in a manner that will restrict movement without jeopardizing potential evidence. Do not use adhesive tape to secure an item into a box as this can damage potential evidence when it is removed. See Figure 3.5 for method to secure items into as box.

Figure 3.5 Securing items into a box

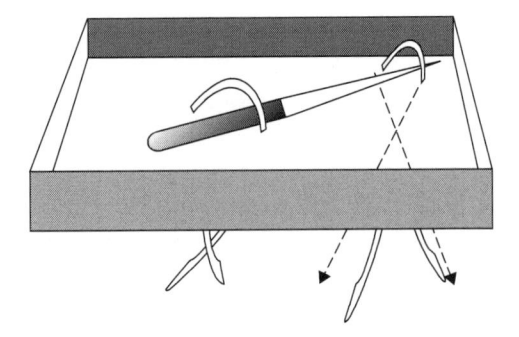

The secured item should then ideally be sealed into a tamper-evident bag or paper evidence sack. The holes made in the box *must* be securely covered with tape on the underside of the box. Forensic material can be microscopic and can be lost from, or indeed added to the exhibit, if these holes are not securely covered. If the box will not be placed into a bag, the lid must be securely taped down and all visible seams of the box taped over. Sign and date across all the taped seals.

> **KEY POINT—PRESERVING DRIED BODY FLUIDS**
>
> If a fragile item potentially bears dried bodily fluids and DNA analysis is required, the item should be placed into a clean plastic or tamper-evident bag before being secured into a box in the manner described above. The exhibit packaging must be labelled with 'biohazard' to ensure those that handle the exhibit are aware of the potential risks to health and safety.

3.4.4 Knife tubes

These are purpose made plastic containers available in a variety of sizes. They can be used to safely package knives and other bladed instruments such as screwdrivers for example, in a manner that protects the evidence and anyone subsequently handling the exhibit. They are also appropriate for packaging items that may be susceptible to damage if packaged in a non-rigid container.

Knife tubes should be sealed with tape to cover the joint of the two parts. Sign and date over the taped join with a permanent marker pen and then ideally place the tube into a paper evidence sack or tamper-evident plastic bag and seal.

If items contain possible body fluids, the exhibit packaging must be labelled as 'biohazard'.

3.4.5 Nylon bags

Nylon bags must always be used where the analysis for the presence of liquid accelerants is required in a case involving suspected arson. The clothing from a suspect believed to be involved in arson and any containers that are believed to have contained accelerant material must be packaged into nylon bags.

The analysis for accelerants involves placing the packaged exhibit into an oven, heat is applied and a fine probe is inserted into the bag to sample the vapour inside. The analysis can, depending on the circumstances, provide information of the chemical nature of any liquid accelerant, establish the amount of accelerant present in the sample and provide comparisons with samples from different locations to potentially link a suspect with the crime scenes. The success or otherwise of the analysis is dependant on the correct packaging of the exhibit.

Liquid accelerant may be present in miniscule amounts, on a suspect's clothing for example, so it is vital that precautions are taken to avoid any contamination and loss of the accelerant.

Nylon bags should be kept in a secure area away from any potential contamination—having such packaging loose in the boot of a police vehicle is not appropriate. The batch number of the bags used for packaging should be recorded and a control sample of the nylon bags must be submitted, to enable a scientist to determine if the bags used for packaging contain any contaminant that may have an effect on the analytical results. Do not use adhesive tapes to seal the bags—the adhesive may 'relax' during heating to allow the vapour to escape, also there is a small chance the adhesive may interfere with the analytical result.

Use the largest size bag available, as both ends of the nylon bag need to be sealed using a 'swan-necking' technique (see Figure 3.6), which will reduce the space available for the exhibit. This technique ensures that any vapour is retained in the event that the seal on the bottom of the bag is breached. It may not always be possible however to 'swan-neck' seal both ends due to size constraints. Double bagging is required in such circumstances where both ends cannot be 'swan-necked' sealed. Where clothing or other textiles such as cloths are wet or damp from suspected accelerant they *must not* be air dried prior to packaging. This is due to liquid accelerants being susceptible to evaporation, which will possibly render any analysis as inconclusive. For this reason, items suspected of bearing potential accelerants must be recovered and packaged at the earliest opportunity to maximize the potential evidence.

Any liquid accelerant must be contained in clean glass or metal containers. Seek the advice of a CSI before decanting any such material from its original container.

Chapter 3: Exhibit Handling

Figure 3.6 'Swan necked' sealing technique to preserve suspected accelerant

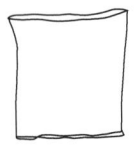

Twist the bottom sealed end of the bag and bend the twisted part over on itself. This is referred to as 'swan necking'. Secure in this position with string or a cable tie, ensuring that there will be enough room in the bag for the item.

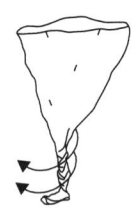

Place item containing suspected accelerant into the bag. Tightly twist the top of the bag to repeat the 'swan necking' procedure. Bend the twisted neck of the bag over on itself and secure tightly with a cable tie or string.

Place the sealed nylon bag into a second nylon bag if appropriate, and repeat the swan necking technique to seal both ends. Double bagging is required if item is wet, there is a strong odour of possible accelerant or if the sealed bottoms of the nylon bags are not 'swan-necked' sealed.

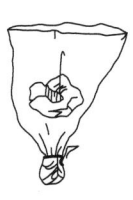

A control sample of the nylon bag must be submitted. Take an empty nylon bag from the same pack and 'swan-neck' seal both ends of the empty bag.

Attach the exhibit label with string or cable tie. Do not use staples or adhesive tapes. A 'flammable' warning should be attached and the exhibit stored in a cool well-ventilated secure store.

To ensure that the packaging is not punctured during storage or transit, it is advisable to place the exhibit into a box or paper evidence sack.

3.5 Exhibit Labels

The exhibit label is the first stage in the continuity audit trail of the item and is used to record the details of the exhibit and its movements during the investigative process. The exhibit label has a key role in the demonstration of the continuity of the item.

Exhibit labels may differ in format; however the key information required is standard.

3.5.1 Identifying reference or exhibit number

An exhibit label must contain a unique identifying reference number, which is the seizing officer's exhibit number. A common format for an exhibit number involves the officer's initials followed by a number—for example, ABC/1 is the first exhibit seized by Arthur Brian Chalk, subsequent exhibits seized by Mr Chalk—in the same case—would be ABC/2, ABC/3 and so on. The numbering of exhibits will recommence at number 1 (eg ABC/1) when the officer deals with exhibits for a different case. Although the officer may seize several exhibits denoted ABC/1 on the same day, the exhibit details such as the location will differ to distinguish the items.

The court number is for the use of the courts only—an officer may have 20 exhibits but the court may require only three of these. Some forces use the case reference number and/or the officer collar/shoulder number in addition to the initials and sequential numbering in differing sequences. The individual force policy on exhibits will detail the force requirements for exhibit numbering.

3.5.2 Item description

The description of the item should note key identifying features; descriptions such as 'brown envelope' are not appropriate. 'Brown envelope addressed to . . .' is much better for continuity and integrity purposes as it distinguishes one brown envelope from the many others that may be submitted for forensic examination and individualizes this particular envelope as the one that was seized.

Avoid stating measurements on exhibit labels, for example 'knife with 5" blade', as this can lead to questions being raised in court if the blade is measured by the defence team and it is not exactly 5" in length. Avoid using the term 'approximately' as this to may lead to unnecessary defence questioning—an approximation can be regarded as a 'guess', and as such is not appropriate for a profession that deals with facts. Where details such as the length of the blade are required, the knife should be photographed next to a scale (ruler), ideally by a CSI and in such a manner as not to jeopardize any further forensic analysis.

Similarly, avoid stating a stain as being 'blood', refer to such stains as 'possible blood', 'apparent blood' or 'presumed blood' which are acceptable terms to use if you believe blood stains are present. For example, 'Shirt containing dark staining (possible blood)' is acceptable. This is due to the fact that only a scientist can state that a substance is blood following analysis of the stain. Describing the stain as 'possible blood' demonstrates that the officer is keeping an open mind as to the origin of the stain, whilst highlighting the potential biohazard risk. The

Chapter 3: Exhibit Handling

key difference between making a descriptive statement regarding the length of a blade and the nature of a stain is that it is necessary for scientific analysis to establish the identity of such a stain.

The same consideration should be observed when making any statements that propose to identify any substance; a gold ring should be described as a 'yellow metal ring' for example. Avoid stating anything on the exhibit label descriptor that you *do not know as an absolute* fact—approximations are not acceptable and can generate unnecessary questioning on the integrity of the item in court.

3.5.3 Time and date

This is the time and date the item was originally seized as an exhibit.

3.5.4 Location details

The location from which the item was seized should be similarly specific, detailing the precise location from which the item was recovered. If an item was recovered from the front passenger side (front near side = fns) footwell of a vehicle, for example, the location details must indicate this and include the make, model and vehicle registration number, eg 'FNS footwell of Vauxhall Vectra, registration "abc123z"'.

If a knife is recovered from the kitchen floor by the fridge, state this detail on the exhibit label stating the address of the premises. The location of any material can be useful in corroborating or refuting allegations and assist in any reconstructions of the incident.

3.5.5 Details of person recovering the exhibit

The person recovering the item must detail their name and sign the exhibit label. If this is a member of the public or victim of crime handing an officer an item, it is the exhibit of that individual and their initials should be used to formulate the exhibit number, their name and signature is required as the person producing the item.

An officer receiving such an item from a member of the public must sign the continuity section of the exhibit label. Where an officer recovers the item, the inclusion of the collar or shoulder number is required.

3.5.6 Continuity record

Any person subsequently taking control of an exhibit must endorse the label with their name, sign and date the exhibit label for continuity purposes. When an officer hands an exhibit to another person, they must ensure that the individual endorses the exhibit label. A note of the time and date and person receiving the exhibit should also be made in the PNB.

3.5.7 Sub-exhibiting

This is the term used to describe circumstances whereby an exhibit consists of several separate items, for example a handbag and contents. It is important when initially seizing an item such as a handbag that contains further property, to state on the exhibit label, 'Handbag and contents'—the individual contents do not have to be listed on the label. Items subsequently removed from the handbag for further examination will require exhibiting separately.

In the case of a mobile phone removed from a handbag which is exhibited as ABC/1, the phone will need to be exhibited sequentially as 'ABC/2—mobile phone recovered from ABC/1'.

It is important to always refer back to the original exhibit to maintain continuity. Many computerized property recording systems, including the Home Office Large Major Enquiry System (HOLMES) cannot easily accommodate sub-exhibit numbering systems that give secondary numbers or letters to denote the item as a sub-exhibit for example, the mobile phone from the handbag being exhibited as ABC1/1 or ABC/1a. This is due to the restricted number of characters available for exhibit numbers on such systems.

If forensic analysis is required, it is likely that different parts of the exhibit will require analysis at different locations which is why items require 'splitting' or sub-exhibiting. Figure 3.7 illustrates the concept of sub-exhibiting and the demonstration of the continuity chain.

The continuity of all property seized must be maintained and sub exhibiting enables an accurate record of all the items seized to be generated and will demonstrate the continuity and integrity of the exhibit(s) throughout the investigation.

3.6 Chapter Summary

The initial recovery of any exhibit in an investigation is perhaps the most important time in the evidential chain. The handling, packaging and subsequent storage of the exhibit can have a huge impact on the investigation as a whole. If an exhibit is recovered, packaged and stored incorrectly there is a real risk that any potential forensic evidence will be lost or that a defence team could suggest that contamination and/or cross-transfer of the material has occurred. The key principles that should be foremost in an officer's mind when handling any exhibits are those of continuity and integrity.

The continuity and integrity of exhibits must be proved beyond reasonable doubt in a court of law and the value of these principles is only ever really appreciated when an exhibit is lost, damaged, destroyed or the evidence is devalued through failure to instigate and maintain the integrity and continuity of the exhibit at each stage.

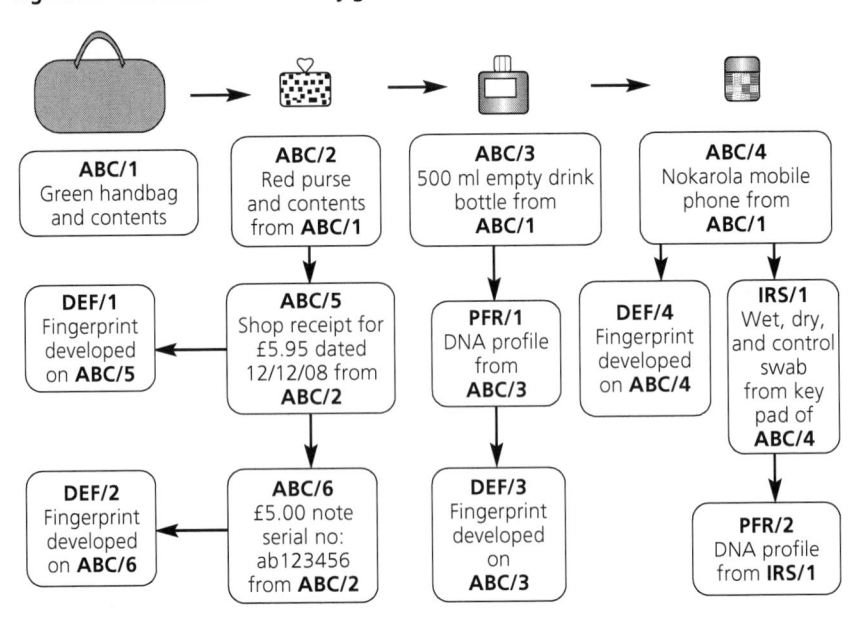

Figure 3.7 The chain of continuity generated from one initial exhibit

```
ABC/1                ABC/2              ABC/3                ABC/4
Green handbag    →   Red purse      →   500 ml empty drink  →  Nokarola mobile
and contents         and contents       bottle from             phone from
                     from ABC/1         ABC/1                   ABC/1
       ↑                  ↓                  ↓                       ↓
DEF/1                ABC/5              PFR/1                DEF/4                IRS/1
Fingerprint      ←   Shop receipt for   DNA profile          Fingerprint          Wet, dry,
developed            £5.95 dated        from                 developed            and control
on ABC/5             12/12/08 from      ABC/3                on ABC/4             swab
                     ABC/2                                                        from key
                                                                                  pad of
                                                                                  ABC/4
       ↑                  ↓                  ↓                                       ↓
DEF/2                ABC/6              DEF/3                                     PFR/2
Fingerprint      ←   £5.00 note         Fingerprint                               DNA profile
developed            serial no:         developed                                 from IRS/1
on ABC/6             ab123456           on
                     from ABC/2         ABC/3
```

Summary of personnel involved in the continuity chain

PC Arthur Brian Chalk recovers a handbag and contents, exhibited as ABC/1. The bag contains a purse, an empty drink bottle (ABC/3) and a mobile phone. The items are sub-exhibited and the following forensic examinations are undertaken.

Daniel Eric Fuller, the fingerprint development officer, recovers fingerprints on some of the items.

The CSI, Imogen Rita Somerton, swabs the mobile phone for possible DNA. The mobile phone is then submitted for fingerprint recovery.

The forensic scientist, Polly Fiona Roberts, generates DNA profiles from the swabs and the water bottle.

Each person must supply a continuity statement detailing their involvement with the exhibit.

It is vital that the continuity and integrity of exhibits can be demonstrated to show that no unaccountable interference with the exhibit could have occurred, accidentally or deliberately—not only for the purposes of the courts, but also for any forensic analysis to be undertaken. The forensic examination of an exhibit may be refused if the examiner or scientist is not satisfied that the continuity and integrity of an item is sufficiently robust. Accurate record keeping and appropriate packaging techniques are the first steps to ensuring the continuity and integrity of exhibits.

Officers must avoid dealing with items from more than one associated scene to prevent cross-transfer of material from a victim, for example, to a suspect. Records of the vehicle used to transport victims or suspects should be recorded

3.6 Chapter Summary

in the PNB. Where possible, items of potential forensic evidence should be left in situ for the CSI to record and recover. If such items must be moved to protect them from loss, damage or destruction their original position should be documented and the CSI informed where appropriate. The packaging of exhibits must protect the item from damage, destruction, contamination and/or cross-transfer and ensure that potential forensic evidence recovery is maximized.

All exhibits must be handled to the same standards irrespective of whether they are recovered during the investigation of a minor or serious offence.

KNOWLEDGE CHECK—EXHIBIT HANDLING

1. What are the key principles to be maintained when handling items of potential evidence?

   The process of demonstrating the continuity and integrity of the exhibit must be instigated by the officer who initially recovers the item.

2. State the ways in which the principles in Q1 can be applied.

   The continuity of an exhibit can be instigated by recording concise and accurate details of the item on the exhibit label and in the PNB. The minimum details required are an identifying reference or exhibit number, a description of the item noting any individualizing features, the time and date seized, the location from where the exhibit was taken and the name and signature of the person seizing the item. The continuity label must be completed by all those who subsequently handle the exhibit.

   The integrity of an exhibit begins with the completion of accurate documentation (continuity) and the application of the correct packaging techniques. The correct handling, packaging and storage of an exhibit can demonstrate that no unaccountable interference can have occurred, whether so caused accidentally or deliberately.

3. Explain the legislative provisions under s 19 PACE.

   PACE, s 19(2) provides that where a police officer is undertaking a search which is being undertaken lawfully under statutory powers, or by consent, they may seize anything on the premises providing that it is reasonably believed that it relates to the offence being investigated, or any other offence and that seizure is necessary to prevent concealment, loss, alteration or destruction of the potential evidence (s 19(3)(b)). This also applies to designated support investigators (CSI or support staff investigators, for example) under the Police Reform Act 2002.

4. State the method for packaging items suspected of containing accelerants.

   Nylon bags should be used in all cases where analysis for suspected accelerants is required. The exhibit is heated in an oven and the vapour analysed to establish

Chapter 3: Exhibit Handling

> the chemical composition of an accelerant, possibly the quantity of accelerant present in the sample and to potentially link it to other samples from different locations. Because it is the vapour that is analysed, nylon bags must be used as they are non-porous and will contain the vapour. The nylon bag must be sealed using the 'swan-neck' technique, and double bagged when the exhibit is wet or damp with possible accelerant, or the odour of accelerant is strong. Adhesive tape must not be used to seal nylon bags.
>
> 5. When should items of potential forensic evidence be moved/recovered by officers?
>
>   When a CSI is unavailable or will not be attending the scene or their attendance is delayed and the item is at risk of being lost, damaged or destroyed if left in its original position. The movement or recovery of such material must be documented and the CSI (if attending) be informed of any actions taken by the officer.

Summary of the National Occupational Standards (NOS) for the Student Officer Learning Assessment Portfolio (SOLAP) relating to this chapter

The table below indicates where it may be possible to demonstrate the achievement of certain performance criteria

NOS unit	Unit descriptor	Performance Criteria, Range, and Knowledge	Activity
1A1	Apply principles of reasonable suspicion or belief	**1A1.1** pc 1, 2, 3, 4, 5, **Range** all **1A1.2** pc 3, 4, 5, 6, 7 **Range** 1a, 1b, 2a, 2b **1A1.3** pc 1, 2, 3, 4, 5, 6, 7, 8 **Range** 1a, 1b, 2a–2d inclusive **Knowledge** 1, 2, 3, 8, 14	Operate within PACE, s 19 with regard to the seizure of items and with regard to ECHR.
2C1	Provide an initial police response to incidents	**2C1.1** pc 1, 2, 6 **Range** 1a–1g inclusive, 2c, 2d **2C1.2** pc 1, 2, 10, 11 **Range** 1a, 1b, 2a–2g inclusive **Knowledge** 1, 2, 3, 8, 19, 21, 22	Initial actions at a crime scene—identify nature of incident and any potential forensic evidence. Take action to ensure that potential forensic evidence is preserved.
2C3	Arrest, detain or report individuals	**2C3.1** pc 6, 8 **Range** 1a–1c inclusive **Knowledge** 2	Exhibit handling to prevent contamination or cross-transfer and with regard to the health and safety of others.
2G2	Conduct investigations	**2G2.1** pc 1, 3, 4, 5, 6, 12, 16 **Range** 1e, 2a–c, 3b, 4a–c inclusive, 5c, 7a, c, f **Knowledge** 1, 3, 14, 15, 16, 17, 19, 20, 24, 26, 27	The identification, recovery and preservation of potential forensic evidential material.

3.6 Chapter Summary

NOS unit	Unit descriptor	Performance Criteria, Range, and Knowledge	Activity
2G4	Finalize investigations	**2G4.1** 8, 12 **Range** 1c, 1e, 3b **Knowledge** 2, 3	Ensure items of potential evidential value are properly packaged and stored to maintain integrity and continuity.
2I1	Search individuals	**2I1.1** pc 10, 11, 13 **Range** N/A **Knowledge** 2, 5, 16 **2I2.2** pc 1, 2, 3, 7, 8, **Range** 1a, 1e, 2a **Knowledge** 2, 3, 4, 21, 22	Avoiding cross contamination or transfer of evidence and maintaining integrity and continuity of potential evidence, search for and appropriately recover items for forensic examination.
2J2	Prepare for court and other hearings	**2J2.1** pc 3 **Range** N/A **Knowledge** 4, 5	Demonstrate the continuity and integrity of relevant exhibits.
2K1	Escort detained persons	**2K1.1** pc 9 **Range** 3a, 3b, 4a, 4b **Knowledge** 12	Avoid cross-contamination or transfer of evidence and maintain integrity and continuity of potential evidence.
2K2	Present detained persons for custody process	**2K2.1** pc 7 **Range** 1d, 2a, 2b **Knowledge** 2, 3, 8	Avoiding cross-contamination/transfer of evidence and maintaining integrity and continuity of potential evidence.
4G2	Reduce the risks to health and safety in your workplace	**4G2.2** pc 3, 4, 5, 8, **Range** 1a **Knowledge** 6, 7, 8, 9, 10	Identify biological and other hazards when handling exhibits and ensuring the correct labelling of items is undertaken to alert others to the potential risks.

Recommended Further Reading

Evidence & Procedure (2008) Johnston, D and Hutton, G.
General Police Duties (2008) Hutton, G and McKinnon, G.
NPIA CSI course notes (2007) NPIA/National Training Centre for Scientific Support in Crime Investigation (NTCSSCI).
PACE—A Practical Guide to the Police and Criminal Evidence Act (2006) Ozin P, Norton H, and Spivey P.
The Police and Criminal Evidence Act 1984 (2007) Zander, M.
The Scenes of Crime Handbook (2004) The Forensic Science Service.

4

Forensic Evidence Recovery from Persons

4.1	Introduction	66
4.2	Forensic Material on Clothing	66
4.3	Recovery of Non-Intimate Samples from Persons in Custody	72
4.4	Firearm and Explosive Residue	78
4.5	Smartwater Recovery	80
4.6	Chapter Summary	82

Chapter 4: Forensic Evidence Recovery from Persons

4.1 Introduction

It is vital that potential evidence is recovered from suspects, victims and witnesses (where a witness may have had physical contact with suspects or victims) in order to corroborate or refute accounts of the incident in question.

There will always be a minimum of two 'scenes' arising from the commission of an offence: the location and the offenders. This number increases where a victim was involved at the time the offence occurred. During the commission of an offence, material will be transferred between the people involved and the location and vice versa.

The types of evidence transferred will depend on the particular offence. Generally, particulates such as glass, fibres, paint flakes, soils and body fluids are the types of potential evidence that may be recovered from victims, scene locations and suspects and where appropriate, witnesses. It is vital that the recovery of such evidence is undertaken in a systematic manner which ensures its integrity, continuity and evidential value.

Although this chapter deals primarily with the recovery of potential evidence and legislative provisions regarding suspects, the principles for recovering evidence are valid for a complainant, victim or witness for non-serious incidents.

The issues of consent regarding victims are such that it is not applicable to recover such samples by force or without consent. For sexual offences, a trained and qualified specialist such as a CSI or specially trained police officer such as a SOLO/SOTI should recover any potential forensic material. Force policies differ on this aspect of evidential recovery so it is important to establish local operating procedures regarding responsibility for recovery of potential forensic evidence from suspects, victims and witnesses.

> **Definition—SOLO and SOTI**
>
> SOLO – Sexual Offence Liaison Officer
>
> SOTI – Sexual Offence Trained Investigator

This chapter covers the practical techniques for the recovery of non-intimate samples for potential particulate evidence such as fibres, glass and soils for example, swabbing for visible body fluids, fingernail clippings and swabs, seizure and packaging of clothing and footwear, all of which are activities that may be undertaken by an officer or designated police staff.

4.2 Forensic Material on Clothing

One area where transfer of material can occur is within custody units, particularly in holding areas where material from one detainee is shed to be picked up on the clothing of subsequent detainees. Whilst it can be difficult to avoid such situations, it is not difficult to minimize the potential for cross-transfer of evidence in such situations by taking suspects believed to be involved in the same incident to different custody units for example. It is therefore vital that any potential evidence is recovered and preserved in a systematic and structured manner, in order to maximize the evidential value of any material recovered.

> **POINT TO NOTE—MINIMIZE TO MAXIMIZE**
>
> Minimize opportunity for transfer of material.
> Maximize the potential evidential value.

Particulate evidence such as glass, fibres, hair or paint flakes and body fluids such as blood or semen for example, can be retained on the clothing, hair and footwear of a person if they have been involved in an offence or been at the crime scene. The *location* of any potential evidence can be valuable in indicating a person's involvement (or otherwise) in an incident and can serve to corroborate or refute allegations. The location of such evidence is important, as illustrated in Chapter 11 with regard to the evidential value of the location of glass fragments on a person, which may indicate their involvement in an incident.

4.2.1 Footwear

Footwear worn by a person can potentially be matched to footwear marks found at crime scenes. The image of the sole of the footwear, or where applicable the footwear item itself, can be examined and potentially matched to footwear marks recovered from crime scenes. This information can be used to link a series of crimes, such as burglaries and can be beneficial intelligence. Although a 'match' between a suspect's footwear and footwear marks at a crime scene will not, on its own, necessarily put the *suspect* at the scene, it can provide intelligence which can lead to further lines of enquiry.

Footwear can also provide an investigator with evidence in the form of particulate traces such as glass, soil, fibres, paint flakes, body fluids and other materials from the crime scene or victim, that may be present on the footwear.

Impressions made by the footwear may be recovered from crime scenes and in some cases from the victim (on their clothing or in the form of bruising). Chapter 10 covers the evidential value and recovery techniques of footwear marks from crime scenes.

4.2.2 Recovery of footwear evidence

Footwear impressions may be taken and stored without a person being arrested, charged or reported for an offence where the impression is to be used for elimination purposes. In such circumstances, written consent from the person must be obtained and the person made aware that the recorded marks will be used in the investigation of crime.

Chapter 4: Forensic Evidence Recovery from Persons

> **POINT TO NOTE—HANDLING FOOTWEAR**
>
> Be aware of health and safety considerations. The shoes may have been contaminated by body fluids, sharp shards of glass and other material that could cause harm.
>
> Ensure gloves are worn when handling footwear and ensure the scanner plate or other area is thoroughly cleaned prior to and following the taking of the impression.
>
> This ensures the decontamination of the scanning area, reducing the potential for suggestions of cross-transfer of evidence and ensures that no grit or other debris creates a distortion of the image.
>
> Gloves should be changed between seizure of each item and packaged and exhibited where body fluids, firearm residue, drugs or explosives are suspected of being present.

The two main methods for the recording of footwear impressions in a custody unit are by the use of a dedicated flatbed scanner, which can enable the image to be sent electronically to the analyst for comparison with marks recovered from crime scenes, or by use of a specialist footwear recovery pad.

Avoid taking footwear impressions if it is suspected that there may be body fluids present on the soles of the footwear—seek advice from the CSI. In these circumstances, the CSI will photograph the footwear to include the sole and upper to record the footwear sole pattern and any other potential forensic evidence.

For a forensic laboratory comparison with footwear marks at crime scenes, the actual footwear item is far more beneficial than a photograph or similar image of the footwear sole.

The use of ink or WD40 applied to the soles of the shoes to capture the impression is not a viable or acceptable method for recovering impressions as it can lead to permanent damage of the footwear.

> **POINT TO NOTE—LEGISLATION COVERING THE TAKING OF FOOTWEAR IMPRESSIONS**
>
> The taking of footwear impressions is covered by PACE, s 61A(3).
>
> This enables officers to take impressions of a detainee's footwear in order to compare them with footwear marks recovered from crime scenes. Section 61 confers the power to specifically record the footwear impression with or without consent—providing that the person has been detained at a police station following arrest for, or charged (or reported) with a recordable offence, and that they have not previously had an impression taken during the investigation.
>
> Code D, para 4.18 allows for reasonable force to be used where appropriate, to take a footwear impression without consent, subject to specific conditions as set out in PACE.

4.2.3 Trace evidence on footwear

To seize footwear for trace evidence two sheets of clean paper are required. With the person standing on one piece, remove the first shoe ensuring the person then places the foot directly onto the second sheet of paper. Repeat the process with the other foot, as illustrated in Figure 4.1.

Figure 4.1 Recovering footwear from persons

This procedure minimizes the risk of any material picked up from the custody unit floor on the shoes being transferred to the sheet on which the person stands for the removal of clothing.

The person should then stand entirely on the second sheet of paper. The shoes and the first piece of paper should be exhibited (one shoe per paper bag, paper sheet as a separate exhibit).

The remaining clothes can then be removed with the person standing on the second sheet of paper which is clear of any possible transferred material from the custody unit floor. See Chapter 3 for appropriate packaging techniques for clothing.

> **POINT TO NOTE—SEIZURE OF SHOES**
>
> Where it is only the shoes that are being seized and not the socks or other clothing, the use of one piece of paper only is appropriate. It is advisable that the person stands on a piece of paper to remove footwear, as the action of removing the shoes can dislodge microscopic material which may provide potential evidence. Any such material will be dislodged onto the paper which can also be forensically examined.

Where shoes are to be searched at the custody desk, stand the person on a sheet of paper as above, and seize the shoes at this point. Provide the person with overshoes to wear to walk them to cells for recovery of clothing. Again, remove the overshoes prior to standing the person on a clean sheet of paper. Retain and exhibit the overshoes.

To seize the shoes of a complainant, the same principle as above can be adopted, however the use of the first piece of paper can be disregarded depending on the circumstances and location when seized, consider the possibility and implications of any potential transference of possible evidence.

The following principles apply to both a suspect and complainant:

- If glass is apparent on the uppers carefully tape over the area to retain the glass in situ. Make a note of any observations in your PNB, and indicate the presence of any possible glass on the exhibit label, for example, '*White "Reebok" trainer, size 9, left foot, with possible glass apparent on upper.*
- If body fluids such as blood are present, the advice of the CSI should be sought. In the first instance, a sketch showing the location of visible stains should be made, which needs to be exhibited. The CSI can photograph the footwear and undertake a presumptive blood test of the stains to establish if it is blood or not.

Dependant on the offence circumstances and in line with force policies, the stains may either be swabbed to recover potential DNA material or the footwear itself may be submitted to the forensic laboratory for analysis.

> **POINT TO NOTE—GLOVES**
>
> Gloves must be worn when recovering forensic samples and where DNA material is required, care must be taken not to breathe directly over the samples. Where possible, wear a disposable mask.
>
> Gloves should be changed between seizure of each item and packaged and exhibited where body fluids, firearm residue, drugs or explosives are suspected of being present.

4.2.4 Procedure for seizing clothing

Outermost layers of clothing should be removed first, as opposed to 'top to bottom' or 'bottom to top' sequences. Where a person is wearing a T-shirt tucked into trousers for example, the trousers should be removed before the top. This approach ensures that any potential forensic material that is trapped in folds of clothing is not dislodged by the action of pulling a T-shirt out from the waistband. See the illustration in Figure 4.2 below which represents an appropriate sequence for clothing removal.

Where it is known that there is a requirement for the clothing to be seized, belts should ideally not be removed when initially booking a detainee into custody. The clothing should, where *applicable and practicable*, be removed as soon as a detainee is put into a cell. There is the potential for a loss of material that could be trapped behind the belt if it is removed from the garment. However, health and safety considerations take precedence. Be mindful that potentially harmful items can also be concealed behind or within belts.

As each item of clothing is removed, where practicable, ask the person to drop each item into an evidence bag. Avoid shaking the garment—this will dislodge and lose potential evidence.

4.2 Forensic Material on Clothing

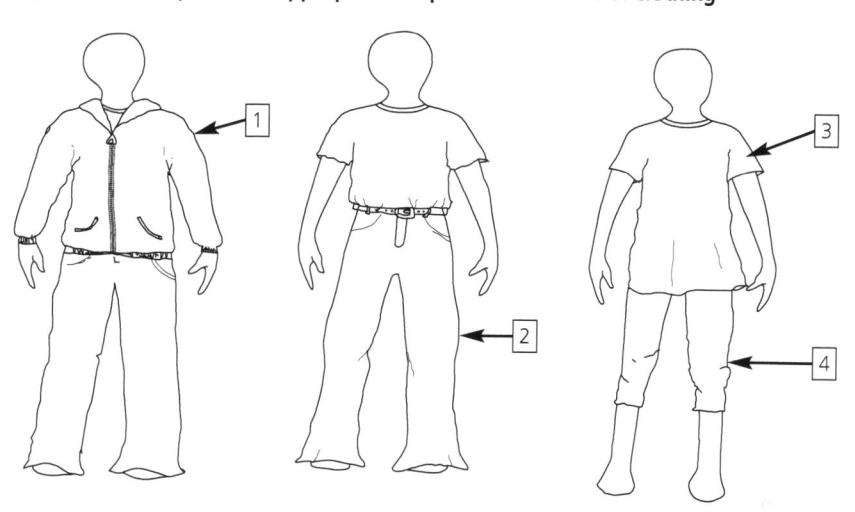

Figure 4.2 Example of the appropriate sequence for seizure of clothing

Where an item has an area of interest, such as a possible blood stain, rip or cut, this information should be recorded to show the location of such marks for the interviewing officers. Details of particular marks can go onto the exhibit label, for example;

'*1 x pair light blue Levi jeans, size 38, with apparent blood stain to lower right front hem*'

A sketch of the location of areas of interest should also be documented in your PNB or on a piece of notepaper which should then be exhibited.

Package items appropriately as per the packaging guidelines outlined in Chapter 3, Exhibit Handling.

> **POINT TO NOTE—INTEGRITY OF SEIZED ITEMS**
>
> Ensure all items seized are sealed in front of the donor to ensure continuity and integrity are maintained.
>
> Remember the defence teams have access to CCTV footage in custody units—it is not advisable to leave the cell area with open bags of clothing.

Where it is deemed appropriate to seize a person's clothing, they must be provided with replacement clothing of a reasonable standard of comfort and cleanliness—PACE, Code C, para 8.5 directs that no person can be interviewed unless adequate clothing has been provided for them. It is common practice within custody units to provide the detainee with paper suits in such circumstances.

4.3 Recovery of Non-Intimate Samples from Persons in Custody

The following techniques will enable recovery of potential evidence from persons, but *must not* be used where firearm residue/explosives residue evidence may be required. Specialist kits are available for the recovery of such evidence and advice of the CSI or designated officer should be sought in such cases, in line with force policy.

There may be occasions when it would be appropriate to take swabs of possible blood, for example, where a suspect is arrested for assault and they have apparent blood on them. This staining may need recovering before the suspect is placed in a cell and has the opportunity to remove it. Figure 4.3 details an appropriate technique for recovery of such visible staining.

Figure 4.3 Swabbing techniques

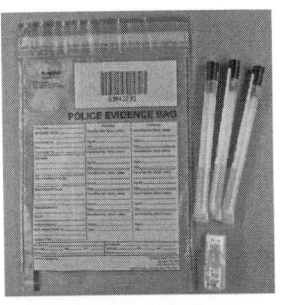

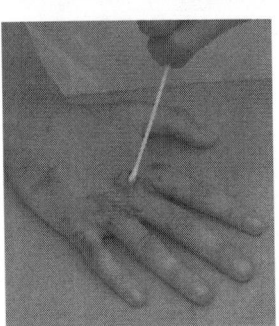

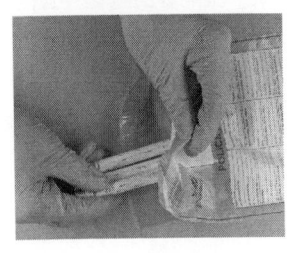

1. Requirements:
   - 3 x swabs
   - 1 x tamper evident bag
   - 1 x ampoule of sterile water
   (do not use water from any other source.)
2. Wearing gloves, snap open the water ampoule and drip 3–4 drops of water onto the swab.
   Drip the water onto the swab—never put swab into water container.
   Replace the moistened swab into the tube—this is your control swab.
3. Using a new swab moisten as in step 2.
   Rub over the stain using small circular movements—ensuring the stain is concentrated on the tip of the swab.
   Replace the swab in its tube and place in a tamper evident bag.
   Repeat the process with a dry swab.

The swab tubes should be individually labelled, for example:
   ABC/1—Control swab (wetted)
   ABC/1—Wet swab from back of right hand
   ABC/1—Dry swab from back of right hand
   All 3 swabs are exhibited as one item, for example
   ABC/1—Wet, dry and control swabs from ......
   Swabs should be stored in a freezer

4.3 Recovery of Non-Intimate Samples from Persons in Custody

Similarly a complainant may have stains upon them which require recovery as soon as possible to prevent loss or contamination of the potential evidence. The techniques illustrated are a basic minimum, force policies differ on the procedure regarding this and referral to a CSI is advisable if in doubt.

4.3.1 Intimate and non-intimate samples

The Police and Criminal Evidence Act 1984 (PACE) divides sample types into two distinct categories—intimate and non-intimate samples. The taking of intimate samples falls under PACE, s 62. This section states that, with the exception of urine, intimate samples must be taken by a registered medical practitioner. Dental impressions are classed as intimate samples and must only be taken by a registered dentist (s 62(9)). The taking of intimate samples will therefore not be covered.

Swabbing for visible body fluids and the recovery of hair and fingernail samples are classed as non-intimate samples, as prescribed by PACE, s 63.

Table 4.1 Summary of intimate and non-intimate samples

Sample type	Description	Conditions for sampling
Intimate samples	Blood, semen, any body tissue, pubic hair or a swab from any body orifice other than the mouth, dental impressions.	s 62 and Identification Code D s 6 PACE. Written consent required. Registered medical professional only to recover. In the case of dental impressions only a registered dentist to recover. Donor to be informed that samples may be subject to a speculative search.
Non–intimate samples	Saliva, hair (not pubic); samples from a nail or under a nail; body fluid traces on skin (non-intimate areas only); swabs from any part of the body including the mouth but not any other body orifice; footprint or similar impression of part of the body other than the hands.	s 63 and Identification Code D s 6 PACE. Can be taken by a police officer or designated police staff. Written consent required or without consent if necessary, with an inspector's authority. Reasonable force may be used. Donor to be informed that samples may be subject to a speculative search.

Figure 4.4 Fingernail sampling kit

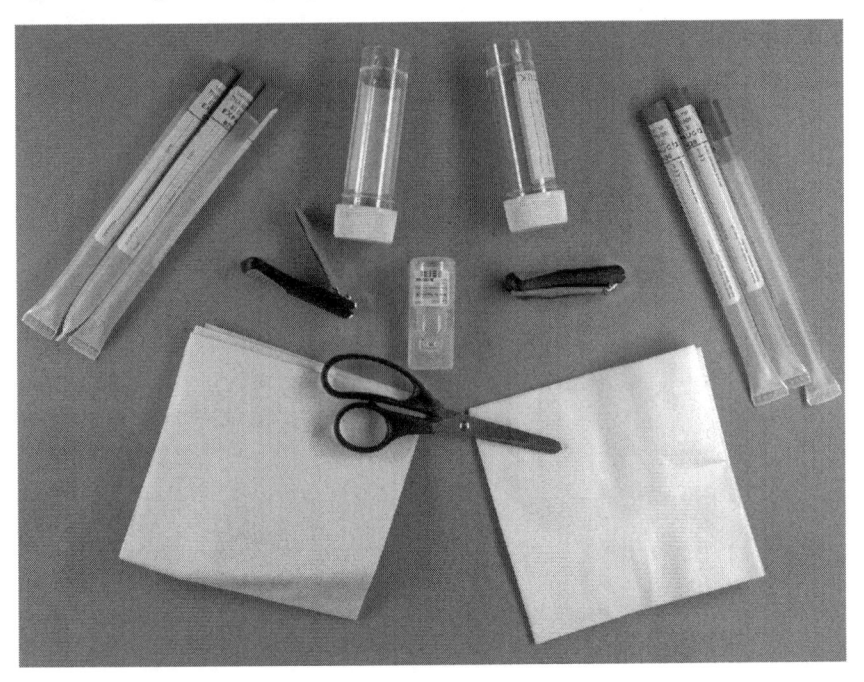

4.3.2 **Samples from fingernails**

Evidence such as body fluids, skin, fibres or paint for example can be recovered from fingernails. In addition, a physical fit of a fingernail may be undertaken where a broken fingernail is found at the scene.

The following techniques will ensure potential evidence recovery from the fingernails is maximized. Modules for this purpose are available from forensic suppliers. Forces differ on where the modules or individual items are kept, however many custody units report holding the items required in the medical examination room. It is advisable to confer with your CSI or forensic submissions officers to establish where the modules are stored within the force.

As a minimum, the requirements for recovery of potential evidence from fingernails should include two pieces of sterile paper, two pairs of fingernail clippers, swabs, water, and scissors and tamper-evident bags for packaging.

4.3.3 **Nail clippings**

Open a pack of clean or sterile paper and lay it out on a clean bench. Place the donor's hand over the paper and using the clippers, clip all the nails of one hand. Some clippers will retain the nails within the body of the clippers.

Return the clippers to the container in which they are supplied and place in a tamper-evident bag as illustrated in Figure 4.5.

4.3 Recovery of Non-Intimate Samples from Persons in Custody

Figure 4.5 Fingernail clipping

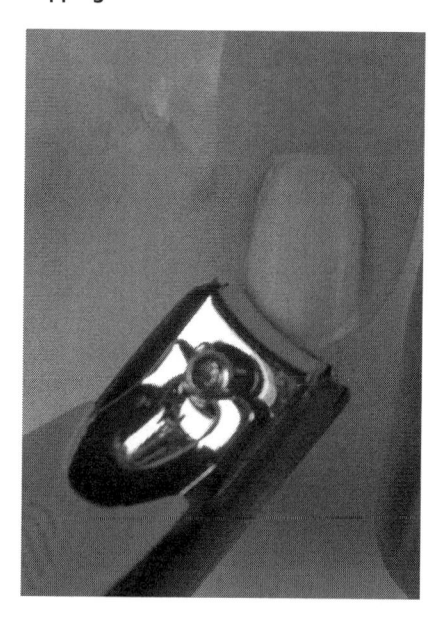

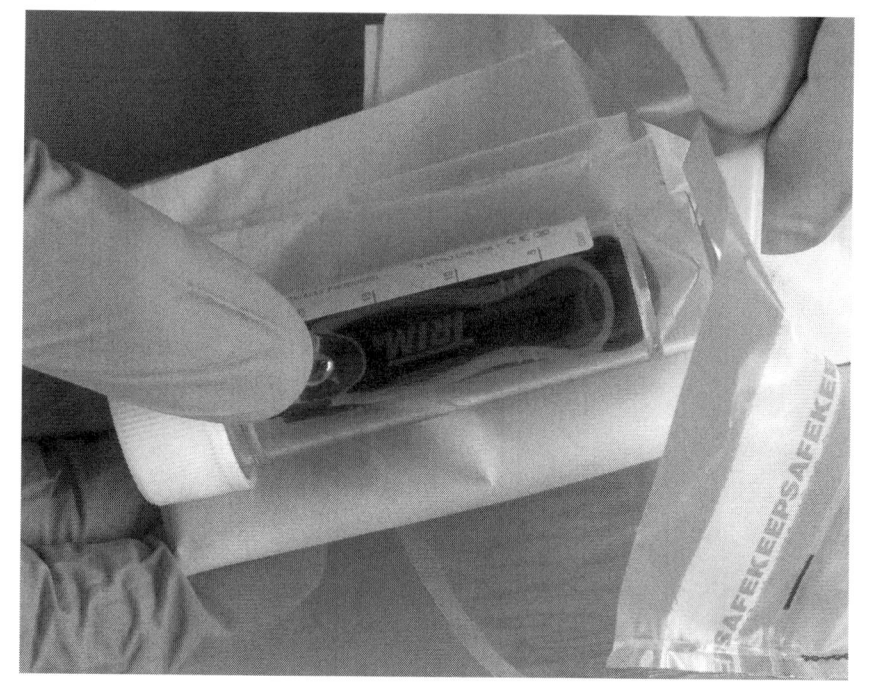

Carefully fold the paper, ensuring you retain any deposited material. Place this in the same bag as the clippers.

75

Exhibit as:

'ABC/1—fingernail clippings and paper cover from left hand of...'

Repeat the process for the other hand, which would be exhibited as, for example: *'ABC/2—fingernail clippings from right hand of...'*

Fingernail clipping exhibits should be stored in a freezer. *Note that if physical fit is required to a broken fingernail recovered at the scene, nails must be cut with scissors.*

Where nails are too short for clipping or it is not deemed appropriate, swabbing is an acceptable method to recover potential evidence.

4.3.4 Swabbing fingernails

You will need one control, one wet and one dry swab (see Figure 4.3 for details on swabbing techniques).

Place the donor's hand over a piece of sterile paper. Using a pointed ended swab moistened with sterile water, run the tip of the swab under each nail rim, the surface of the nails and around the cuticles, as illustrated in Figure 4.6. Use the edges of the swab as well as the tip of the swab to maximize the available surface area of the swab.

Repeat the process with a dry swab.

Package in tamper-evident bag and label as for example,

'ABC/3—Wet, dry & control swabs from fingernails of left hand of...'

Carefully fold the paper cover, ensuring you retain any debris, and place into a tamper-evident bag with the swabs. Repeat this process with the other hand if applicable.

The nail swabs exhibit should be stored in a freezer.

Figure 4.6 Fingernail swabs

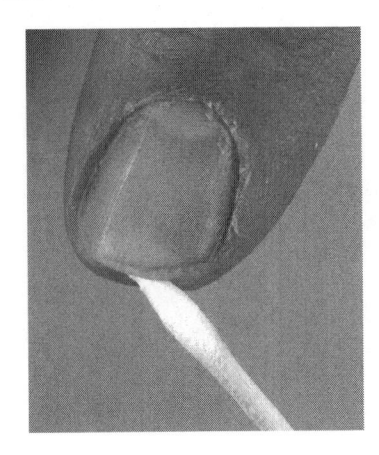

4.3 Recovery of Non-Intimate Samples from Persons in Custody

4.3.5 Hair collection modules

Hair can hold valuable evidence such as fibres, glass and body fluids as well as being useful for comparison with hairs recovered at a scene. Hair combings should be done prior to removal of any outer clothing in order to minimize any loss of potential evidence and transference onto lower clothing.

Figure 4.7 Hair sampling kit

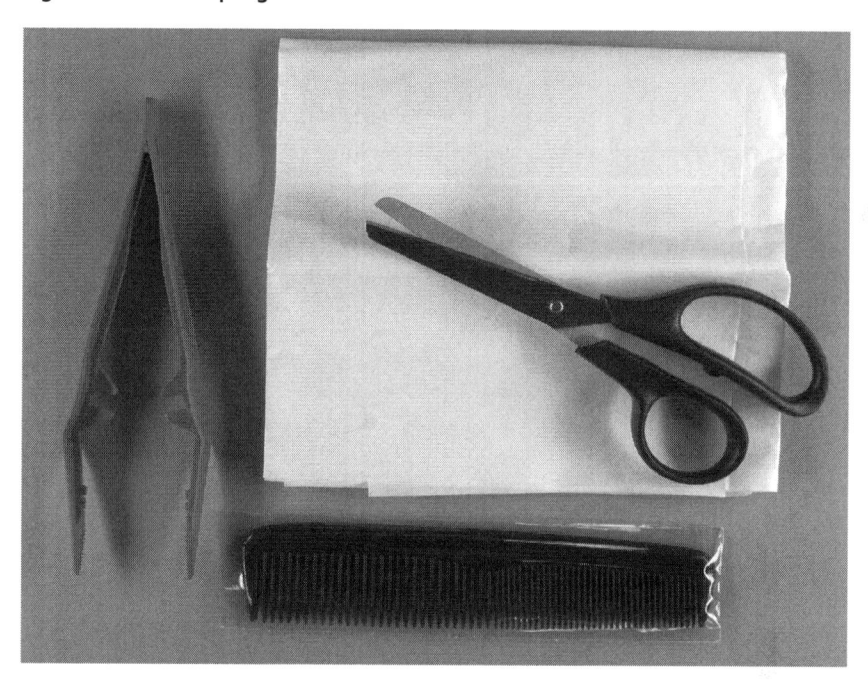

As a minimum, you will require:

- Sterile tweezers to remove visible foreign matter (fibres, etc).
- Comb.
- Sterile paper pack.
- Scissors.
- Swabs and water (if required).
- Tamper-evident bags, one for each exhibit to be taken.

For all recovery techniques from hair, place the piece of paper on a bench and ensure the donor's head is placed above the paper.

Recover any visible potential evidence such as fibres or glass for example, using tweezers or gloved fingers and place onto the paper sheet.

Comb through the hair using the comb or fingers of a gloved hand to loosen any particles. Any material should be collected on the paper cover, which should be carefully folded to retain the collected material.

Exhibit the paper and tweezers, scissors and/or comb (whichever has been used) in the same bag as one exhibit.

It is advisable to exhibit the gloves you have worn as a separate exhibit by placing them into a tamper-evident bag.

Depending on the offence/evidential needs, there different techniques for recovering certain materials from hair.

Body fluids

For the recovery of body fluids (blood or semen, for example) from hair, swabbing techniques can be used to recover any visible stain or the stained area cut out using scissors. Package swabs, paper and scissors if used in tamper-evident bag and store in freezer. (See Figure 4.3 for swabbing technique.)

Glass, fibres and other particulate material

For the recovery of glass, paint flakes or fibres for example, remove any visible material with tweezers or gloved fingers and place on the paper cover. Comb the hair over the paper cover to recover remaining material.

Carefully fold the paper to ensure any debris is retained and place into a tamper-evident bag with the tweezers and/or comb if used. It may also be useful to undertake a taping of the head using a low tack adhesive tape which is then secured to an acetate sheet. For tapings, the items can generally be obtained from your CSI. Exhibits should be stored in a dry store.

Hair comparisons

To recover a sample to be used to compare with hair recovered from a scene or for drug analysis, cut a minimum of 25 hairs, as close to the scalp as possible, from different places on the head. This ensures a representative sample of lengths and colours is obtained. Do not use tweezers to remove hair for comparison purposes as these may cause crushing to the surface of the hair.

Place the hair onto the paper cover. Carefully fold the paper containing the hair sample and place in tamper-evident bag. The exhibit should be stored in a dry store. Chapter 12 details the evidential potential of hair comparison.

4.4 Firearm and Explosive Residue

Firearm residue can be present on the hands and clothing of suspects. Force policies differ on who may recover such potential evidence, and in many cases such a process *must* be undertaken by a CSI or specifically trained specialist officer.

The techniques outlined are suitable for the recovery of firearm discharge residue from a suspect; however it is recommended that you seek advice from your CSI on the local policy for recovery of such material. Officers must not attempt to recover such residues unless they have received specialist training.

4.4 Firearm and Explosive Residue

Firearm residue can be present on the hands, face, hair and clothing of a person who has discharged a firearm or has been in close proximity to a discharged firearm. Chapter 9 outlines the potential evidence available regarding firearm and ballistic material.

> **POINTS TO NOTE—USE OF FIREARM RESIDUE KIT**
>
> - The sampling kit must be sealed prior to use—never use a kit that has previously been opened.
> - Any officer who has handled or been in the immediate vicinity of firearms, ammunition or explosives within the previous seven days must not recover samples or have contact with recovered items. Also consider whether you have visited the force armory or been in face to face contact with firearms officers in that period, as this may impact on the recovery of samples from a suspect. Do not use the kit if you are a regular user of firearms or explosives.
> - Samples need to be recovered as soon as possible after detention of a suspect and prior to fingerprint processing.
> - Consider cross-contamination and transfer—use different officers and locations where there is more than one suspect.
> - Roll up sleeves and thoroughly wash hands and forearms and wear a disposable overall prior to opening the kit.
> - Read and prepare the included paperwork within the kit before beginning the sampling process.
> - You *must* only use the items supplied in the kit. Make a note of the serial or batch number of the kit in your PNB.
> - Follow the instructions in the kit carefully.
> - Be aware that some people hold cultural beliefs that forbid contact with alcohol. It may not be applicable to use the solvent based kit in such situations. Kits which use a low tack adhesive material to collect the particles are available from forensic suppliers. Seek advice of the CSI manager or force diversity officer.

4.4.1 Using the firearm and explosive sampling kit

Depending on the incident being investigated, force policy will direct whether the sampling should take place in a specially prepared cell that has been deep cleaned.

It is advisable to wear a disposable paper scene suit for the sampling process to reduce the risk of cross-contamination. Thoroughly wash and dry hands and forearms. Open the kit and remove the paperwork. Prior to starting the sampling, ensure the paperwork is completed with the relevant details.

> **SAMPLING TECHNIQUE**
>
> - Put on the gloves supplied in the kit.
> - Take one swab and rub it over the front and back of the gloves you are wearing, replace the swab into its tube and label this as 'Control Swab'. This is to enable a scientist to check for any background contamination which may have come from the gloves or your hands as you put them on. Place swab into exhibit bag.
> - Using a second swab, rub over the face and neck of the suspect, including the eyebrows. Take care not to get the solvent from the swab into the eyes of the suspect. Replace the swab into its tube which should be labelled with the words 'FACE' and 'NECK'. Place swab into exhibit bag.
> - Comb through the hair and any beard or moustache with the supplied comb. The comb will have a piece of material threaded through it that has been pre-wetted with solvent. Where a suspect has no hair, or it is difficult to comb, wipe the sides of the comb with the swab material over the head. Replace the comb, with the swab material attached, back into the plastic bag it came in. Place this into the exhibit bag.
> - Using a clean swab, rub the front and back of the suspect's right hand—paying particular attention to the web of the thumb, between fingers and underneath any jewellery. (Watches and rings should have been removed and exhibited separately.) Label the swab as being from the right hand. Place swab into exhibit bag. Repeat the process for the left hand.
> - Remove the nail scraper and gauze from its bag. Taking one finger at a time, hold the finger over the gauze and scrape the debris from the nail, wiping the scraper on the gauze after each nail. Replace the gauze and scraper into the bag it came in and place this into the exhibit bag.
> - Ensure each item is properly sealed before sealing the exhibit bag.
> - Remove gloves when sampling is complete, these can be placed into a separate bag and exhibited.

4.5 Smartwater Recovery

Smartwater is a solution which contains a unique code specific to a particular location. The Smartwater system is a product of the Forensic Science Service (FSS). The solution, called Index solution can be used in a sprinkler type system which can be activated in the event of a burglary, for example. Anyone and anything in the immediate vicinity will be sprayed with the uniquely coded solution.

Once dry the solution is only visible by ultraviolet light, where it will fluoresce as blue/white or green/yellow colour (depending on the product). In custody units equipped with ultraviolet light, spray patterns of the Index solution may be visible on a suspect's clothing, skin and hair.

In addition to Smartwater Index solution, a product which can be applied to property of value is Smartwater Tracer. This uniquely identifies the property much as a fingerprint or DNA profile can identify a person, due to the unique properties of the Tracer. Smartwater Instant is a recent development to the Tracer, for the identification of property. This contains particles containing unique combinations of numbers which can be viewed by officers with a good quality magnifier.

4.5.1 Recovery of Smartwater from scenes and suspects

Where Smartwater activation has occurred at premises, the CSI will thoroughly examine the area with an ultraviolet light source, to search for any footwear patterns and fingerprints that may be present. The CSI will photograph and/or video the scene and recover samples from key areas. The activated canister must be recovered in order for the scientist to establish the link between the scene and any suspects.

Samples of Tracer on larger, less portable items can be recovered from stolen property by the CSI who can either swab or take scrapings from the stained area, although ideally the entire item should be submitted to the scientist for examination where possible.

The recovered samples will be examined and identification made as to the registered owner of the property from which the Smartwater product originated. The comparison of the samples enables a link to be established between suspects and scenes.

The unique serial numbers in the product can then be forwarded to the FSS who can check the database and identify the registered user and establish where the property originated.

Where Smartwater products are located on a suspect, the following points require consideration:

- The fluorescence under ultraviolet light must be recorded by photography or video by the CSI or suitably qualified specialist photographer, prior to the recovery of clothing.
- Other substances can cause fluorescence, such as the whitening products in some washing powders, urine and semen for example.
- Areas of skin that display Smartwater fluorescence should be swabbed with the appropriate Smartwater swabbing kit. Smartwater products are not water soluble; therefore using water to swab the area will not successfully recover the required material. Swabbing should be undertaken by a CSI or specifically trained officer.
- Clothing should be packaged as per the guidance in Chapter 3, taking into consideration any other potential forensic evidence. Clothing containing Smartwater products must always be packaged in brown paper evidence sacks.
- The use of ultraviolet light for the examination and recording of Smartwater products should ideally be undertaken by a CSI or other suitable trained person due to the potential for the risk of harm from the incorrect use of ultraviolet light sources.

> **POINT TO NOTE—HUMAN RIGHTS LEGISLATION: ECHR CONSIDERATIONS**
>
> It is important to be conscious of the provisions of the Human Rights Act 1998 when conducting the searching and seizure of possessions, in particular
>
> - Article 1 of the 1st protocol—'Every natural or legal person is entitled to the peaceful enjoyment of his possessions.' Therefore officers must ensure that they can justify, with lawful reason, the seizure of detainees' possessions.
> - Article 3 ECHR directs that 'No-one shall be subjected to torture or to inhuman or degrading treatment or punishment.' It is important to ensure a person is not put in a position where embarrassment could be caused by removal of clothing.
>
> Officers must be able to justify their actions and ensure such are necessary, legal and proportionate. It is also important to be aware of cultural issues and show sensitivity to ensure that a person's beliefs or religious beliefs are not unnecessarily compromised.

4.6 Chapter Summary

People who have been involved in an incident will have material upon them that can link them to the location and to others involved in the incident. By considering suspects, victims and where appropriate, witnesses as crime scenes, the potential for the recovery of forensic material is maximized.

Witnesses who have given first aid to an injured victim or who have held on to a suspect for example may have potential forensic material upon them. It is always worth considering this potential where the circumstances of the incident dictate.

As Locard's 'Principle of Exchange' is based on the assumption that 'every contact leaves a trace', it is important that officers consider the impact of their actions when dealing with persons involved in incidents.

A lot of forensic material is microscopic and can easily be transferred. It is imperative therefore that steps are taken to minimize any cross-transfer by dealing with only one aspect of the incident where evidence of contact is required. Officers who deal with a victim must not then deal with a suspect during that particular shift for example.

The methods for the recovery of firearm or explosive residues can only be undertaken by a CSI of specifically trained officer to ensure the integrity of any potential evidence recovered.

> **KNOWLEDGE CHECK—FORENSIC SAMPLING OF PERSONS**
>
> 1. A suspect is arrested for criminal damage to a vehicle by spraying paint onto the vehicle and breaking the windows with a piece of rough wooden fencing post. The piece of wood and spray paint can are recovered at the scene.

4.6 Chapter Summary

> What potential evidence could be available to link this suspect with the crime scene?
>
> Glass on footwear (soles and uppers) and clothing and possibly in hair from the vehicle.
> Paint on the suspect's hands/clothes can be compared with paint at the scene.
> Fingerprints of the suspect on the paint can and/or on the vehicle.
> Comparison of wood fragments on the suspect with the fencing post.
> Fibres from the suspect's clothing on the vehicle/paint can/fencing post.
> It must be considered that in many cases the potential evidence recovered may not be submitted for forensic analysis.
>
> 2. In the scenario given in Q1, what items would you consider for recovery from the suspect, as a minimum?
>
>   Footwear, hair combings, outer layers of clothing for examination for glass, paint and possibly wood fragments, photography of any paint on hands by CSI, fingerprints and DNA.
>
> 3. What samples can you recover as non-intimate samples with regard to PACE, s 63?
>
>   Hair (not pubic), urine, swabs from skin from non-intimate areas, swabs from any part of the body, including the mouth but not any other body orifice, saliva.
>
> 4. Who can take intimate samples in accordance with PACE, s 62?
>
>   Registered medical professional or, registered dentist for dental impressions.
>
> 5. Who can take non-intimate samples in accordance with PACE, s 63?
>
>   Police officers or designated police staff.

Summary of the National Occupational Standards (NOS) for the Student Officer Learning Assessment Portfolio (SOLAP) relating to this chapter

The table below indicates where it may be possible to demonstrate the achievement of certain performance criteria.

NOS unit	Unit descriptor	Performance Criteria, Range, and Knowledge	Activity
2C1	Gather information and plan a response	**2C1.1** pc 1, 3 **Range** 2c **2C1.2** pc 1, 2, 8, 10 **Range** 2a–2g inclusive **Knowledge** 1, 2, 3, 7, 8, 16, 21	Liaison with CSI. Liaison with CSI, preservation of the scene.

Chapter 4: Forensic Evidence Recovery from Persons

NOS unit	Unit descriptor	Performance Criteria, Range, and Knowledge	Activity
2C3	Arrest, detain or report individuals	**2C3.1** pc 1, 3, 4, 5, 6, 8. **Range** 1a **Knowledge** 1, 2, 3, 4, 7	Take forensic samples within legislative boundaries.
2G2	Conduct investigations	**2G2.1** pc 1, 2, 3, 4, 5, 6, 12, 13, 15, 16 **Range** 1e, 2a –2c, 3b, 4a, b, c, 5c, 7a, c **Knowledge** 1, 3, 9, 10, 15, 16, 17, 18	The identification and recovery of appropriate forensic samples in line with the circumstances of each case.
2G4	Finalize investigations	**2G4.1** pc 2, 7, 8, 9, 11, 12 **Range** 1c, 3b **Knowledge** 1, 2, 8	Ensure items of potential evidential value are properly packaged and stored to maintain integrity and continuity.
2I1	Search individuals	**2I1.1** pc 4, 10, 11 **Range** N/A **Knowledge** 1, 8, 16	Avoid cross-contamination or transfer of evidence and maintain integrity and continuity of potential evidence.
2K1	Escort detained persons	**2K1.1** pc 9 **Range** 3b **Knowledge** 12	Avoid cross-contamination or transfer of evidence and maintain integrity and continuity of potential evidence.
2K2	Present detained persons for custody process	**2K2.1** pc 7 **Range** 1d, 2b **Knowledge** 8	Avoid cross-contamination or transfer of evidence and maintain integrity and continuity of potential evidence.
4G2	Reduce the risks to health and safety in your workplace	**4G2.2** pc 2, 5 **Range** 1a **Knowledge** 1, 2, 4, 6, 8, 10	Identifying biological and other hazards when sampling persons and ensuring the correct labelling of items is undertaken to alert others to the potential risks.

Recommended Further Reading

PACE—A Practical Guide to the Police and Criminal Evidence Act (2006) Ozin P, Norton H, and Spivey P.
The Police and Criminal Evidence Act 1984 (2007) Zander, M.
The Scenes of Crime Handbook (2004) The Forensic Science Service.

5

Fingerprints

5.1	Introduction	86
5.2	Types of Fingerprint Evidence at Crime Scenes	86
5.3	The Role of the CSI in the Recovery of Fingerprint Evidence	88
5.4	Chemical Development Techniques for Fingerprint Recovery	89
5.5	The Role of the Fingerprint Identification Officer	93
5.6	National Fingerprint Database—Ident 1	94
5.7	Taking Fingerprints	97
5.8	Chapter Summary	102

Chapter 5: Fingerprints

5.1 Introduction

Fingerprints may be considered as the most important type of forensic evidence as they are both individualizing and identifiable evidence—it is possible to identify a person by their fingerprints. Fingerprints are routinely used to compare marks at crime scenes with those on the national database to potentially identify a suspect, in the identification of an unknown deceased, to eliminate persons from an investigation, and as means of confirming or establishing identity for immigration purposes.

The skin on the underside of the feet and the palms and fingers of humans and other primates is ridged to ensure a better gripping surface, and the patterns created by these ridges are referred to as 'friction ridge details'. The patterns formed by the ridges contain individual characteristics which has enabled the development of a robust classification system for the comparison of fingerprints. The patterns and characteristics that are created by friction ridge skin are developed in the womb, remaining unchanged throughout life, and in some circumstances for some time after death. No two people have been found to have the same fingerprints in over 100 years of the fingerprint classification system being utilized, thus fingerprinting is a widely accepted means of identification.

When an item is handled a transfer of materials secreted from the skin occurs to leave a contact pattern that can potentially be developed to enhance the visualization of fingerprint ridge details, thus making fingerprints an ideal form of forensic evidence to link a suspect to a crime scene. In addition, fingerprints are routinely used to establish and/or confirm the identity of deceased persons.

The skin on the underside of the feet contains friction ridge skin and can be used for comparison purposes but as yet there is not a national database for comparison or identification purposes. If required, comparisons can be made between a suspect's bare footprint and a bare footprint found at a crime scene.

This chapter will cover the use of fingerprint evidence in the police service, the types of potential fingerprint evidence typically found at crime scenes, the techniques used to recover such fingerprints and the procedures and legislation for taking fingerprints for comparison purposes.

5.2 Types of Fingerprint Evidence at Crime Scenes

The recovery of finger or palm print evidence at a crime scene can establish the identity of persons involved. Palm prints are now routinely used in the same way as fingerprints; throughout this chapter the references to fingerprints includes palm prints.

It is important to be aware that whilst a fingerprint recovered on a surface is evidence that a particular person has touched the surface *at some time*, the absence of fingerprints does not mean that a person *has not* touched the item. A person may handle an item and leave no recoverable fingerprints, due to the many variables that can affect the amount of secretions available to transfer to a surface. The amount of residue available tends to be depleted for each successive touch meaning a transferred latent fingerprint will become progressively weaker and more difficult to recover. Some people may not secrete sufficient amounts of specific materials required for the recovery techniques to be successful. The pressure used and the surface handled are also variables affecting the potential recovery of fingerprints.

There are broadly three categories of fingerprint evidence typically recovered from crime scenes.

5.2.1 Latent

'Latent' means 'invisible' and such marks cannot be readily seen with the naked eye. Latent fingerprints are made up of the secretions of perspiration from the sweat pores situated along the ridges. Research by Fortunato et al, reported that the perspiration from the sweat glands on the ridged skin of the hands and feet consists of 99.0–99.5% water and 0.5–1.0% organic and inorganic substances such as salts, amino acids, fats, and urea. The deposits left by a fingerprint are typically in the region of a tenth of a milligram, according to research by Menzel et al. When the water constituent in the print evaporates this leaves, at best, nanograms of material for a CSI to detect and recover. Sebaceous oils from the face and hair may also be present in latent prints where a person has touched their face or hair prior to handling an item or surface.

This type of fingerprint requires some form of process to enable it to be visualized. At the scene, a CSI can use powders on clean, dry, smooth non-porous surfaces as the powders adhere to the fats, oils and water contents left behind. This enables the resulting marks to be lifted with a low tack adhesive tape which can then be secured to a clear acetate sheet. These are referred to as fingerprint lifts which are then forwarded to the fingerprint officers (FPOs) for comparison with marks available on the national database, Ident 1.

Chemical development techniques are available for the recovery of potential fingerprints where powders may not be the appropriate method to employ.

5.2.2 Visual marks

This type of fingerprint generally is deposited in a substance that contrasts with the surface on which it is deposited. Such marks are found where a substance such as paint, ink, cosmetics or blood for example, is transferred by the fingers onto a suitable surface. These marks can be photographed and the photograph be forwarded to the FPO. In some cases the mark may be subject to further development in order to improve the contrast between the mark and the surface it is on and potentially develop further details which are not always visible. Where possible the item containing the mark should be recovered and exhibited.

5.2.3 Impressed marks

These are three-dimensional marks which do not rely on the deposition and transfer of a substance. They are formed when a three-dimensional impression of the ridge skin is made in a suitably soft material such as putty, wax, chocolate or part dried paint, for example. Such marks can be photographed and then photographs forwarded to the fingerprint identification team for comparison and identification. Where possible the item containing the mark should be recovered and exhibited.

5.3 The Role of the CSI in the Recovery of Fingerprint Evidence

The examination for any potential evidence will be undertaken with regard to employing the appropriate recovery methods in a sequence that begins with the least destructive method being utilized first. This is referred to as sequential processing, which will typically follow the following steps:

A. Visual examination

  Following a visual search to locate the potential evidence, including a search with the appropriate light sources, the CSI will record an accurate description of the location of any visual marks, including measurements which show the position of the fingerprint in relation to a fixed point in the scene notes.

B. Photography

  A photograph of the mark in situ may be taken prior to any further process being undertaken. This is particularly useful for visible marks that could be destroyed/altered by further processing techniques, for example where the mark is in a substance believed to be blood. Following photography, swabs can be taken from an area of the fingerprint that is not necessary for comparison purposes. A presumptive blood test can be undertaken to establish the likelihood of the substance being blood. It is vital in such circumstances that a photographic record is made prior to and following the swabbing or other technique utilized at each stage in order to demonstrate the integrity and continuity of the mark.

C. Processing

  The CSI will employ the most appropriate technique for the recovery of the fingerprint(s). If the surface is clean, dry, inflexible and non-porous such as a window pane or gloss painted door, the CSI will generally use powders to search for and recover marks. The powdered marks when located, may be photographed in situ prior to being recovered either on a low tack clear adhesive tape which is then transferred onto a clear acetate sheet or the mark can be lifted onto a gelatine lifter, depending on the surface. Where appropriate, the item containing the mark should be recovered and exhibited.

5.4 Chemical Development Techniques for Fingerprint Recovery

The CSI has a range of different powders that will be effective in various circumstances and will utilize the most appropriate technique. Where fingerprints cannot be recovered using powders, such as on porous surfaces like writing paper, cardboard or pliable items such as plastic bags for example, the CSI will submit these items for chemical development of potential fingerprints (see section 5.4 below for the chemical development techniques available).

5.4 Chemical Development Techniques for Fingerprint Recovery

Items recovered from a scene can be submitted to the chemical fingerprint development laboratory, or equivalent, which will utilize the application of chemical techniques to recover fingerprints and other marks, such as footwear from submitted items. Whilst this is a key role of most in-force police laboratories, other techniques may be available within your own force laboratory, for example—the examination of documents for indented writing and/or alterations, the initial screening for body fluids or fibres utilizing light sources, and recovery of erased marks

One of the least destructive methods for locating fingerprints is a search utilizing high intensity forensic light sources. The light sources are an excellent screening tool when searching for body fluids such as semen (see Chapter 6) and can also be utilized where other techniques are not appropriate to detect traces of fluorescent material that may have been deposited from the hands.

Case study—Locating fingerprints with light sources

Stolen property was recovered from a burglary of a manor house. Many of the items recovered were of extremely high monetary value and rarity, which excluded any use of the traditional fingerprinting techniques such as powders or chemicals.

Some of the items were examined with a range of forensic light sources and areas of ridge detail were located and photographed. These areas were then swabbed to recover any potential DNA material. The light sources enabled a targeted approach to the recovery of potential evidence without causing any damage to the items examined.

5.4.1 Chemical development techniques

The laboratory technicians are trained to examine items to establish the most appropriate techniques to use, with regard to the nature of the items submitted, the requirements of the case and with full regard for other potential forensic evidence types. The same principles of sequential processing as those used by a CSI are followed—employing the least destructive method first. The techniques applied will be in line with the Home Office Scientific Development Branch

(HOSDB) guidelines for approved methods of fingerprint recovery as outlined in this section.

The methods utilized will be dependant initially on the type of surface of the item to be examined. Items received into the laboratory typically fall into two distinct categories of surface type—porous and non-porous—which initially determines the process used.

5.4.2 Porous items

Items such as paper (bank notes, envelopes, etc), plasterboard, uncoated cardboard, raw untreated wood, etc can be submitted for examination. Following a visual examination and appropriate photography of any marks, the following techniques are available:

- 1,8 Diazafluoren-9-one (DFO) and ninhydrin

These two reagents react with the amino acid secretions in latent fingerprints and can also be useful for developing marks in blood. The use of both these techniques, in sequence, can lead to the development of more fingerprints than may be possible with just one of the methods. DFO must be used before ninhydrin if both methods are to be employed. For the development of blood marks, DFO can be used for porous surfaces only whereas ninhydrin may be used on porous or non-porous surfaces.

- Physical developer

This technique can be used after the application of DFO and ninhydrin. The physical developer reacts with non-soluble sebaceous materials, which can generally be recovered after an item has been wet. It is important to inform the laboratory technicians when it is known an item has been recently wet, so that they can apply the appropriate technique.

5.4.3 Non-porous items

Items in this category include bottles, vehicle cowlings and plastic bags. The techniques available for these items are as follows:

- Vacuum metal deposition (VMD)

This process is the most effective single process that can be employed for recovering fingerprints on many non-porous items even when the fingerprints are very old and small deposits of secreted or deposited material are present. It can also be successfully employed on items that are known to have been wet. It is a relatively expensive process, and not every in-force laboratory will have the capability to undertake this process. This process is generally utilized for serious cases rather than for routine volume crime work.

- Superglue (cyanacrolate fuming)

The item is placed into a purpose built humidifying cabinet with a foil dish containing a small amount of superglue. The superglue fumes bind to the aqueous

5.4 Chemical Development Techniques for Fingerprint Recovery

(water) components of a fingerprint to form a hard white coloured crust on the available ridge details. This can then be stained with a fluorescent dye and any viable marks photographed. As superglue adheres to the aqueous component in a fingerprint it cannot be used to successfully develop fingerprints on items that have been wet. The use of the superglue should be undertaken as soon as is practicable—prolonged storage of an item may result in the evaporation of the water and therefore a reduction in the opportunity to recover viable fingerprints.

- Sudan black

Sudan black is a dye which stains the fat content of latent fingerprints and is particularly useful for the development of greasy marks such as those on food packaging such as takeaway boxes, crisp packets and the dried residues of soft drinks on cans or bottles.

- Small particle reagent (SPR)

This adheres to the fatty components in a fingerprint secretion and can be used where an item has been previously wet. It is more effective on recent marks rather than older ones.

- Powder suspensions

This technique is a simple and effective technique, particularly useful for recovering fingerprints on the sticky side of adhesive tapes, and can be used on items that have been wet.

- Gentian violet

This process is effective for the development of latent marks on the sticky side of adhesive tapes and on surfaces contaminated with oils and grease. As gentian violet contains a toxic chemical—phenol—the use of large quantities is to be avoided.

5.4.4 Marks in blood

When an item is received in the laboratory, and there is no prior forensic confirmation that the stain is blood, a presumptive test for blood may be undertaken. Depending on the circumstances of the case, the laboratory technician may contact the investigating officer in the case to inform of the possible presence of blood. If deemed appropriate, there are chemical development techniques available for the development of marks in blood, as detailed in Chapter 7.

Where an item contains potential body fluids, the outer packaging must be clearly labelled to indicate a biohazard may be present.

> **POINT TO NOTE**
>
> It is vital that you indicate where known, if an item *has been* previously wet, even if dry when you recover it. Be aware that substantial moisture (dew) can be absorbed

Chapter 5: Fingerprints

> by a porous item if left out overnight even when the weather conditions are dry. Please mark on the packaging if the item is known to have been wet—this will maximize the chance of developing marks.

Some items will not fall neatly into one category, for example a cardboard box that has a shiny surface and an interior of matte porous cardboard. The laboratory team will ensure that the sequence in which items are processed will maximize the forensic potential.

5.4.5 The impact of chemical development techniques on other forensic evidence types

When an item is received into the chemical development laboratory, it should be closely examined for any other potential forensic evidence such as the presence of fibres, body fluids such as blood and any other evidential material that may be appropriate to the investigation. In many cases the laboratory technician will recover such material in the appropriate manner in consultation with the CSI or OIC.

When an item is recovered that bears possible body fluids, it is important that consideration is given to whether any possible DNA material needs to be recovered. Swabbing an item to recover DNA material can destroy any latent fingerprint ridge detail that may be present on the item, so the issue of maximizing potential evidence requires consideration prior to submitting for chemical development techniques.

Research reported by Lee and Gaensslen (2001) and the Home Office Scientific Development Branch (HOSDB) has shown that DNA material can be recovered from blood and latent fingerprint secretions on items following one single chemical development technique. Where an item is to undergo any chemical development techniques and DNA analysis is required, it is important to discuss the particular case with the appropriate forensic science service provider who will advise on the best sequence to follow. Where chemical development techniques are utilized prior to DNA analysis it is vital that the forensic service provider receives the item as soon as possible following a chemical development process in order to maximise the potential for recovery of DNA material.

Case study—Chemical fingerprint process and DNA recovery

Several self seal plastic bags containing white powder were recovered and exhibited by police officers. The exhibits went first to the forensic service provider to establish the identity of the powder in the bags with a request to 'preserve packaging for fingerprints' made on the submissions form.

The forensic service provider decanted the powder from the self seal bags, which were sub-exhibited and returned to the in-force laboratory for fingerprinting.

> The superglue technique was employed on the self seal plastic bags and areas of ridge detail were developed. Unfortunately the quality of the developed ridge detail was insufficient for the fingerprint officers to make a comparison.
>
> The bags were then returned to the forensic service provider with a request that DNA analysis be undertaken on the developed areas of ridge detail. The developed ridge detail enabled the scientist to target the search for potential DNA material with the result that two DNA profiles were recovered from these areas.
>
> Ideally DNA analysis should be undertaken first with the request to 'preserve for fingerprints' made on the submissions form. The forensic service provider will perform their analysis and either undertake the fingerprint recovery process or return the item to the force for fingerprinting.
>
> Consultation with the CSI or laboratory technician and the forensic service provider is recommended to establish the sequence to be followed to maximize the recovery of all potential evidence.

Many of the chemicals used to develop fingerprints can be hazardous to health, and it is important to be aware of the force policy in place regarding the return of items to the lawful owner after such processes have been employed. Some forces have a blanket policy which dictates that no items can be returned to the owner after chemical development techniques have been utilized. It is recommended that a victim of crime is made aware that such processes can lead to the item being permanently damaged. Recovered stolen property may have sentimental value to the owner and it is important that care and consideration is shown with how this is processed. Ensure the laboratory technicians are aware of any such issues in order that consideration can be given to employing less destructive methods where appropriate.

It is possible for many of the chemical development techniques to be utilized at a crime scene by fully trained operatives. However, there are health and safety implications with such procedures including the requirement to decontaminate any premises in which chemical development techniques are utilized. Such examinations would typically be used for serious incidents and may require the authorization of a senior investigating officer.

Once fingerprints have been recovered, either by a CSI at the crime scene or by the use of chemical development techniques, the next stage is to submit the marks to the fingerprint identification officer for the comparison and identification procedure.

5.5 The Role of the Fingerprint Identification Officer

The fingerprint identification officer will receive the fingerprints lifted, or scanned directly from the crime scene and photographs of any chemically developed fingerprints from the chemical development laboratory. These marks will be checked against any elimination marks provided and then, if not eliminated and of sufficient quality, they are scanned onto the national fingerprint database known as Ident 1 (formerly known as NAFIS—National Automated Fingerprint Identification System).

When a fingerprint identification officer receives a fingerprint mark, by means of an electronic image, fingerprint lift or photograph, the individual characteristics present in the mark are located and the mark is then scanned or transferred onto the database. The Ident 1 system searches the database to present the fingerprint identification officer with a list of 15 possible suspects. It is then down to the expertise of the fingerprint identification officer to determine which, if any, of the suspects presented by the database has left the crime scene mark. Where identification is made, it will then require a rigorous system of triple checking by a further two fingerprint identification officers who are fully qualified fingerprint experts. Only where all three fingerprint identification officers independently agree will a notification of identification be given.

5.6 National Fingerprint Database—Ident 1

The national fingerprint database is a fundamental part of the criminal justice system and as such, all forces have a duty to populate and maintain the database by providing high quality fingerprint sets and accurate information of those fingerprinted. Fingerprints of those arrested and charged, reported or summoned for a recordable offence will have their fingerprints taken to confirm their identity where the person is already on the database. If they are not shown on the database, where appropriate their fingerprints are taken and added to the database. These can be searched against all the unidentified crime scene marks in what is termed a speculative search. Taking fingerprints from persons is also the method employed to prove previous convictions of those arrested, warned, cautioned, reprimanded or invited into a police station in connection with all recordable offences.

The fingerprints of those in custody are placed onto Ident 1 via Livescan or by the scanning of inked ten print forms. Fingerprints recovered from crime scenes are compared with those held on Ident 1 and can potentially lead to the identification of an individual. Figure 5.1 summarizes the procedure typically utilized in the comparison and identification of fingerprints.

The national database holds approximately seven million 'ten print' sets of fingerprints at the time of writing, and is an extremely valuable tool used to assist in establishing the identity of individuals and those who have left marks at crime scenes.

POINTS TO NOTE—FINGERPRINTS

The presence of a fingerprint on a surface is conclusive evidence that a person has, at some time, touched the item in question.

5.6 National Fingerprint Database—Ident 1

> There is currently no scientifically accepted method to state when such contact was made. The investigator can narrow down potential time frames by asking questions as to when the surface from which the fingerprint was recovered was last cleaned.
>
> The absence of fingerprints on an item is not conclusive evidence that a person has not handled an item. There are many factors concerning whether a fingerprint is deposited, including successive handling of items, leading to the depletion of substances to transfer onto a surface and the fact that some people do not leave prints that are developed with the different mediums.

It is important to consider the presence or absence of any fingerprint evidence in the context of the investigation.

5.6.1 Searching for fingerprints on Ident 1

When taking fingerprints from persons, it is important to ensure that the fingerprints submitted for comparison purposes are of a high standard. Some of the marks submitted to the fingerprint officers are not found on Ident 1 due to a number of factors including:

- The system may attribute characteristics differently from a fingerprint identification officer. Due to the potential for such variance, the system is not 100% accurate and a suspect may not be found. The main reason for the disparity between the system and fingerprint identification officer attributing different characteristics is due in part to poor quality sets of ten prints held on the system. It is vital that the ten prints submitted by officers are of the best possible quality and clarity.
- The suspect may not have been fingerprinted in connection with any offence and is therefore not on the database at the time of an offence. Fingerprint identification officers regularly undertake 'back searching' where all unidentified scene marks are compared against Ident 1 to ensure a fuller report of a suspect's previous criminal activity is available.
- Fingerprints recovered may belong to the victim or those with 'legitimate access' and so they may not be on the national database. The submission of elimination fingerprints of those with legitimate access to the scene is required where possible, to enable the fingerprint identification officer to work more efficiently. The elimination fingerprints enable the fingerprint identification officer to verify that such marks do not belong to a possible suspect, thus such marks can be discounted from any back searching.

Up until 2001, only the fingerprints of those convicted of an offence were retained on the database and there was a numerical standard in place for the identification of a fingerprint to be confirmed. This required that a minimum of 16 points (characteristics), all in agreement and none in disagreement were present in order for an identification to be confirmed. Since 2001, fingerprint

Chapter 5: Fingerprints

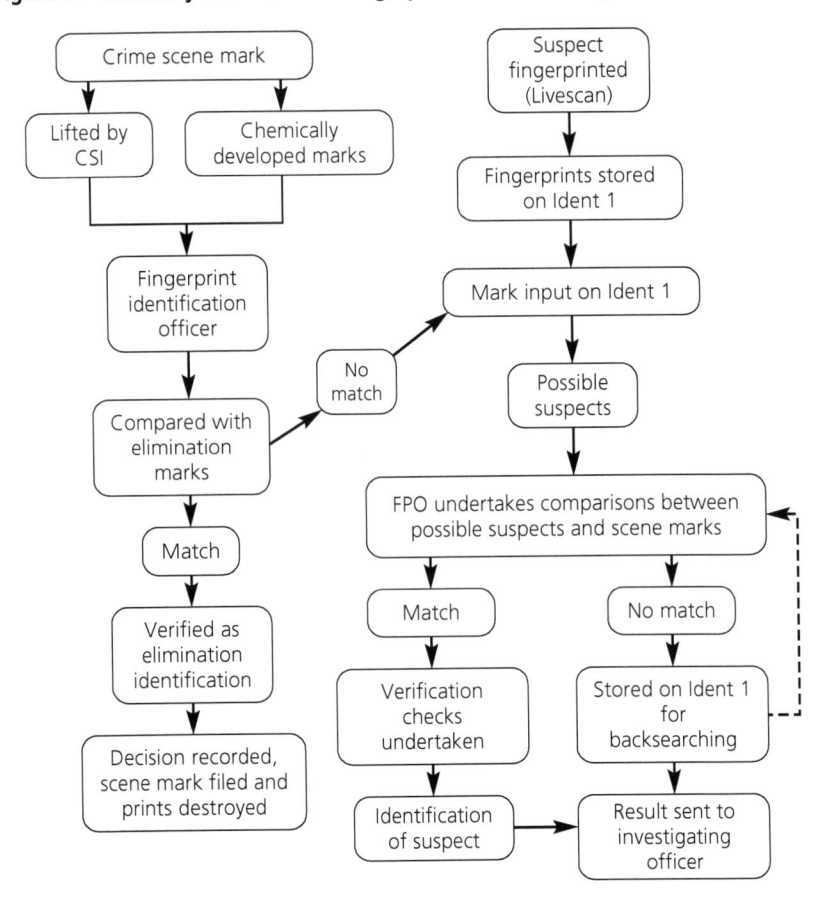

Figure 5.1 Summary of crime scene fingerprint identification procedure

```
                                        ┌─────────────────┐
┌──────────────────────┐                │    Suspect      │
│  Crime scene mark    │                │ fingerprinted   │
└──────────────────────┘                │   (Livescan)    │
     │         │                        └─────────────────┘
     ▼         ▼                                 │
┌─────────┐ ┌──────────────┐                     ▼
│Lifted by│ │ Chemically   │            ┌─────────────────┐
│  CSI    │ │developed marks│           │Fingerprints stored│
└─────────┘ └──────────────┘            │   on Ident 1    │
     │         │                        └─────────────────┘
     └────┬────┘                                 │
          ▼                                      ▼
   ┌──────────────┐                    ┌──────────────────┐
   │ Fingerprint  │                    │ Mark input on    │
   │identification│                    │    Ident 1       │
   │   officer    │      No match      └──────────────────┘
   └──────────────┘  ─────────────►             │
          │                                     ▼
          ▼                            ┌──────────────────┐
   ┌──────────────┐                    │    Possible      │
   │ Compared with│                    │    suspects      │
   │ elimination  │                    └──────────────────┘
   │    marks     │                             │
   └──────────────┘                             ▼
          │                   ┌─────────────────────────────────┐
          ▼                   │ FPO undertakes comparisons      │
   ┌──────────────┐           │ between possible suspects and   │◄──┐
   │    Match     │           │ scene marks                     │   │
   └──────────────┘           └─────────────────────────────────┘   │
          │                       │                   │             │
          ▼                    Match               No match         │
   ┌──────────────┐               ▼                   ▼             │
   │  Verified as │        ┌──────────────┐  ┌──────────────────┐   │
   │ elimination  │        │ Verification │  │  Stored on       │   │
   │identification│        │    checks    │  │  Ident 1 for     │---┘
   └──────────────┘        │  undertaken  │  │  backsearching   │
          │                └──────────────┘  └──────────────────┘
          ▼                       │
   ┌──────────────┐                ▼
   │Decision recorded,     ┌──────────────┐   ┌──────────────┐
   │scene mark filed│      │Identification│──►│ Result sent to│
   │and prints destroyed│  │ of suspect   │   │ investigating │
   └──────────────┘        └──────────────┘   │   officer     │
                                              └──────────────┘
```

identification officers no longer have to rely on the comparison of friction ridge detail characteristics alone and other information is now accepted in the identification process, such as the general direction or 'ridge flow' of the ridges, the overall pattern type, positioning of pores (referred to as third level detail) and features such as creases or scars.

5.6.2 Police elimination database (PED)

This is a local database which is not linked to the national criminal database. All newly recruited police officers and designated police support staff are required to have their fingerprints taken to be used as a means to compare any unidentified marks from a crime scene with those of the officers attending the scene.

The police elimination database is an important tool in many ways. The identification process is a painstaking task, if a mark can be identified as belonging to a police officer or support staff member, it will save a lot of time and effort for the investigation team. It also means that such marks are not loaded onto the national database as an outstanding crime scene mark. Fingerprints from a crime scene that are unidentified can cause problems for the investigation if the case is to go to court, as the defence team may imply that the investigation has not been thorough and the fingerprint is that of the 'real' offender.

5.6.3 Retention of fingerprints on the national database

The Criminal Justice and Police Act 2001 (CJPA) abolished the requirement for the fingerprints and DNA profiles of those who were not convicted of an offence to be removed from the national database. CJPA 2001, s 82 provides that where fingerprints are taken in the investigation of an offence where a person has been:

- arrested and subsequently cleared of an offence; or
- a decision not to prosecute is made,
- fingerprints taken for elimination purposes, for example from the homeowner who has been the victim of a burglary,

must be destroyed once they have fulfilled the purpose for which they were taken. They cannot be retained on the database unless the person has given explicit consent for them to be used in this way.

Fingerprints recovered from a crime scene are generally retained by the investigating police force for a minimum of six years before they are destroyed, except in serious cases such as murder. The ten print sets of fingerprints taken from suspects are retained on the Ident 1 until the 100th birthday of the individual.

The taking of a detainee's fingerprints and DNA Buccal swab samples is now a routine aspect of detainee processing within custody. The reasons for the taking of such samples is primarily for identification purposes, and samples are also used to compare with samples from crime scenes and are subject to speculative searching on the appropriate databases. The appropriate methods and considerations to be made for the taking of fingerprints and DNA PACE samples are detailed below.

5.7 Taking Fingerprints

Fingerprints can be taken for identification purposes from those in custody, from those with lawful and legitimate access to a crime scene for elimination purposes, for immigration purposes and to establish or confirm the identification of a deceased person. It is essential that the fingerprints taken are of the highest quality possible as poor standard fingerprints can lead to a missed identification.

The procedure for taking good quality prints is the same whether fingerprints are taken electronically on a Livescan system or whether inked marks are taken. The success of the national database in identifying persons is reliant on the consistent good quality of the fingerprints and the accuracy of the relevant information loaded onto it. The following guidance is applicable whether fingerprints are taken electronically on Livescan or whether inked impressions are taken.

> **Checklist—Considerations for taking fingerprints**
>
> - For inked prints, only a thin layer of ink should be applied to the inking block—too much ink will cause the fingerprint to be overloaded and the resulting impression will be too dark and/or smudged.
> - Recover any other potential forensic evidence such as swabs of possible blood stains and any fingernail samples (where applicable) prior to fingerprinting a person.
> - Ensure you have the lawful authority to take the fingerprints.
> - Check the hands of the donor for any injuries. If open injuries are present it is important to assess whether prints can be taken. Be mindful of health and safety issues and the contamination of equipment with body fluids.
> - Ensure the donor's hands are clean. If it is necessary for the donor to wash their hands, consider whether any other potential evidence may be recovered first, for example swabbing for body fluids, nail scrapings, etc.
> - If the skin of the donor's hands is very dry, a small amount of moisturiser can be applied to the hands.
> - If the donor's hands are moist, use a tissue to wipe the hands. Repeat this process between taking each impression if the hands are excessively sweaty.
> - Take control of the process—do not allow the donor to dictate the pressure and movement during the taking of impressions.
>
> Where a finger cannot be printed due to injury or amputation, this must be recorded on the form.

5.7.1 Types of impressions required

Rolled impressions

This is where the finger is rolled from one side of the nail edge to the other. It is vital that the finger does not slip during this process as it will cause smudging to the fingerprint. Repeat this process with each finger and the thumbs.

Plain impressions

This is where all four fingers are printed simultaneously to ensure that the individual rolled impressions are in the correct box, for example to check that the fingers from the right hand have not been placed into the boxes for the left hand, or that the impressions have not been taken out of sequence.

The plain impressions require all four fingers to be placed into the appropriate box. It may be necessary to place the fingers at an angle in the box as shown in Figure 5.4. A light pressure can be applied to the fingers if required.

5.7 Taking Fingerprints

Figure 5.2 Good and poor fingerprint impressions

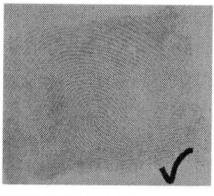

A good mark will be even in tone and appear squared in the centre of the box.

The overlaying of a mark can occur where the finger slips or there is a hesitation during the rolling process. This mark would not be useable.

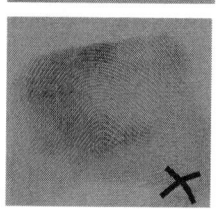

This mark is uneven in appearance due to the difference in the amount of ink on the finger and/or uneven pressure when rolling. Ensure the finger has an even coating of ink before taking the print—the print should not be too dark or too light.

Figure 5.3 Taking a rolled fingerprint impression

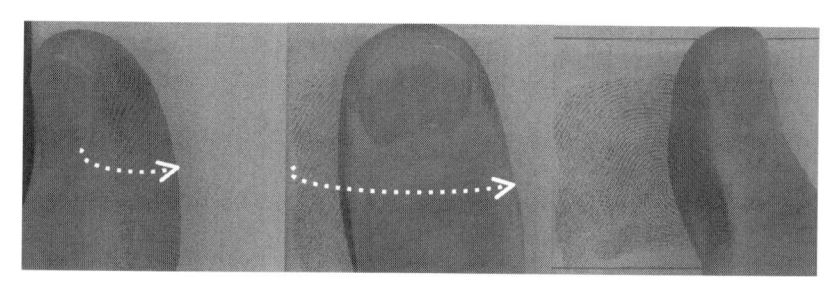

Figure 5.4 Plain impressions

Example of good set of plain impressions

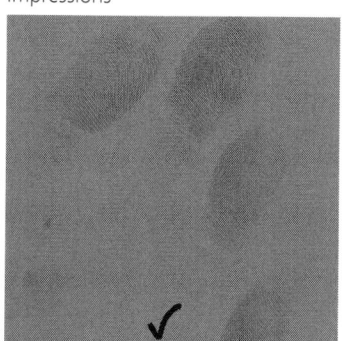

Example of a poor set of plain impressions

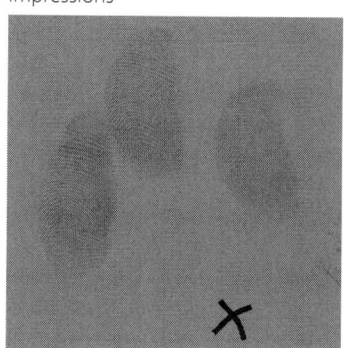

99

Chapter 5: Fingerprints

Palm impressions

Ensure that clothing is not obscuring any part of the palm. Start taking the impression by placing the wrist at the bottom of the box and lower the palm in a smooth movement from wrist to fingertips. Apply a light even pressure to the back of the hand to ensure the natural hollow present in the centre of the palm is captured. A good quality palm print will capture the area of the palm from the base of the fingers to the wrist.

Figure 5.5 Good and poor palm prints

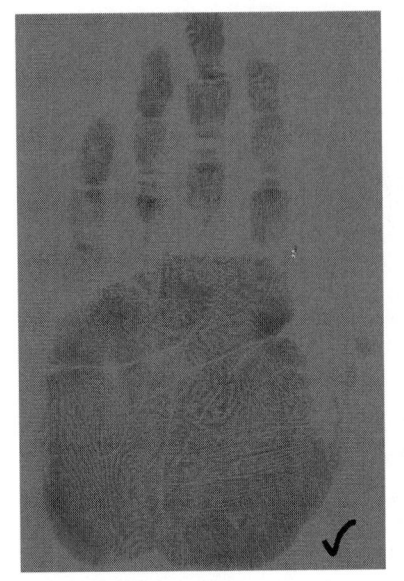

This print has captured the bottom of the palm and the centre area and has a good, even application of ink.	This is a poor quality palm print as there are areas missing due to an uneven pressure when taking the print. The bottom edge by the wrist has not been captured.

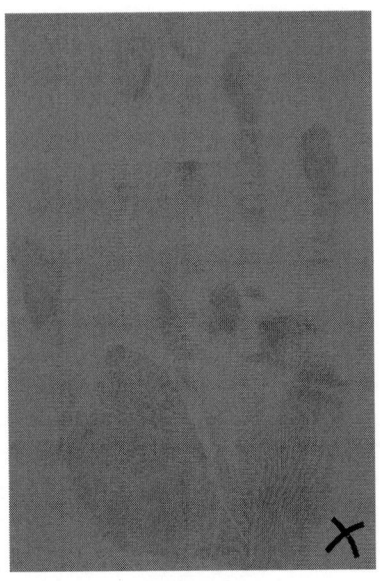

The side or edge of the palm must be taken where applicable. Livescan has a space for this, but it may not be possible on forms used for inked prints.

The side edge of the palm is known as the hypothenar or 'writer's edge or chop' impressions and is commonly found where a person has shielded their eyes with the hands to peer through windows, referred to as 'look–in marks' at crime scenes.

It is important to ensure that the palm edge is centralized within the box when taking such impressions and that the palm is not tilted too far towards the back of the hand. It is the ridge details that require capturing and if the hand is tilted too far back there is a risk such details will not be captured.

5.7 Taking Fingerprints

The importance of taking good quality prints cannot be overstated; the potential consequence of submitting poor prints is a missed identification.

5.7.2 Legislation and fingerprinting persons

Code D, para 4.1 and PACE, s 65(1) defines a fingerprint as a record produced by any method of the skin pattern and other physical characteristics or features of a person's fingers or palms.

PACE and subsequent amendments by the Criminal Justice and Police Act 2003 has conferred powers on the police to take finger and palm prints of persons over the age of ten years old under certain circumstances.

> **POINT TO NOTE—LEGISLATION AND FINGERPRINTING OF PERSONS**
>
> PACE, s 61 is the main overarching legislation regarding the taking of person's fingerprints. PACE, s 61 states that fingerprints of a person may only be taken with consent and when taken at a police station, such consent must be in writing in accordance with s 61(2); Code D, para 4.2.
>
> Fingerprints can be taken without consent under the powers as laid out in s 61(6) and Code D, paras 4.3 and 4.4 which enables reasonable force to be used where necessary. Section 61(6) states that fingerprints can be taken without consent from persons who have been convicted of a recordable offence, or who have received a caution for a recordable offence to which they have admitted, or where they have been reprimanded or warned under the Crime and Disorder Act 1998, s 65 for a recordable offence.
>
> Fingerprints can be taken without consent in line with the amendments provided by the Criminal Justice Act 2003 (CJA), s 9(2). The CJA provides that fingerprints can be taken without consent from any person arrested for a recordable offence without the need for authorization from an inspector. This amendment prevents people avoiding detection by giving a false name and address, and enables checks to be made as to whether the person is wanted in connection with other offences. Where utilizing Livescan technology, a person's fingerprints can be checked against the national database to confirm the person's identity whilst in police detention. This is referred to as a 'live ID'.
>
> The Police Reform Act 2002 confers on designated support staff the power to take fingerprints under PACE, s 61.
>
> Under the Criminal Justice and Public Order Act 1994 persons who have their fingerprints taken must be informed that these may be the subject of a 'speculative search'. This is a search of the appropriate databases to see if their fingerprints can be identified against any crime scene marks.

5.8 Chapter Summary

Fingerprints are a key method of identification. The comparison of fingerprints recovered from a crime scene can be made against those held on the national database—Ident 1. Fingerprints can also be used to confirm the identity of persons arrested, for immigration purposes and to establish and/or confirm the identity of deceased persons.

Fingerprints are laid down when material present on the ridged skin is transferred to a surface or where the ridged skin creates an impression in a suitably soft medium. The presence of fingerprints on a surface is conclusive evidence showing that, at some time, a particular person has touched that surface. The absence of fingerprints on a surface however is not evidence that a person has not touched the surface—some people may not deposit sufficient material to be recovered by certain means. Fingerprint evidence needs to be considered carefully in the context of the investigation as it is not scientifically possible to 'age' a fingerprint and say precisely when it was deposited. At a burglary scene, for example, asking the victim when the area was last cleaned and obtaining a statement to that effect can narrow down the time scales.

Fingerprints are unique to each individual—no two people have been found to have the same fingerprints in over 100 years of the system being utilized. There are many techniques available for the recovery of fingerprints from the crime scene and related items, all of which the CSI and the chemical laboratory technicians are trained to use. The recovery of DNA material is possible after the use of one single fingerprint recovery technique. It is important to seek the advice of the CSI or laboratory technician and/or forensic scientist if DNA and fingerprints are required in order to establish the best possible sequence to maximize the recovery of potential forensic material.

It is vital that fingerprints taken from persons for comparison purposes are of a high standard, as poor quality fingerprints can lead to an identification not being made even if a person is on the system. It is extremely beneficial for elimination sets of fingerprints to be taken from those who have had lawful access to crime scenes where the CSI has recovered fingerprints. This enables the fingerprint identification officers to concentrate on establishing the identity of those who have not had lawful access.

> **KNOWLEDGE CHECK—EXHIBIT HANDLING**
>
> 1. What are the reasons for taking a person's fingerprints?
>   Fingerprints can be taken for identification purposes from those in custody, from those with lawful and legitimate access to a crime scene for elimination purposes, for immigration purposes and to establish or confirm the identification of a deceased person.

5.8 Chapter Summary

2. State the definition of a fingerprint.

   PACE, s 65(1) defines a fingerprint as a record produced, by any method, of the skin pattern and other physical characteristics or features of a person's fingers or palms.

3. What would be the chemical development technique used to recover fingerprints from a plastic bag brought to the scene by an offender, which is found inside a premises at a dwelling burglary?

   The superglue technique would be the most appropriate if the bag was dry. If the bag was known to have been wet, then the laboratory technicians need to be made aware of this.

4. Fingerprints are recovered from the plastic bag referred to in question 3 above, and are identified on Ident 1. What would be the evidential value of the fingerprints?

   The fingerprints will determine that a particular person touched the plastic bag at some time, but not necessarily place them at the crime scene as the bag is an easily transportable item.

5. State the reasons why fingerprints may not be found on Ident1.

   There are several reasons why a fingerprint identification officer will not find a person's fingerprints on the national database:

- The main reason for the system and the fingerprint identification officer attributing different characteristics is due in part to poor quality sets of ten prints held on the system. It is vital that the ten prints submitted by officers are of the best possible quality and clarity.
- The suspect may not have been fingerprinted in connection with any offence and is therefore not on the database at the time of an offence. Fingerprint identification officers regularly undertake 'back searching' where all unidentified scene marks are compared against Ident 1 to ensure a fuller report of a suspect's previous criminal activity is available.
- Fingerprints recovered may belong to the victim or those with 'legitimate access' and so they may not be on the national database. The submission of elimination fingerprints of those with legitimate access to the scene is required where possible, to enable the fingerprint identification officer to work more efficiently. The elimination fingerprints enable the fingerprint identification officer to verify that such marks do not belong to a possible suspect, thus such marks can be discounted from any back searching.

Chapter 5: Fingerprints

Summary of the National Occupational Standards (NOS) for the Student Officer Learning Assessment Portfolio (SOLAP) relating to this chapter

The table below indicates where it may be possible to demonstrate the achievement of certain performance criteria.

NOS unit	Unit descriptor	Performance Criteria, Range, and Knowledge	Activity
1A1	Apply principles of reasonable suspicion or belief	**1A1.3** pc 2, 3, 4, 7, **Range** 1a, 1b, 2a–2d inclusive **Knowledge** 1, 2, 3, 8, 14, 18	Operate within PACE, s 61 and the Criminal Justice Act 2003 with regard to the taking of fingerprints from persons.
2C1	Provide an initial police response to incidents	**2C1.1** pcs 1, 2, 3, 6 **Range** 1a–1g inclusive, 2c, 2d, 2e **2C1.2** pc 1, 2, 8, 10, 11 **Range** 1a, 1b, 2a–2g inclusive **Knowledge** 1, 2, 3, 8, 18, 19, 21, 22	Initial actions at a crime scene— identify nature of incident and any potential fingerprint evidence. Take action to ensure that potential fingerprint evidence is preserved.
2C3	Arrest, detain or report individuals	**2C3.1** pc 1, 2, 3, 5, 6, 8 **Range** 1a–1c inclusive **Knowledge** 1, 2, 4, 6	Fingerprint persons in compliance with legislation.
2G2	Conduct investigations	**2G2.1** pc 1, 3, 4, 5, 6, 8, 9, 12, 15, 16 **Range** 2 a–c, 3b, 4a–c inclusive, 5a, b, c and e, 7a **Knowledge** 1, 3, 14, 15, 18, 19, 24	The identification, recovery and preservation of potential fingerprint evidential material.
2G4	Finalize investigations	**2G4.1** 11 **Range** 1c, 1e, 3b **Knowledge** 3	Ensure items of potential evidential value are properly recorded to maintain integrity and continuity. Disposal of items subject to chemical development techniques with regard to health and safety.
2J2	Prepare for court and other hearings	**2J2.1** pc 3, 4 **Range** N/A **Knowledge** 4, 5	Demonstrate the continuity and integrity of relevant exhibits and their value to the investigation.
2K2	Present detained persons for custody process	**2K2.1** pc 7 **Range** 1d, 2a, 2b **Knowledge** 2, 3, 8 **2K2.2** 2, 3 **Range** 2a, d, e **Knowledge** 8, 11	Avoid cross-contamination or transfer of evidence and taking of fingerprints in line with legislation.

5.8 Chapter Summary

Recommended Further Reading

Advances in Fingerprint Technology, 2nd edn (2002) Lee HC and Gaensslen RE.
Manual of Guidance for Fingerprint Development (2004) HOSDB.
PACE—A Practical Guide to the Police and Criminal Evidence Act (2006) Ozin P, Norton H, and Spivey P.
The Police and Criminal Evidence Act 1984 (2007) Zander, M.

References

Advances in Fingerprint Technology, 2nd edn (2002) Lee HC and Gaensslen RE, CRC Press: London.
'Development of latent fingerprints from skin' Fortunato SL, Journal of Forensic Identification, 48 (6) (1998) pp 704–17.
'Fingerprint detection by laser' Menzel ER, (1980) Marcel Dekker: New York.

6

DNA—Deoxyribonucleic Acid

6.1	Introduction	108
6.2	What is DNA?	109
6.3	The National DNA Database (NDNAD)	115
6.4	Sources of DNA	119
6.5	Recovery and Preservation of DNA Material	122
6.6	DNA Samples from Persons	123
6.7	Chapter Summary	128

Chapter 6: DNA—Deoxyribonucleic Acid

6.1 Introduction

The application of DNA technology has without a doubt had a huge impact on the investigations of crime. The scientific advances have enabled the relatively quick and efficient means of identification of offenders due to the development of a national DNA database (NDNAD). Investigators of cases, both current and historical, have access to this key tool for the potential identification or elimination of offenders or victims and to establish links between different scenes.

The technological advances have enabled DNA profiles to be obtained from increasingly small samples. As the sensitivity of the techniques improves, so do the risks of transfer and contamination. It is vital that material that could potentially bear DNA is handled carefully and with due regard to the risks of contamination and cross-transfer.

Definition box—DNA

A DNA profile is essentially the sequence in which the combination of certain areas of the DNA occurs.
In simple terms it can be compared to a bar code on retail goods—the overall appearance of bar codes is the same, but individual differences occur to individualize one bar code from another.

A key disadvantage to the technological advances is that it can lead to investigators becoming overly reliant on forensic evidence. Whilst forensic science undoubtedly offers huge benefits, investigators must not neglect other aspects of the criminal investigation. There can be numerous defences regarding the presence of forensic material and it is imperative that an investigator is aware of potential defences and ensures a thorough and robust investigation is undertaken in order to put any forensic evidence into context.

At the level of genes and DNA we have individual differences which can enable the identification of an individual from their DNA material. Currently, the coding system used enables scientists to calculate a *probability* of two individuals having the same DNA codes and the likelihood of individuals being the donor of a profile from a crime scene stain. There is not yet a procedure that enables every difference between the whole of the DNA structure to be compared, which would be able, theoretically, to give a much more conclusive result. The DNA 'markers' used are those that have been found to offer distinguishable differences in the population.

DNA material recovered from crime scenes is in the form of body fluids or biological matter. Health and safety precautions must be taken at such scenes due to the associated risks of biohazards. Disposable gloves as minimum must always be worn when handling items that potentially contain body fluids. The profiles from crime scene stains can be compared with the DNA profiles of suspects. DNA samples taken from persons in custody are loaded onto the national database to be searched against any unidentified crime stains. The procedure for taking DNA samples from persons is detailed in this chapter.

Whilst the potential for DNA material to be recovered from body fluids is perhaps the most obvious evidential consideration, there are other investigative benefits in the examination of certain body fluids. The distribution of blood at a crime scene for example, can be useful in establishing what has happened and can corroborate or refute versions of events.

6.2 What is DNA?

Deoxyribonucleic acid (DNA) is the type of forensic evidence most often considered where body fluids and biological matter are located at a crime scene. It is a genetic coding material which determines physical characteristics such as hair and eye colour. DNA remains unchanged throughout life and can remain long after death.

We inherit half our DNA from our mother and half from our father, with siblings (sisters and brothers) inheriting different combinations of the DNA sequence from the same parents. DNA profiles of siblings will have similarities; however their individual profiles will be different. With the exception of identical twins, triplets, etc who will have the same DNA profiles, individual DNA profiles are now widely accepted as being unique to each individual.

6.2.1 Nuclear DNA

The nucleus of the cells contains 22 pairs of chromosomes (half from each parent) plus the two sex chromosomes (males have xy and females xx chromosomes) which hold our DNA material. It is from the cell nucleus that nuclear DNA can be extracted to provide a 'profile' suitable for searching on the national DNA database (NDNAD).

Figure 6.1 Diagrammatic representation of the structure of a cell

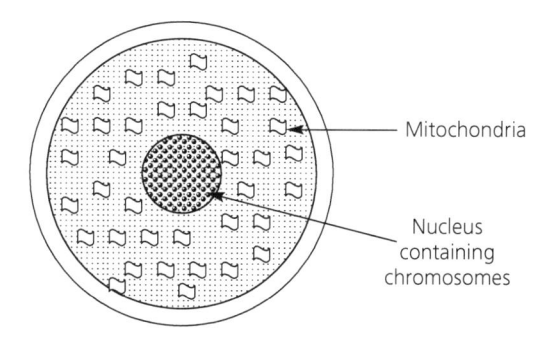

6.2.2 Mitochondrial DNA (MtDNA)

Mitochondrial DNA is present in large amounts within a cell, but has fewer features, which makes it unsuitable for searching on the national DNA database (NDNAD). The fewer points for comparison essentially mean that many people will have the same features within their MtDNA, so it is not highly discriminating.

MtDNA is passed to children via the maternal line, so whilst males have mitochondrial DNA, only females can pass it on to their children. Mitochondria are essentially the energy source of the cell. During conception the female egg containing mitochondria is fertilized by the sperm which only contains mitochondria in the tail. As the sperm enters the egg, the tail falls away leaving only the head of the sperm to fertilize the egg, which is why males do not pass on their mitochondria to their children.

Brothers and sisters will have the same MtDNA as their mother and all their relatives linked through the maternal line. As so many related individuals will share the same MtDNA profiles, this system can not be used for searching on the NDNAD.

The process does have benefits in a forensic capacity however, and has been used successfully for the identification of degraded and old human remains and bodies involved in mass disasters and familial searches. The technique has been very valuable for cold case reviews where there are only old, degraded samples to work with.

6.2.3 DNA profiles

In summary, the DNA material, when extracted, will show as a series of 'bars' of differing length and width—similar to the barcodes on retail goods. These are then analysed further by a computerized system which accurately measures the 'bars' to produce a series of graphs which show the corresponding lengths and widths of each bar. The graphical and numerical data produced is analysed by the scientists to determine the amount of the specific sections of the DNA that are present and enable them to make an interpretation of the results.

Standard DNA profiling, which uses an analytical process generally referred to as SGMplus (Second Generation Multiplex) examines 10 pre-selected sites of the DNA strand plus the sex chromosomes. The examination of the sex chromosomes means a scientist can determine whether the donor was male or female. The discrimination potential for such profiles averages one in a billion, however it must be remembered that a 'match' between profiles is that of probability and is not an absolute certainty, which is why DNA evidence alone will not be admissible as the sole evidence—it must be supported by corroborative evidence.

There is not yet the capability to look at every area of the DNA. The areas of the DNA examined are those that have been found to have the best potential for variation between people. This enables the comparison profiles from different individuals to establish a link or to eliminate persons from an enquiry.

6.2.4 Initial laboratory submission and analysis results

Where material potentially bearing DNA is recovered from a crime scene, it should be sent to the forensic service provider laboratory in order for any DNA to be extracted and subsequently profiled where appropriate. There are two routes to making a laboratory submission. One is the route used where a crime stain has been recovered and requires a profile to add to the database for searching to establish the identity of the donors. This route requires the completion of a standard form 'GF111—Submission of crime stains (DNA) for the national database' or equivalent. This is a simple, one-page form to be used for example, where a cigarette butt has been recovered from a crime scene and the identification of the donor is unknown.

The second route is used for comparison purposes, for example, where a crime stain (DNA) or other forensic material such as glass, drugs, fibres requires comparison with other samples of the same type recovered from another scene such as a suspect for example. The form required for comparison work is the MGFSP (or equivalent)—'Submission of work for scientific examination'. This form requires more detail than the GF111 and it is important that it is completed as fully and accurately as possible. The details of the subjects are required and an account of the incident under investigation, the accounts given by any suspects and any other information that would be beneficial for the scientist to be aware of (these are termed 'critical success factors' and a summary of the appropriate success factors should be available alongside the forms in force). The form also requires details of the points to prove. Bear in mind that these forms are read by persons who were not at the incident and who rely only on the information you provide. It is important that you state your rationales for the submission fully and be clear on what you would like to achieve from the examination. The MGFSP form (or equivalent) should also be used for the examination of other forensic material such as drugs, fibres, paint and the like to establish the identity or constituents of the samples.

> **Scenario 1—Forensic submission routes**
>
> An assault has occurred whereby a person has been hit in the face and upper body with a broken bottle. Witnesses state the offender was seen standing outside the victim's home smoking a cigarette. The victim has sustained deep gash wounds and is bleeding heavily. Medical attention is arranged for the victim and their clothing is seized. There are no suspects at this time. A cigarette butt and broken bottle are recovered from the location of the assault.
>
> (For the purpose of this scenario, fingerprint analysis of the bottle is not viable.)

> - What would be your first consideration for a laboratory submission?
>
> The cigarette butt would be sent by means of the GF111 route for any DNA profile recovered to be loaded onto the NDNAD to ascertain if an identification of the donor can be established. Bear in mind a profile and any subsequent identification will only show who smoked the cigarette, this may not be the person who committed the assault.
>
> A possible suspect is named by the victim and is arrested an hour after the assault. The suspect fits the descriptions given by witnesses in physical appearance and the clothing worn. There is possible blood staining on the suspect's clothing and they have a deep cut on their right hand.
>
> - What are the potential forensic links?
>
> Possible blood on the suspect's clothing would require profiling, to establish if it is that of the victim. The victim's clothing could be examined to establish if the possible blood came from the suspect, and to ascertain if any glass fragments are available for comparison with the glass fragments on the suspect's clothing to establish a link. The broken bottle recovered from the scene can be compared to the glass fragments on the subject's clothing to establish if it was the one used in the attack. Any blood on the broken bottle could be profiled to establish the donor.
>
> There are potential forensic links between the victim, the suspect and the location through the transfer of the possible blood and glass fragments, as illustrated in Figure 6.2 below.

Submission results

Once a sample has been received into the laboratory any potential DNA material needs to be extracted from the sample to obtain a profile of the DNA in the first instance. Once the sample has had any DNA extracted from it, the scientist will then be able to analyse the profile. The investigating officer will be informed of the success (or otherwise) of obtaining any viable DNA material (see Table 6.1).

The sample has to be of sufficient quality in order to be loaded onto the NDNAD and not every sample can be loaded for searching and comparison on the database. It may however be possible to compare a named suspect sample with a crime stain, or to undertake further analytical processing which may enhance insufficient samples gained through standard processes. These possibilities can be discussed with the scientist or forensic submissions department; however the authorization of further work will be subject to the circumstances of the case.

6.2.5 Low copy number (LCN)

This system is much more sensitive than the standard techniques such as SGM-plus, and can be utilized where very few cells or partly degraded cells are present.

6.2 What is DNA?

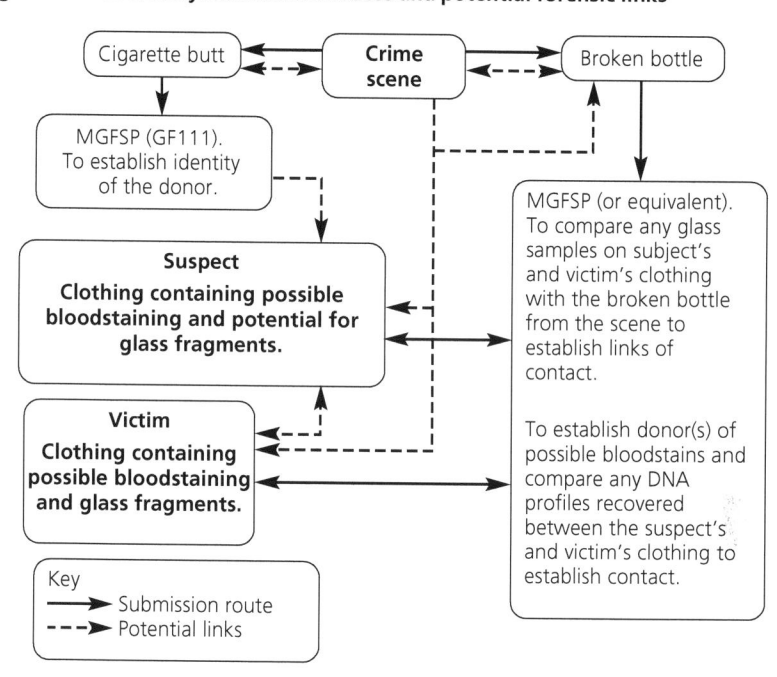

Figure 6.2 Laboratory submissions routes and potential forensic links

```
    Cigarette butt  ←----→  Crime  ←----→  Broken bottle
         ↓                  scene              ↓
    MGFSP (GF111).            |                |
    To establish identity     |                |
    of the donor.             |                |
                              |          MGFSP (or equivalent).
         ↓                    |          To compare any glass
       Suspect                |          samples on subject's
  Clothing containing possible          and victim's clothing
  bloodstaining and potential for ←--   with the broken bottle
  glass fragments.                       from the scene to
                                         establish links of
         ↓                               contact.
       Victim
  Clothing containing                To establish donor(s) of
  possible bloodstaining ←--         possible bloodstains and
  and glass fragments.               compare any DNA
                                     profiles recovered
                                     between the suspect's
  Key                                and victim's clothing to
    ——→ Submission route             establish contact.
    ---→ Potential links
```

Table 6.1 Summary of the possible initial analysis results

Reported results	Loadable to NDNAD	Note
Full profile—suitable	Yes	All areas analysed are present in the profile.
Partial profile—suitable	Yes	Not all areas analysed are present but are above the minimum required.
More than 1 person—distinguishable	Yes	A mixed profile where the individual profiles can be distinguished.
Partial profile—unsuitable	No	The sample does not contain the minimum number of areas required. Can be subject to a one-off speculative search at police request or re-analysed with a more sensitive technique.
No profile	No	There may not be sufficient material present to obtain a profile.
More than 1 person—indistinguishable	No	A mixed profile where individual profiles cannot be separated.
No body fluids present	No	No material is present for the extraction of DNA.

113

The sample will be analysed with the standard technique first and, if applicable the LCN process (or equivalent) can be used to further 'amplify' or copy the small amounts of material present in order to provide sufficient material to obtain a profile. The LCN process is potentially capable of producing a profile from a single cell and from samples previously found to be negative by the routine process. The main issue with LCN is that the amplification process can also increase any background contamination proportionately. The interpretation of the profile can be more problematic than where standard profiling techniques are utilized.

The LCN technique (or equivalent) can be used to obtain profiles from cells that are left behind in a fingerprint or the skin cells that may be present in sweat. There have been successes in obtaining profiles from items that have been handled by offenders such as tools, weapons and from clothing grabbed by an offender.

Due to the sensitivity of the LCN process, the risk of contamination and cross-transfer is especially high. Profiles obtained by the LCN process have the same discriminatory power of those obtained by the standard process, approximately one in a billion. Essentially this means that where the scene profile matches that of the profile of the suspect, the chances of that profile belonging to anyone else is one in a billion.

Case study—The Omagh bombing appeal

The low copy number (LCN) DNA technique was recently highlighted in the national media with regard to the release of Sean Hoey as a result of the Omagh bombing appeal. LCN DNA played a key role in the conviction of Sean Hoey, accused of the bombing that claimed the lives of 29 people in Omagh.

Several issues are highlighted within the judgment, most significantly the interpretation of the LCN evidence and the handling, recording and storage of exhibits that potentially contained DNA material.

It was shown during the appeal that the interpretation of the evidence could not be relied upon due to the failure of the scientists to provide robust evidence as to the reliability of their findings. Essentially, more weight was attributed to the evidence in the initial trial than could be substantiated.

The LCN evidence was further undermined with respect to issues of continuity and integrity. Officers (police, army and CSI) involved in the case were shown to not have been wearing any protective clothing such as masks, scene suits and gloves when examining the scenes. Items bearing potential forensic evidence were not packaged and sealed at the time of recovery. The subsequent handling of the exhibits at the forensic laboratory was also found to be unsatisfactory.

DNA evidence was not considered during the recovery and subsequent handling of exhibits at the scene. There was a catalogue of systemic and procedural failures which cast doubt on the integrity and continuity of the exhibits examined for LCN DNA, throughout the whole process from recovery at the scene through the analytical process.

> The Association of Chief Police Officers (ACPO) in consultation with the Crown Prosecution Service (CPS) recommended a temporary suspension on the use of LCN DNA analysis technique in criminal investigations following this judgment. The temporary suspension was in order for a review of the process and the procedures to be undertaken.
>
> The CPS reviewed current cases involving the use of LCN DNA analysis and found that the problems highlighted in the review had been satisfactorily rectified and concluded that the use of LCN analysis should remain available for the recovery of potential evidence.
>
> The interpretation of the strength and weight of such evidence remains a key consideration regarding the way it is presented and tested in the light of all the other evidence.

The Omagh case highlights the need to ensure any items bearing potential forensic evidence, especially but not exclusively DNA, are handled with care, packaged and stored correctly and accurate continuity records maintained. It is the responsibility of the prosecution to demonstrate, beyond reasonable doubt, that any forensic evidence relied upon in court must be reliable and has been handled in a manner in which no contamination could have occurred accidently or deliberately. Due to recent appeal cases such as this, the systems in place to ensure the continuity and integrity of forensic evidence will be increasingly scrutinized. As forensic techniques become increasingly sensitive the risk of contamination increases.

6.3 The National DNA Database (NDNAD)

The national database was launched in April 1995 and without a doubt has proved to be an effective tool for police investigators. It currently holds approximately four million profiles, a number that is increasing daily.

DNA profiles obtained from the suspect samples taken in custody are loaded onto the database which is continually updated. All samples are compared with the unidentified profiles obtained from materials recovered at crime scenes.

All suitable profiles obtained from crime scenes are also compared with each other to ascertain if the same profile is present at different scenes. This enables an investigator to link the scenes associated with that profile.

6.3.1 Volunteer/elimination samples

There will be occasions where the DNA material recovered is there from those who have lawful access to the crime scene. As with fingerprints, it is necessary to take a sample from a victim where appropriate, to ensure any profile obtained does not belong to them.

As with fingerprints, if the profile cannot be eliminated it will be loaded onto the database as an unidentified crime scene profile. This can cause costly and time consuming investigations to be undertaken unnecessarily. If the scientist can compare the profiles of those with lawful access to that of the crime scene stain, it will prevent the database being loaded with unnecessary profiles and save investigative time. An unidentified profile can cause problems with defence teams who could suggest that the unknown profile is that of the true offender. Investigators must ensure that samples are taken for elimination purposes where material containing potential DNA has been recovered from the scene. Section 6.6 details the procedures for DNA sampling of persons.

6.3.2 The police elimination database (PED)

Within the database framework there is a police elimination database (PED) which holds profiles of police officers and operational staff. This is *entirely separate* from the main suspect or crime stain database.

As with the police fingerprint elimination database, the PED is an essential tool to ensure that any profiles put on the main crime database are those from genuine suspect samples. The increasing sensitivity of the techniques used means that contamination of samples is a real issue.

A search of the PED can only be authorized at the request of an SIO, and the search is limited to the comparison of the profiles of those officers who had access to the scene or exhibits in question, with the profile of the unidentified crime scene profile. It must be demonstrated that there are genuine grounds for believing that contamination by an officer has occurred. The profiles on the PED cannot be speculatively searched against the NDNAD.

6.3.3 NDNAD search results

When a profile is obtained that can be loaded onto the database, the results from this will indicate the evidential strength of any 'match'. Officers will only be notified where a match between profiles has been made and not where a sample has been loaded but no subsequent match occurs.

Where profiles are compared, the strength of the match between them will be reported to the investigating officer. It must be remembered that a 'match' between profiles is that of probability and is not an absolute certainty, which is why DNA evidence alone will not be admissible as the sole evidence—it must be supported by corroborative evidence.

6.3.4 Non-routine database searches

In addition to the standard routine searching of the NDNAD for matches between crime scene and suspect profiles, there are other methods that can be utilized for serious cases where the routine searching does not produce a result.

6.3 The National DNA Database (NDNAD)

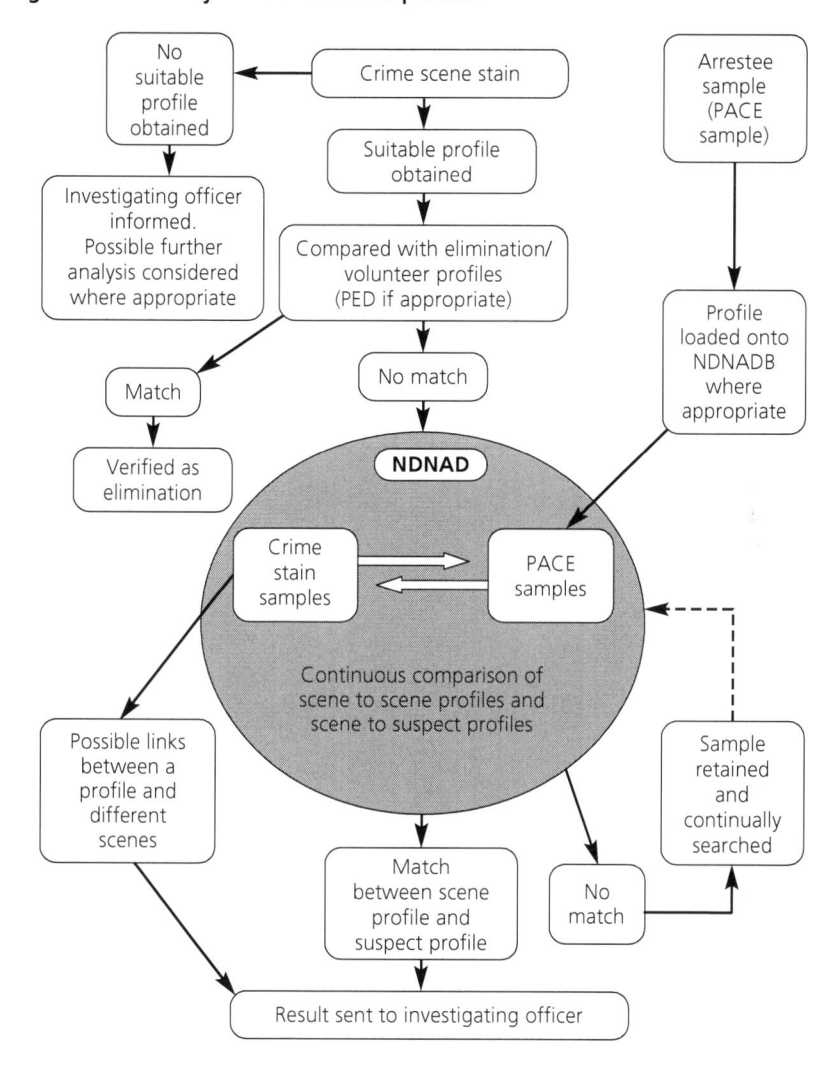

Figure 6.3 Summary of routine NDNAD process

```
                     Crime scene stain
                            │
         ┌──────────────────┼──────────────────┐
         ▼                  ▼                  
   No suitable        Suitable profile      Arrestee sample
   profile obtained   obtained              (PACE sample)
         │                  │                     │
         ▼                  ▼                     ▼
  Investigating      Compared with          Profile loaded
  officer informed.  elimination/           onto NDNADB
  Possible further   volunteer profiles     where appropriate
  analysis           (PED if appropriate)
  considered where          │
  appropriate         ┌─────┴─────┐
         │            ▼           ▼
         │          Match      No match
         │            │           │
         ▼            ▼           ▼
                Verified as    [NDNAD:
                elimination    Crime stain samples ⇄ PACE samples
                               Continuous comparison of scene to
                               scene profiles and scene to
                               suspect profiles]
                                   │              │
                     ┌─────────────┤              ▼
                     ▼             ▼        Sample retained
              Possible links   Match          and continually
              between a        between scene  searched
              profile and      profile and         ▲
              different        suspect profile     │
              scenes               │           No match
                     │             │
                     └──────┬──────┘
                            ▼
                  Result sent to investigating officer
```

Familial searching

This search technique can be used where a full DNA profile has been recovered from a crime scene stain that does not produce any matches when loaded onto the database.

Based on the knowledge that close genetic relatives will share similarities in their DNA profiles, a search of the database can be made for the profiles that most closely match the crime stain. Such a search can produce hundreds of possible profiles which are then narrowed down by utilizing search parameters such as geographic locations and existing intelligence.

Chapter 6: DNA—Deoxyribonucleic Acid

Table 6.2 Match report results

Reported results	What it means
Conclusive association	The crime stain and suspect sample match across all of the comparison markers.
Strong support for association	The crime stain and suspect sample have some areas of comparison. *Discuss the strength of potential evidential value with a scientist.*
Some support for association	The crime stain and suspect sample have very few areas of comparison match.
Inconclusive	Insufficient material or poor quality sample for comparison purposes.
Some support for elimination	The crime stain and suspect sample have some areas of comparison.
Strong support for elimination	The crime stain and suspect sample have very few areas of comparison. *Discuss the strength of potential evidential value with a scientist.*
Conclusive elimination	The profile crime stain and suspect sample are not alike.

Case study—Familial searching

Michael Little was killed when a brick was thrown into the cab of his lorry from a footbridge on the M3. Mr Little suffered heart failure after the brick struck him in the chest.

The brick was recovered and using LCN, a partial profile was obtained which was also linked to blood found on a vehicle nearby that the offender had attempted to steal prior to throwing the brick.

The profiles did not produce a match when searched on the database, nor was a result gained following an intelligence led screening in the locality. Familial searching was utilized to see if any individuals on the database closely matched the profile obtained from the scene. The search was limited to white males, under 35 years old living within specified geographic parameters.

The search produced a list of 25 names with the most closely matching profile having 16 out of 20 areas of comparison matching the crime stain profile. This was the profile of a family member of the offender, whose DNA profile was analysed and was found to be a match with the crime stain.

Craig Harman was sentenced to six years for the manslaughter of Michael Little.

Pendulum list search (PLS)

This can be used where a mixed profile has been obtained. This occurs when the profiles of two people are present, such as may occur if two people share a cigarette, they may both leave cellular material on the cigarette butt which, when analysed, will produce a mixed profile.

The PLS system produces a list of the possible profiles that could theoretically be present in the mixture; these theoretical profiles are speculatively searched against the NDNAD. Where such profiles match any of those on the database, an intelligence report detailing the match will be made available, enabling investigating officers to focus further investigation. The process can be used for both volume and serious crimes.

6.4 Sources of DNA

Deoxyribonucleic acid (DNA) is present in almost every cell in the body with the notable exception of red blood cells which do not carry DNA material.

There are many items that can be recovered from crime scenes that will potentially bear DNA—only 'potentially' as there are several factors that mean a sample may not yield a profile. DNA can be degraded by environmental factors and it is also possible that there may not be enough DNA-bearing cells present in the recovered stain.

Millions of skin cells are shed from the body every day, and these will be inevitably contained in other bodily secretions such as saliva, mucus and sweat—it is the skin cells within these fluids that contain the DNA in the form of the skin cells.

The most commonly encountered biological samples recovered for DNA analysis include the following.

6.4.1 Blood

Most cells within the body carry DNA with the exception of red blood cells. The role of the red blood cell is to carry oxygen and other nutrients around the body. It is the white blood cells that are required for DNA analysis. It is often thought that where a large pool of blood is present, a DNA profile will most certainly be obtained.

When a person bleeds, the first defence of the body is to try and stop the loss of blood—white blood cells rush to the wound and are washed out, with damaged skin cells, in the initial flow. Latter bleeding may not contain as high a concentration of white cells or skin cells and therefore a profile may not be obtained. A CSI will therefore generally look for the site of the initial blood loss as this is most likely to contain a higher concentration of the white blood and skin cells and thus potentially lead to a full DNA profile.

All the blood stains present will be sampled however, as this is a general 'rule' and subject to many variables. It is likely that latter blood stains will yield DNA, however the concentration of the white blood cells present may be one factor in a sample not producing a useable DNA profile.

On locating a stain that appears to be blood, a CSI should undertake a presumptive blood test if there is sufficient material available. The presumptive blood test will establish if the stain is not blood. However a positive result does not necessarily mean the stain is blood, but a positive test will warrant the recovery of the stain for analysis. Such tests cannot distinguish between human and animal blood.

On backgrounds that may obscure blood, the CSI can utilize a forensic light source to search for potential blood stains. Blood will not fluoresce under the light source but will absorb the light to show as darker than the background. There are also chemical screening techniques that can be utilized to locate non-visible blood staining such as Luminol.

When seizing clothing, if staining is noted that could potentially be blood, officers must note the location of the stain on their exhibit label and ideally produce a sketch diagram showing the location of the stain as this can be of tremendous use to the interviewing officers.

Blood can be transferred onto parts of clothing after an attack, for example blood on offenders' hands can be transferred to the insides of pockets or on underwear. Be mindful that blood may not always be readily visible. Gloves must always be worn if the presence of blood is suspected even if it is not obviously visible.

6.4.2 Semen

Semen is a good source of DNA material which is present in the heads of the spermatozoa. There are a number of techniques that can be utilized for the analysis of semen for DNA.

Laser microdissection

Where a sample is likely to contain female cellular material in addition to sperm cells, a technique known as laser microdissection can be used to separate the male cells from any female cellular material. This technique enables the male only cells to be targeted and analysed. Once sufficient sperm cells have been recovered the LCN process is used to extract the DNA profile.

Fluorescence in situ hybridization (FISH)

This process enables the extraction of non-sperm male cells where semen may not contain any sperm, for example as a result of vasectomy. The technique targets the sex chromosomes, identifying the Y (male) chromosomes. Laser microdissection is then used to recover the identified male cells to produce a DNA profile.

Both the LMD and FISH techniques can produce profiles that are compatible with the NDNAD.

Identification of semen

Semen stains can be searched for by utilizing a forensic light source which will cause the stain to fluoresce as a pale white or yellow stain against the background.

Where such stains are located, a presumptive test for semen can be undertaken by the CSI providing sufficient material is present.

It used to be the case that at least five sperm had to be present in a stain for it to be confirmed as semen by a scientist. It is now possible to identify a stain as semen where no sperm are present. Scientists can analyse the sample for seminal acid phosphotase (SAP) or a protein specific antigen (PSA) or P30.

6.4.3 Saliva

Items such as cigarette butts, drinking vessels, swabs of lick or bite marks for example, can be sent for analysis. It is the skin cells sloughed off from the inside of the mouth (buccal cells) which are the focus of analysis. In addition, lots of cells are continually lost from the lips; contact such as occurs when smoking a cigarette, chewing gum, or drinking from a bottle, will dislodge cells which then adhere to the cigarette filter or bottle opening.

Be mindful that some drinks may degrade any DNA material which may be present on the mouth of a bottle—acidic and sugary carbonated drinks are believed to be particularly damaging to any DNA material and their presence may affect the quality of the resulting profile. Smooth surfaces are not generally good for retaining cellular material. The best area for DNA on a drinking bottle is the ridged type tops/caps, as the twisting action required to remove them from the bottle effectively sloughs of skin cells which then adhere to the ridged material.

A presumptive test for saliva is available for use by the CSI.

6.4.4 Sweat

Sweat is a liquid secretion which does not carry cellular material in its pure form. As with saliva, sloughed skin cells may be present within the sweat stain. Examples where such skin cells may be present are in the armpits of close fitting clothing and headbands of hats. Any area on an item of clothing that has had close contact with skin may potentially hold enough skin cells to yield enough material for DNA analysis.

6.4.5 Mucus

Mucus can be a good source of DNA, especially if a used handkerchief is recovered. The force of sneezing, coughing or blowing the nose means a good concentration of skin cells from the lining of the nose can be present. Mucus material that was swabbed from the pavement (where the suspect was seen to spit mucus) yielded a full profile for a suspect in a series of sexual offences who was wanted in three force areas. This was the only forensic material that had been recovered from the numerous scenes for which this person was believed to be responsible.

6.4.6 Urine

Urine will not be routinely submitted for analysis as there is unlikely to be enough cellular material from the urethra present to extract sufficient DNA. However, in serious cases it is worth seeking advice from the forensic scientist as the technology is always improving.

6.4.7 Hair

Hair shafts contain dead cells and so are not suitable for analysis for the crime stain database, but may be suitable for MtDNA analysis. In order to recover sufficient cellular material for nuclear DNA analysis, hair with a root is required. Hair has three distinct growth phases, with the root gradually reducing in size until the hair falls out naturally. This is generally the type of hair found in hats or on vehicle seats for example, that have been shed naturally. The presence of a good root on the hair generally requires some force to remove it (see Chapter 12 for the forensic potentials of hair).

6.4.8 Faeces

Faeces contain a lot of bacteria which can degrade any DNA material that may be present and is not generally suitable for the general DNA profiling unless blood is visible. MtDNA may be able to be extracted from faeces. There are studies being currently undertaken utilizing LCN analytical techniques that have proven successful for the recovery of nuclear DNA material, these procedures may be routinely available in the future. It is important to discuss any forensic potential of faeces with the forensic scientist or CSI.

6.4.9 Dandruff and skin

Dandruff and surface layers of skin are not routinely used for standard DNA profiling techniques as it is basically dead skin cells.

The skin cells mentioned in previous sections are 'live' at the time they are removed or sloughed off by some form of friction contact (eg skin under fingernails where the victim has scratched the offender in a struggle deep enough to draw blood or the unscrewing of a bottle cap or the rubbing action of a headband on the forehead, etc). Dead skin cells which are shed naturally are not suited for the routine analysis. However, in serious offences, further techniques may be available.

6.5 Recovery and Preservation of DNA Material

The sensitivity of the DNA profiling techniques mean that contamination and cross-transfer are very real risks, particularly to those items potentially bearing DNA material. The role of the investigating officer is to preserve the scene in order to maximize the potential evidence available for the CSI to recover. Where possible, the item bearing the stain should be photographed in situ before being recovered by CSIs, who have a range of equipment and methods available to them for the recovery of potential DNA material.

Where DNA material is recovered from a crime scene stain and a profile gained which is loaded on to the NDNAD, it can then be searched against the samples from other unidentified crime scene stains and compared to the samples taken from suspects.

Table 6.3 Summary of sample types and DNA recovery potential

Sample type	Source of DNA	Comments
Blood	White blood cells	Good source of DNA.
Semen	Sperm cells Non-sperm male cells	Good source of DNA.
Hair with roots	Hair follicle cells	Good source of DNA.
Skin/dandruff	Skin cells (dead)	Not a good source for routine analysis.
Shed hair shafts (dead)	Adhering dead skin/follicle cells	Not a good source for routine analysis. MtDNA may be obtained.
Sweat stains	Sloughed skin cells contained in fluid	Can be a good source.
Vaginal fluids	Mainly fluid but may contain sloughed mucosal skin cells	Good source of DNA.
Nasal secretions	Mainly fluid but may contain sloughed mucosal cells	Good source of DNA.
Urine	Mainly liquid but may contain sloughed mucosal cells	Not routinely used as so few cells generally present. Seek advice in serious cases.
Faeces	Sloughed intestinal skin cells	Not usually a good source of nuclear DNA. MtDNA may be used for serious cases.

6.6 DNA Samples from Persons

There are two routes for taking DNA samples from persons for comparison against profiles recovered from crime scenes. The PACE kits (K505) are for taking samples from arrestees and the volunteer kits (K515) are for those samples taken from victims, for elimination purposes and for those involved in intelligence led screens.

The PACE kits have a barcode with the first two digits starting from '96 ******' therefore any barcode beginning with 96 or upwards can be used for PACE sampling.

Chapter 6: DNA—Deoxyribonucleic Acid

6.6.1 DNA status on the police national computer (PNC)

Prior to taking a DNA PACE sample from an arrestee, the person's status should be checked against the police national computer (PNC) to establish if they are already recorded on the system. The following list in Table 6.4 is a summary of the results from a PNC DNA status check.

Table 6.4 Summary of status codes on the PNC

Status	Comment	New PACE sample required (Y/N)
Blank	No DNA records held	Y
'C' – Confirmed (DC)	A DNA profile is held on the NDNAD, indicating a conviction has been obtained at court.	If there is no DC marker, take sample in accordance with PACE. If there is a DC marker, a second sample should be taken in certain circumstances (Table 6.5).
'P' – Profiled (DP)	A profile is held on the national database.	As per 'DC' guidance above.
'T' - Taken	A sample has been taken but not yet profiled or loaded onto the national database.	N
'D' – Destroyed	A sample was held but has now been destroyed.	Y
'F' – Taken but held in force	A sample has been taken but is being held in force.	N
'S' – Rejected	A sample has been taken but rejected due to poor quality of submission.	Re-sample if sample was failed or unsatisfactory due to sample being lost, destroyed, contaminated, damaged or laboratory analysis proved unreliable (Criminal Justice Act 2003) and Code D para 6.6 and 6B.
'R' – Rejected	A sample has been taken but no profile obtained.	As for 'S' rejected samples.
'M' – missing	A sample barcode is held on PNC but the sample has not yet been received by the forensic supplier.	N

6.6.2 New PACE sampling considerations

Consideration must be given as to when a DNA PACE sample was added to the national DNA database (NDNAD), as indicated by the first two numbers on the barcode. This is due to the upgrading of the technology—all samples taken with the older kits now require upgrading to the new standard in order to be evidentially viable, which is why swabs need taking from persons on the database who were initially sampled prior to the '96' barcode being utilized. All samples taken with the PACE K505 kit (with barcodes of 96 and upwards) can be used for evidential purposes and a second reference sample will not be required for evidential purposes.

Where the donor has an older profile (pre-'96' numbered barcode) on the NDNAD a new sample is required. Where a direct comparison is required to a particular profile from a crime stain and the donor has a pre-'96' numbered barcode a new sample is required and should be marked as 'Casework' with the exhibit number and job reference of the crime stain profile clearly stated on the paperwork. Older profiles (pre-96 barcodes) cannot be used evidentially to compare with the crime stain profile.

Table 6.5 Taking of new samples

DNA PNC Status	Confirmed 'DC'	Profiled 'DP'	Comparison with DNA crime stain profile required
Pre-96 barcode	Yes	Yes	Yes—mark as 'Casework'. No—Retake as PACE sample.
Post-96 barcode	No Yes	No Yes	Take PACE sample. No requirement to take sample.

6.6.3 Reasons for sample rejection

Samples can be rejected by the laboratory for analysis for several reasons, all of which can be readily avoided by taking care when undertaking the sampling process. The most common reasons for sample rejection are as follows:

> **Checklist—Possible reasons for sample rejection**
>
> - Where tamper-evident bags are not used or poorly, incorrectly or not sealed bags are used.
> - The required forms are missing, incomplete or incorrectly completed.
> - Where barcodes on the form do not match the barcodes on the tubes.
> - If two swabs are placed in one tube.
> - If swabs are missing.
> - If part of the swab stick is left on the swab.
> - Where the swab containers are damaged or unsealed.

- If foreign material is found in the container.
- The swab is upside down in the container.

Where samples are rejected due to administrative or paperwork errors, it may be possible that these can be rectified, however this will incur unnecessary delays and have possible cost implications. Samples that have been rejected for reasons other than administrative errors cannot be resubmitted, and it may not be possible in law to retake samples. It is vital that procedures are followed and the relevant paperwork completed accurately.

6.6.4 Taking a DNA sample from persons

The DNA sample is taken from the skin cells inside the cheeks, known as buccal cells. Before using any sampling kit, ensure the expiry date, printed on the outer bag, has not been passed.

Checklist—Taking a buccal swab DNA sample

- Ensure that the person has not eaten or drunk anything in the 20 minutes prior to the sample being taken. If they have, officers must ensure that 20 minutes elapse before taking the sample.
- Make sure the swabs and containers in the kit are fully sealed and undamaged. If they show damage, discard and begin with a new kit.
- Wear the disposable gloves provided and avoid talking or coughing for example, over the swabs and containers.
- Take one of the two swabs and hold by the stem end. Use the ridged end of the swab to firmly scrape the inside of the cheek of the donor, for at least six passes.
- Open one of the flip top containers, press down on the stem end of the swab to eject the ridged swab piece into the container. Be careful not to bend the swab stem.
- Once the sample has been ejected into the flip top container, seal the top, attach one of the provided barcode labels to the container and place this into the bag provided.
- Repeat this process using the second swab on the other cheek of the donor.
- With both sealed containers in the tamper-evident bag provided, seal the bag in front of the donor.
- Complete the DNA sample form included in the kit in black ink using block capitals. If this is incomplete the sample will be rejected by the laboratory.

6.6 DNA Samples from Persons

- Place the form, the bag containing the two samples and spare barcodes into the larger tamper-evident bag, seal and place in the freezer for storage.
- It is advisable to make a record of the barcode used in the pocket notebook and on the custody record where appropriate, for continuity purposes.

Volunteer sampling

Samples may be required from victims, for elimination purposes or during intelligence led screens. The procedure for taking the sample is the same as above, but a volunteer kit (K515) must be used. These have a barcode which begins at number '5' upwards.

Written consent is required in these situations both for the sample to be taken and if appropriate, any profile obtained to be loaded onto and retained on the national database. Such samples can also be the subject of a speculative search against the database. Once consent has been given for the sample to be loaded onto the database it cannot be withdrawn. It is important that those giving the voluntary sample (whether victim or suspect) are fully informed of the reasons for taking the sample and the consequences of any consent given. Where consent is not given to load any profile onto the database, samples will be destroyed following the completion of the purpose for which they were taken.

POINT TO NOTE—LEGISLATION AND DNA SAMPLES

A DNA buccal swab is classed as a non-intimate sample as defined by PACE, s 65.

PACE, s 63 is the main overarching legislation regarding the taking of an arrestee's DNA. PACE, s 63(1) states that the DNA of a person may only be taken with consent and, where at a police station, such consent must be in writing in accordance with s 63(2); Identification Code D, s 6.

DNA buccal swabs can be taken without consent with the authority of an inspector or above for a recordable offence and where there are reasonable grounds to believe that the sample will serve to confirm or eliminate the suspect's involvement (s 63(3),(4)). The person must be informed that authority has been given to take a sample without consent and the grounds and nature of the offence in which the suspect is believed to be involved (s 63(6)).

Amendments made by the Criminal Justice Act 2003 extend the powers for taking DNA samples without consent, without the authority of an inspector or above, in the following circumstances:

- from a person in police detention, arrested for a recordable offence;
- who has not had a sample of the same type, from the same part of the body taken during the investigation, or;
- where a sample has been previously taken that has proved insufficient.
- The power is available irrespective of whether or not the sample is required for the investigation of the offence for which the suspect is arrested.

> Samples taken under this power can be taken for the purpose of adding the person's profile to the NDNAD. The power confers the same responsibility for informing the person of the reason for taking the sample, but does not require the nature of the offence to be stated.
>
> The Police Reform Act 2002 confers on designated support staff the power to take DNA PACE samples under PACE, s 63.
>
> Under the Criminal Justice and Public Order Act 1994, persons who have their DNA sample taken, with or without consent, must be informed that these may be the subject of a 'speculative search'. This is a search of the appropriate databases to see if their DNA profile can be identified against any crime scene marks.
>
> Reasonable force may be used to take a non-intimate sample by virtue of Code D, para 6.7.

6.7 Chapter Summary

The use of DNA profiling has, without a doubt been a tremendous tool in the investigation of crimes. However, as the technology has advanced to enable DNA profiles to be gained from increasingly smaller amounts of material, so the risks of contamination and cross-transfer have risen.

Where DNA material may be required from an exhibit, care must be exercised in the handling, packaging and storage of such. Officers must always wear disposable gloves when handling items containing body fluids and must avoid talking, coughing and sneezing over samples.

DNA material recovered from crime scenes and those taken from persons are processed to obtain a profile. Where the profile is of suitable quality, it can be loaded onto the national DNA database (NDNAD) where crime stain profiles are searched against profiles gained from PACE samples of those arrested. A match between profiles can be in the form of a scene to scene match, enabling investigators to link a series of incidents committed by the same person or between a scene profile and a suspect's profile.

A match between a scene profile and a suspect is not however conclusive evidence on its own that the suspect committed that particular crime. The evidence that can be gained from a DNA profile is based on a probability match between the suspect sample and the crime scene sample, and the likelihood of anyone else having the same profile. For this reason it is important that other corroborative evidence is available to support the DNA identification and place it into the context of the case.

6.7 Chapter Summary

KNOWLEDGE CHECK—DNA

1. What is DNA?

    Deoxyribonucleic acid (DNA) is the genetic coding found in most of the cells of the body, with the exception of red blood cells. We inherit half our DNA from our mother and half from our father which means that an individual's DNA is unique with the exception of identical twins, triplets, etc who share the same profile.

2. What is a DNA profile?

    A DNA profile is the unique sequence and combinations of certain areas of the DNA at specific points. It can be compared to a barcode found on retail goods, inasmuch as barcodes all have a similar overall appearance but the location, sequence and size of the bars means that they can be identified as being individual. The analysis of a person's DNA profile enables scientists to establish links or eliminations between a profile at a crime scene with a suspect's sample.

3. State the two types of DNA material that can be recovered from cells and their uses and limitations.

    Nuclear DNA comes from the cell nucleus and if a suitable profile is obtained it can be loaded onto the national database and searched against unidentified crime scene profiles and profiles of persons. A DNA match however is based on probability and is not an absolute certainty so additional corroborative evidence is required if it is used evidentially.
    Mitochondrial DNA (MtDNA) can be recovered from bones, teeth and hair shafts. It is inherited down the maternal line only and has low discriminatory value which means it is unsuitable for searching on the NDNAD. It can be used to identify old, degraded human remains and in mass disaster circumstances where nuclear DNA may not be suitable.

4. Under what circumstances can the police elimination database (PED) be searched?

    The PED holds the DNA profiles of police officers and operational support staff who will have access to crime scenes and recovered forensic evidence.
    It can be searched at the request of an SIO where a profile from a crime stain remains unidentified, if there is a genuine belief that the profile may belong to a member of the police. The search must be limited to comparing the unidentified crime stain with the profiles of the officers who had access to the scene or exhibits. Profiles on the PED cannot be searched on the NDNAD.

5. Where DNA material does not produce a match on the NDNAD or is unsuitable for searching, what options are available to an investigator?

> Where a profile is insufficient to search on the database, the low copy number technique can be used in an attempt to recover a usable profile. This is a highly sensitive technique that can provide DNA profiles from extremely small amounts of material. It is generally only used in serious cases.
>
> If a profile is obtained that is suitable for searching, but no match is produced the techniques of familial searching can be undertaken to potentially identify close genetic relatives. This is generally used for serious crimes.
>
> A pendulum list search can be used where there is a mixed profile, to establish the theoretical profiles present in the mixture. These theoretical profiles can be searched on the NDNAD and where matches occur these are reported for intelligence purposes which can help inform further investigations. This technique can be used for volume and serious crimes.

Summary of the National Occupational Standards (NOS) for the Student Officer Learning Assessment Portfolio (SOLAP) relating to this chapter

The table below indicates where it may be possible to demonstrate the achievement of certain performance criteria.

NOS unit	Unit descriptor	Performance Criteria, Range, and Knowledge	Activity
1A1	Apply principles of reasonable suspicion or belief	**1A1.3** pc 2, 3, 4, 7, 8 **Range** 1a, 1b, 2a–2d inclusive **Knowledge** 1, 2, 3, 8, 14, 18, 21, 22	Operate within PACE, s 63 and the Criminal Justice Act 2003 with regard to the taking of DNA samples from persons and the recording of such decisions and actions.
2C1	Provide an initial police response to incidents	**2C1.1** pc 1, 2, 3, 6 **Range** 1a–1g inclusive, 2a, 2c, 2d, 2e **2C1.2** pc 1, 2, 8, 10, 11 **Range** 1a, 1b, 2a–2g inclusive **Knowledge** 1, 2, 3, 8, 18, 19, 21, 22	Initial actions at a crime scene—identify nature of incident and any potential DNA evidence. Take action to ensure that potential DNA evidence is preserved.
2C3	Arrest, detain or report individuals	**2C3.1** pc 1, 2, 3, 5, 6, 8 **Range** 1a–1c inclusive **Knowledge** 1, 2, 4, 6	DNA sampling of detained persons in compliance with legislation.
2G2	Conduct investigations	**2G2.1** pc 1, 3, 4, 5, 6, 8, 9, 12, 15, 16 **Range** 2a–c, 3b, 4a–c inclusive, 5a, b, c, e, 7c **Knowledge** 1, 2, 3, 14, 15, 16, 17, 18, 19, 20, 22, 24	The identification, recovery and preservation of potential DNA evidential material.

6.7 Chapter Summary

NOS unit	Unit descriptor	Performance Criteria, Range, and Knowledge	Activity
2G4	Finalize investigations	**2G4.1** 11 **Range** 1a, b, c, e, 3b **Knowledge** 1, 3	Ensure items of potential evidential value are properly recorded to maintain integrity and continuity. Disposal of items subject to chemical development techniques with regard to health and safety.
2J2	Prepare for court and other hearings	**2J2.1** pc 3, 4 **Range** N/A **Knowledge** 4, 5	Demonstrate the continuity and integrity of relevant exhibits and their value to the investigation.
2K2	Present detained persons for custody process	**2K2.1 pc** 7, 9 **Range** 1d, 2a, 2b **Knowledge** 2, 3, 8 **2K2.2** pc 2, 3 **Range** 2a, d, e **Knowledge** 8, 11	Avoid cross-contamination or transfer of evidence; taking of DNA samples in line with legislation.

> **Recommended Further Reading**
>
> *DNA Good Practice Manual* (2005) ACPO.
> *PACE—A Practical Guide to the Police and Criminal Evidence Act* (2006) Ozin P, Norton H, and Spivey P.
> *The Police and Criminal Evidence Act 1984* (2007) Zander, M.
> <http://www.forensic.gov.uk> For case studies and DNA fact sheets.

7

Blood Pattern Analysis

7.1	Introduction	134
7.2	Principles of Bloodstain Pattern Analysis	134
7.3	Transfer Bloodstains	141
7.4	Preserving Items for BPA	143
7.5	Health and Safety Considerations	144
7.6	Chapter Summary	144

7.1 Introduction

The analysis of the stain patterns created by blood during an assault, referred to as blood pattern analysis (BPA), can only reliably be undertaken by a suitably qualified and experienced scientist. The following is a basic overview into what the analysis of bloodstain patterns can offer police investigators.

The shape, sizes, location and distribution of bloodstains at a crime scene can provide investigators with information that can serve to corroborate or refute the accounts given and provide an interpretation and possibly a reconstruction of the events that occurred.

BPA is based on the physical properties of blood and how it reacts under certain circumstances, which enable the identification of attack sites, establish the locations of items or persons during the attack, aid a reconstruction of the sequence of events, determine the level of force used and, in some circumstances, indicate the type of weapon used.

Investigators should be mindful of the potential that BPA can offer the investigation both at crime scenes and when recovering the clothing of suspects or victims. It is worth bearing in mind that witnesses close to the attack may have bloodstaining on their clothing, and the location of such staining may provide supportive evidence into the sequence of events.

Bloodstaining should be accurately recorded by a CSI by photography or video. In the case of serious incidents it is beneficial for a scientist to attend the scene to undertake the BPA rather than relying on the photographic record.

When seizing clothing from persons, if staining is noted that could potentially be blood, officers must note the location of the stain on their exhibit label and ideally produce a sketch diagram showing the location of the stain as this can be of tremendous use to the interviewing officers.

Blood can be transferred onto parts of clothing after an attack. For example, blood on offenders' hands can be transferred to the insides of pockets or onto underwear. Be mindful that blood may not always be visible and DNA analysis may be required. Bloodstains that are not visible to the naked eye can be located by the use of chemical development techniques.

Gloves must always be worn if the presence of blood is suspected, even if it is not obviously visible.

7.2 Principles of Bloodstain Pattern Analysis

The direction in which blood has travelled can be useful in establishing the location of the victim when the blood was shed. When a drop of blood hits a surface at a 90° angle it will generally leave a circular stain. As the angle of impact onto the surface changes, so does the shape of the resulting blood stain, which will become more elongated in appearance. The viscosity of blood means that the elongated tail of the drop points in the direction of travel. This property enables a scientist to determine the location from where the blood originated.

7.2 Principles of Bloodstain Pattern Analysis

Blood will begin to dry quickly when exposed to air and within a minute an outer crust will begin to develop around the edge of the stain. Attempts to wipe away the blood will typically leave the encrusted outer ring which remains as a skeletal outline and can be indicative of the time frames of actions.

There are broadly three categories of bloodstain, generally referred to as passive, projected and transfer bloodstains.

7.2.1 Passive bloodstains

Passive bloodstains are formed when a drop of blood falls onto a surface without any force other than gravity acting upon it. For example, blood dripping from the blade of a weapon that is not moving would drip from the end of the blade to leave circular stains as illustrated in Figure 7.1, where the blood hits the surface at a 90° angle.

Figure 7.1 Typical passive bloodstains

The surface onto which the blood drips can alter the appearance of the outer edges of the bloodspot, with hard non-porous surfaces producing a stain with smoother edges as in Figure 7.1.

Textured or porous surfaces can produce a blood spot with scalloped distortion apparent around the edges as illustrated in Figure 7.2. The level of distortion around the edges of a bloodstain is wholly dependant on the surface texture.

The diameter of the circular stain created by a free falling drop of blood will increase according to the distance it has fallen, up to a height of 48 inches. Above this height the diameter of the bloodspot would remain fairly constant. Generally, the diameter of a passive dripping blood spot is 4 mm or above.

Figure 7.2 Blood spot with scalloped edges

7.2.2 Projected bloodstains

Projected blood marks will occur where the blood is moving under some force, which can be external or internal in origin. The force of such movement will cause the blood to be expelled or projected onto a surface. An indication of the force used to project the blood can be determined by a scientist by the analysis of the size, shape and quantity of the projected stains. This can enable the amount of force required to create the stain to be established.

When a drop of blood hits a surface at an angle other than 90°, the resultant stain will be elongated. The more acute the angle of impact onto the surface, the longer the stain will become. The resultant 'tail' of the elongated bloodstain will indicate the direction of travel, as shown in Figure 7.3. This information can aid investigators in determining the location of the victim and/or suspect during an attack and serve to corroborate or refute allegations.

Figure 7.3 Direction of travel as indicated by the tail of bloodstain

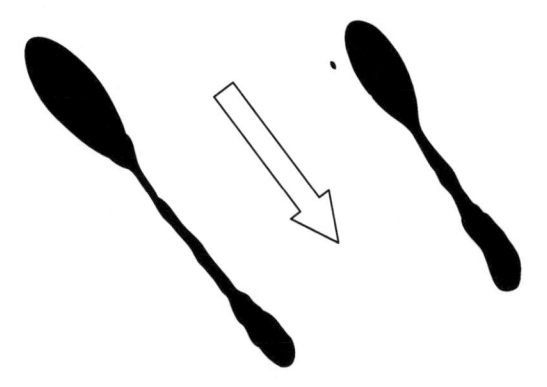

A scientist specializing in BPA can determine the origins of bloodstains by the application of mathematical formulae. The calculations take into account the physical properties of blood which dictate that a drop of blood in flight will take on a spherical shape, resulting in an oval shaped staining on impact with a surface (see Figure 7.4). The width of the stain will be equal to the diameter of the drop before it hit the surface. The length of the resulting stain is dependant on the diameter of the original drop and the angle of impact onto the surface.

7.2 Principles of Bloodstain Pattern Analysis

Figure 7.4 Angle of impact of projected blood drop and resulting stain

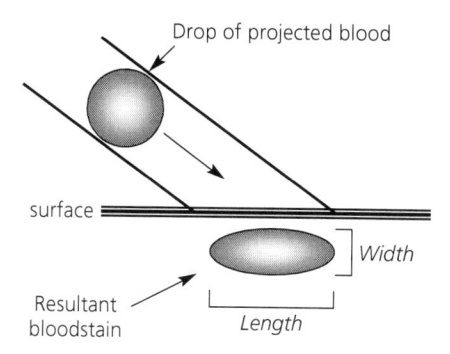

When the direction of travel and the angle of impact of a group of stains have been established, it is possible for the scientist to determine the location from which the stains originated.

This can assist an investigator in establishing where a victim or offender was during the attack and their positioning, for example whether the victim was lying down or standing up during the attack.

Projected bloodstain patterns can be separated broadly into three categories: arterial spurt, cast-off stains and impact patterns.

Arterial spurt

When an artery is breached, blood is forced from the body under the force of the pumping of the heart. Arterial spurts will typically display a wave-type, zig-zag pattern caused by the pressure changes of the heartbeat.

Cast-off stains

When an object strikes the skin with enough force to cause bleeding, the initial blow may split the skin; the immediate reaction of the body is for the capillaries to tighten in an attempt to prevent blood loss. There will be a delay between the splitting of the skin and the blood rising to the surface.

On the second blow, blood will have begun to pool on the surface of the skin, which will then be transferred onto the weapon. This blood is then thrown, or cast from the weapon when it is in motion as illustrated in Figure 7.5.

Cast-off marks will generally form drops of blood that are deposited in a linear manner, as illustrated in Figure 7.6. The number of cast-off marks may indicate a minimum number of blows. As a general rule, the principle of 'first bash–no splash' can be applied. Figure 7.6 shows three distinct lines of cast-off staining, which may indicate a minimum of four blows.

137

Figure 7.5 Blood patterns created from medium velocity impact

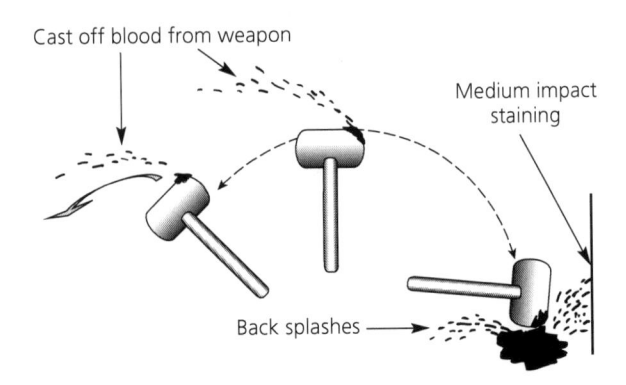

The first blow will not create a cast-off mark as there is no blood on the surface of the weapon. Blood will be picked up on the second and subsequent blows. Where there are two distinct cast-off marks for example, this may indicate at least three blows have been struck.

Figure 7.6 Typical linear pattern of cast-off stains

Impact patterns

These are caused when a force is applied to wet blood which causes the blood to disperse in small droplets. The size, shape and dispersal patterns of the drops

7.2 Principles of Bloodstain Pattern Analysis

can indicate the level of force used. There are three general categories of impact indicated by blood patterns: low, medium and high velocity impact stains. The size of bloodspots can be indicative of the force of impact. Generally, the greater the impact velocity, the smaller the drops produced will be.

> **POINTS TO NOTE—CATEGORIES OF IMPACT**
>
> - Low velocity stains are created by passive blood drops which are usually about four millimeters in diameter.
> - Medium impact velocity will result in stains two to four millimeters in diameter and would typically be caused by blunt force trauma, cutting or stabbing for example.
> - High velocity impact stains are typically less than two millimetres in diameter and are generated as a result of incidents such as gunshot trauma or high speed machinery injury. Such stains appear as a fine spray or mist.

Aspirated bloodstains occur where blood is projected through the action of coughing or gasping for example, when blood is present in the mouth or airways. In such instances, blood is projected and dispersed in small droplets similar to that which occurs with high velocity impact wounding.

Aspirated blood can generally be distinguished from high velocity impact stains as it will often be diluted with saliva which leads to a weaker colouration. Small air bubbles present in aspirated blood may be visible as small rings within the stain where the bubbles have burst, although these may only be noticeable on smooth non-porous surfaces.

Case study—Interpretation of blood patterning

Billie Jo Jenkins was a teenage girl who was battered to death by being beaten with an 18-inch tent peg on the rear patio of her home. She was the foster daughter of Sion Jenkins who was sentenced to life for her murder in July 1998.

The blood of Billie Jo was found on the jacket, trousers and shoes worn by Sion Jenkins on the day of the murder. The blood that was located on Mr Jenkins' clothing was not readily visible and was present as a fine spray of small drops. Similar blood patterning was located on the front of the leggings worn by Billie Jo.

The size and distribution of the blood spots located on the clothing of Billie Jo and Mr Jenkins was reported to be consistent with his being the attacker. Forensic scientists stated that the blood patterns on his clothes were what would be expected if a person was to inflict blows onto wet blood whilst standing over the victim.

The defence team put forward the argument that the blood was as a result of exhalation from the deceased. It was stated that the bloodstains were present due to the fact that when Mr Jenkins discovered the body of Billie Jo, he went to tend to her prior to

Chapter 7: Blood Pattern Analysis

calling for help. It was as a result of moving Billie Jo, the defence argued, that a passive exhalation occurred, depositing blood onto his clothing.

Scientists undertook several experiments in order to replicate the effects of the aspiration of blood and analyse the resultant patterns. It was found that exhaled (aspirated) blood can cause a pattern similar to that which would be created with a high velocity impact.

The bloodstain evidence in this case played a key role in the trial and research was undertaken by forensic scientists to establish whether the bloodstains could be as a result of impact or aspiration. The jury had the task of deciding which of the complex arguments for either position was correct.

The conviction against Sion Jenkins was quashed in July 2004 and Sion Jenkins was released on bail pending a retrial. Mr. Jenkins was acquitted of the murder of Billie Jo in February 2006 following two appeals and three trials.

This case highlights the issue that forensic evidence can, and will, be interpreted in different ways. It is vital investigators retain an open mind and consider all the possible scenarios for the presence of forensic evidence. To have any value in a case such evidence must form part of a thorough investigation to put the forensic material into context.

In addition to the basic patterns that can be observed, there are other characteristic marks that can assist in the reconstruction and interpretation of events. Trail patterns may be evident at crime scenes where blood has fallen in drips from an injury, object or where a bleeding body has been carried. The trail of blood drops can enable a scientist to establish the direction and speed of travel by assessing the elongation of the individual blood drops and the distance between them. As the velocity of the blood source increases, the elongation and distance between the spots will also increase.

Scenario 1—Observation of absence

The absence of bloodstaining in an area can indicate that something was shielding the area from the bloodstains, and that the object has subsequently been removed.

For example, consider a room, the scene of a fatal assault with medium impact staining on the wall and horizontal surfaces such as tables and chairs. It is observed that there is a small rectangular area on a coffee table that is clean, although the rest of the table surface is covered with medium impact blood patterning.

It is not known what was on the table, but it is clear that it would have blood upon it.

A suspect, a known associate of the deceased, is arrested. The suspect has a mobile phone of the same shape as the clear area (void) on the coffee table.

> Forensic analysis established that the mobile phone, which appeared clean to the naked eye, contained the blood of the victim on the front outer cover of the phone.
>
> The suspect put forward the argument that he found the victim after the attack, tried to rouse him and then tried to call for help and that is how the victim's blood came to be on the phone.
>
> **How does the application of BPA corroborate or refute this version of events?**
>
> The phone physically fits the area on the table that is clear of the projected blood patterns and traces of the victim's blood were found on the outer cover and not on the keypad. This is supportive of the proposition that the mobile phone was on the coffee table during the commission of the attack.

7.3 Transfer Bloodstains

A transfer bloodstain is created when a surface containing wet blood comes into contact with another surface: for example, a footwear mark in blood created from blood on the sole of the shoe being transferred onto the floor or other surface. It can be possible for a distinct and recognizable image of the item to be observed. Other transfer marks include wipe, drag or swipe marks which can also be used in the interpretation and reconstruction of events.

7.3.1 Location and recovery techniques for blood at crime scenes

Minute traces of blood may be present that are not readily observable. This may be due to attempts to clean an area following the commission of an act resulting in bloodshed. There are a number of techniques available to a CSI or forensic scientist for locating such marks.

The initial technique utilized should be the use of high intensity light sources to search for possible bloodstains. An examination with a fluorescent light source may locate possible bloodstaining; although blood will not fluoresce, rather it will absorb the light to show as darker than the background surface. Where a stain is located that is believed to be blood, a presumptive test should be undertaken. The presumptive test reacts with the haemoglobin constituent of blood, it will not conclusively identify a stain as blood, but it will indicate where a stain is not blood. Presumptive blood tests cannot distinguish between animal and human blood.

Any stain that indicates a positive result with a presumptive blood test should be recorded and recovered for examination and analysis by a scientist. Where BPA is required it is advisable for the scientist to visit the scene if appropriate, as it is difficult to undertake such analysis from photographs and/or video. The entire item bearing the stain should be submitted to the forensic service provider where possible. The CSI can recover the stain by swabbing, scraping or cutting out the area containing the stain if appropriate.

7.3.2 Chemical development techniques

Bloodstaining may not be visible to the naked eye and the use of chemical reagents can enable non-visible blood to be located and developed to enable the recovery of further potential evidence.

Luminol

Luminol is a chemical that reacts with blood to give off a faint light, referred to as chemiluminescence, which can be recorded by photography. Luminol is a useful screening tool when searching large areas such as rooms, for traces of blood that are not visible or where it is believed an attempt to clean up any bloodstaining has been made.

Luminol is a very sensitive technique and can detect minute traces of blood even following attempted cleaning. The main disadvantage with the Luminol technique is that it must be undertaken in darkness in order to see the faint light given off by the chemical reaction. Luminol can also react with other substances to give false positive results. A confirmatory test utilizing another type of presumptive test for blood should also be undertaken where a positive reaction with Luminol is encountered.

Luminol is best utilized on porous surfaces such as carpets and clothing as its aqueous nature means it will run off non-porous surfaces and can wash away any potential stains and any detail that may be present in the form of footwear patterns. It is useful as a screening tool to detect minute traces of non-visible blood; however to develop fine detail such as fingerprints in blood, different chemical development processes are required.

Development techniques for marks in blood

The chemical development techniques that can be used to develop fingerprints and footwear marks in blood include protein stains such as Acid Black 1, Acid Yellow 7 and Acid Violet 17. Table 7.1 summarizes the chemical development techniques that are approved for use by the Home Office Scientific Development Branch (HOSDB). These applications can be undertaken within a laboratory and at crime scenes, by trained personnel.

A key consideration where the use of chemical development techniques may be required for the enhancement of marks in blood, is to establish the need for any DNA profiling to be undertaken on the bloodstains.

The most appropriate route should be discussed with the CSI or forensic scientist in context of the circumstances of the case and with a view to maximizing all the potential evidence.

Table 7.1 Chemical development techniques for recovery of marks in blood

Chemical technique	Applications
Acid Yellow 7	Can be used for very light stains on non-porous surfaces. Marks can only be visualized utilizing a fluorescent light source, which requires a darkened area to be effective.
Acid Black 1	Produces a visible impression on porous surfaces.
Acid Violet 17	Produces a visible impression on all types of surface.
DFO	Reacts with amino acids and will develop marks or fingerprints in blood on most surfaces. Marks can only be visualized utilizing a fluorescent light source, which requires a darkened area to be effective.
Ninhydrin	Reacts with amino acids and will develop marks or fingerprints in blood on most surfaces.

7.4 Preserving Items for BPA

As BPA is a non-destructive technique, it should always be undertaken before any other examination. As the scientist will be assessing the size, location and distribution of bloodstains it is vital that the stains are not altered by inappropriate handling, such as the folding of wet bloodstained clothing for example, which will cause the transfer of bloodstains to other areas of the item not originally stained.

Ideally, if BPA will be a requirement, it is advisable for a CSI to recover the material. BPA is not generally utilised for volume crime incidents, therefore it is likely that if it is required it will be a serious case, whereby a CSI will be in attendance to record and recover the items as appropriate.

Footwear marks will be present at every crime scene, although they may not be visible. Care must be taken when entering scenes where there is significant bloodshed not to destroy potential footwear marks. CSI may use stepping plates to traverse across the scene in order to preserve any potential footwear marks.

A particular phenomenon occurs in carpeted rooms where officers stand on an apparently clean area close to a bloodstain. The 'wick effect' occurs where there is a visible bloodstain on a carpet; the blood seeps through to the underside of the carpet and disperses underneath it, unseen. When pressure is applied to a clean area near to the bloodstain, this can draw blood up from beneath the carpet to the surface to create an image of the item creating the pressure, such as the footwear marks of investigation personnel.

Such a footwear mark may only become visible following the application of Luminol or other such chemical screening technique. If the blood has seeped onto the surface of the carpet due to the wick effect, there will be traces of blood on the soles of the officers' footwear, which can then be transferred to other areas.

The best way to avoid such contamination and transfer of material at crime scenes is to stay out unless there are preservation of life considerations. (See

143

Chapter 2 for guidance on the preservation and management of crime scenes.) As with other types of evidence, outdoor scenes present the bigger risk to the potential BPA evidence due mainly to environmental factors. The scene must be preserved and managed as outlined in Chapter 2.

7.5 Health and Safety Considerations

When dealing with scenes containing bloodstaining, whether the scene is the location, victim or suspect, care must be taken with a view to minimizing the risk from potential blood borne infections.

> **Checklist—Health and Safety considerations when dealing with blood**
>
> - Always wear gloves when handling items or persons containing blood or other body fluids. It is advisable to retain and exhibit the gloves worn after handling items containing body fluids.
> - Dried blood will become airborne as fine dust particles which can enter the body via mucus membranes. Wearing a disposable mask ensures that the dried blood particles are not inhaled. Avoid unnecessary movement of bloodstained items to prevent dislodging any dried blood.
> - Any items exhibited must be clearly labelled on the outer packaging as 'BIOHAZARD'
> - Be aware that you may have walked through bloodstains that were not visible. It is advisable to decontaminate the soles of boots following attendance at scenes where bloodstaining is present in large amounts. This can prevent the transfer of possible blood to other scenes.

7.6 Chapter Summary

Blood pattern analysis (BPA) can assist investigators to establish a sequence of events and the types of actions involved during an attack involving bloodshed. The information from such an examination can serve to corroborate or refute allegations or differing versions of events.

BPA can only be undertaken by a scientist, usually a biologist, who specializes in the analysis of bloodstains as it is a complex process with many variables. As seen with the Billie-Jo Jenkins case, the interpretation of the staining and how it was formed was a key point during the court procedures. There will inevitably be different interpretations that could apply in a case and investigators must keep an open mind as to the possibilities of differing interpretations being presented.

7.6 Chapter Summary

BPA relies on the knowledge of the physical properties of blood and how it reacts under different circumstances. The scientist will examine the bloodstaining, recording the size, shape, locations and quantity of bloodspots to establish the possible location from which the blood originated, the relative positions of persons involved, possibly the type of weapon and the level of force used where appropriate.

Bloodstaining may not be visible to the naked eye and the use of chemical processes can assist in the locating of minute traces of blood. Care must be taken to ensure that contamination and transfer of blood stains is avoided.

Health and safety precautions must be observed when dealing with bloodstained items or persons due to the risk of blood borne infections. Any items exhibited must be labelled 'biohazard' on the outer packaging.

KNOWLEDGE CHECK—BPA

1. Describe the three basic types of projected bloodstain.

   Impact stains occur when an item such as a weapon impacts into wet blood. Impact stains can establish whether the force used was of low, medium or high velocity.

   Cast-off stains are linear stains which occur as wet blood is flung from an object in motion.

   Arterial spurt stains form wave or zig-zag patterns when an artery is breeched. The pattern created is due to the pressure of blood rising and falling with the heart beat.

2. What information can potentially be gained from the number of cast-off marks at a scene?

   It can be possible to establish the minimum number of blows that were struck due to the number of linear cast-off stains present. The principle of 'first bash, no splash' may apply where the initial blow does not impact into wet blood, subsequent blows into wet blood will transfer blood onto the object which will then be flung or cast off as the object is moving.

3. How can the direction a blood stain has travelled be established?

   A drip of blood falling onto a surface at a 90° angle will generate a circular stain. As the angle of impact decreases, the resulting stain becomes more oval and elongated in shape. The narrower tail end of such an elongated bloodstain will point in the direction of travel. The angle of impact can be determined mathematically using measurements of the width and length of the stain.

4. State the procedures that can be used to locate blood at a crime scene.

   BPA should be undertaken (where appropriate to the case) where visible bloodstaining is present.

Chapter 7: Blood Pattern Analysis

> The CSI should examine the area with a high intensity light source to search for blood. Blood does not fluoresce but will absorb the light to appear darker than the surface background. Once located any possible blood should be tested with a presumptive blood test kit. Chemical development techniques such as Luminol can be used to search for non-visible blood traces. Fingerprints and other marks in blood can be developed by using chemical development processes.
>
> The need for DNA analysis should be considered prior to the application of any chemical processes.
>
> 5. What does a positive result of a presumptive blood test indicate?
>
> A positive presumptive blood test indicates that the stain may be blood, as the test targets the haemoglobin in blood. It cannot distinguish between animal or human blood.
>
> A positive test will warrant the recovery of the stain for further confirmatory testing by a scientist, as no single test is 100% specific for blood. A negative result means the stain is not blood.

Summary of the National Occupational Standards (NOS) for the Student Officer Learning Assessment Portfolio (SOLAP) relating to this chapter

The table below indicates where it may be possible to demonstrate the achievement of certain performance criteria.

NOS unit	Unit descriptor	Performance Criteria, Range, and Knowledge	Activity
2C1	Provide an initial police response to incidents	**2C1.1** pc 1, 2, 3, 6 **Range** 1a–1g, 2a, 2c, 2d, 2e **2C1.2** pc 1, 2, 7, 8, 10 **Range** 1a, 1b, 2a–2g **Knowledge** 1, 3, 6, 8, 19, 21	Initial actions at a crime scene—identify nature of incident and any potential BPA evidence where appropriate. Take action to ensure that potential BPA evidence is preserved and risks to health and safety are minimized.
2G2	Conduct investigations	**2G2.1** pc 1, 2, 4, 5, 13 **Range** 2a, c, 3b, 4a, 5a–e **Knowledge** 3, 9, 14, 15, 16, 17, 18, 19, 20, 22, 23, 24	The identification and preservation of potential BPA evidential material and actions to preserve such.
2K2	Present detained persons for custody process	**2K2.1** pc 7 **Knowledge** 8	Record possible blood staining on the clothing of a person by documenting with a sketch diagram and notes as to the location and nature of the stain for use by interviewers.

Recommended Further Reading

Bloodstain Pattern Analysis with an Introduction to Crime Scene Reconstruction, 2nd edn (2001) Bevel, T and Gardner, RM.
Criminalistics, 8th edn (2004) Saferstein, R.
Forensic Science (2004) Jackson, ARW and Jackson J.
Interpretation of Bloodstain Evidence at Crime Scenes, 2nd edn (1998) James, SH and Eckert, WG.
Manual of Guidance for Fingerprint Development (2004) HOSDB.
R v Sion David Charles Jenkins [2004] EWCA Crim 2047.

8

Sudden Deaths

8.1	Introduction	150
8.2	Post-Mortem Changes	150
8.3	Decomposition	155
8.4	Cause of Death Indicators	158
8.5	Drowning	161
8.6	Role of First Officers at Scenes of Sudden Death	163
8.7	Chapter Summary	167

8.1 Introduction

When police officers are tasked to attend scenes involving deceased persons, the incident can take a number of forms. It can include fatal road traffic collisions (RTCs), suicides, murders and other unexpected deaths such as drug-related deaths. CSIs will attend the scenes of all suspicious deaths. Suicides and non-suspicious accidental deaths such as fatal RTCs are generally attended by CSIs who will record the scene and collect evidence on behalf of the coroner. The criteria for CSI attendance at non-suspicious deaths is dependant on force policies and the circumstances surrounding the case. The key issues to be addressed at such scenes are to identify the deceased and establish the circumstances surrounding the death. Establishing the time that has elapsed between the death and the discovery of the body (the post-mortem interval—PMI) can be of benefit to investigators.

This chapter will give a basic overview of the changes that occur in a body after death that can aid an estimation of the time that has elapsed since death occurred and the deceased being discovered. The main considerations when dealing with the deceased are the risks to health and safety. The presence of body fluids can present biological hazards with the risk of infection. The minimum requirement is to wear disposable gloves and mask when required to handle a cadaver under non-suspicious circumstances (suicide for example).

Where the deceased is known to have an infectious disease such as HIV or hepatitis B it is vital that this fact is relayed immediately to those who will subsequently be handling the body including the CSI, pathologist and undertakers for example.

In addition to the physical hazards present when dealing with the deceased, there is the impact it may have on the mental health of officers. Such scenes can be distressing and upsetting. It is not inappropriate for such incidents to have an impact on officers. Occupational health units and trauma counsellors are available in-force for officers affected by any incident. Do not be afraid to seek support if adversely affected by any incident.

8.2 Post-Mortem Changes

The amount of time that has elapsed between a person's death and the discovery of the body can have a great impact on the investigation. There is currently no singular scientific method available that can accurately establish the time since death or post-mortem interval (PMI) due to the number of variables that can affect the outcome. In the absence of a witness to the death occurring, it can be difficult to pinpoint an exact time that death occurred.

Changes that take place in a body after death can be used to indicate an approximate time frame and the more observations the pathologist can utilize, the better the determination of the PMI. The combination of observed conditions such as rigor mortis, body cooling, livor mortis and the states of decomposition can lead to a narrower estimated time frame provided that the necessary records have been made on the initial attendance at the scene, in particular the recording of environmental factors such as the temperature. The presence or otherwise of any insect activity can also provide valuable information in estimating the PMI. The sooner after death that a body is discovered, the narrower the time frame will be.

8.2.1 Body cooling (algor mortis)

A body will lose heat following death until it is at an equal temperature to the immediate environment. The rate of cooling can be a useful indicator in establishing the PMI. The environmental temperatures should be recorded where appropriate on at least two occasions by the CSI if the body temperature is to have any meaning. The temperature should be taken from an area close to the body, and the times of each reading recorded.

It is important that the temperature around the body is not altered significantly. At indoor scenes, ensure windows, doors and heating systems for example, remain as they were on discovery of the body. If doors or windows are left open following discovery of the body this will alter any temperature readings taken, often to the point that they are no longer representative. Where heating systems are on a timer and the body has lain for a few days, it is worth recording the timer settings where possible.

The rate of cooling is subject to many variables including the immediate environmental conditions, body mass, body temperature at time of death and the amount of clothing worn. Generally a clothed body will lose heat at about 1.5°C per hour for the initial six to eight hours and will generally feel cold to the touch after 12 hours. The numerous variables concerning cooling rates make it an unreliable singular method of determining PMI.

8.2.2 Rigor mortis (rigidity)

Rigor mortis is the process whereby the muscle groups stiffen after death. This occurs due to the biochemical changes within the muscles and has an immobilizing effect on the joints. Rigor mortis begins at the same time throughout the body, but is first observed in the head and jaw, it appears to traverse downwards towards lower extremities due to the differing sizes of the various muscle groups. The observation of the stiffening is first apparent in the smaller muscle groups such as in the jaw, neck and fingers. Once a body stiffens it will remain in that position until rigor passes or is 'broken' when a joint is forcibly moved. Rigor mortis is a temporary condition which will subsequently disappear leaving the body limp. Once rigor mortis has fully developed and then subsequently departed it will not recur.

Chapter 8: Sudden Deaths

As a general rule, the stages of rigor mortis are that it:

- begins within two to four hours after death;
- is completed within eight to 12 hours;
- begins to reduce between 18 and 36 hours;
- will have disappeared completely within 48 to 60 hours and will not return.

Because of the numerous variables that influence the onset and subsequent departure of this condition, these timings can only be rough guidelines. Factors that can affect the status of rigor mortis are the temperature of the environment and the internal body temperature immediately prior to death (heat can accelerate the onset and the subsequent dissipation of the condition). Persons with reduced muscular development, for example the elderly or young, may have little if any, apparent rigor mortis.

The numerous variables concerning the onset and dissipation rates of rigor mortis make it an unreliable singular method of determining PMI. A condition which can be mistaken for rigor mortis can occur immediately after death. This condition is referred to as a 'cadaveric spasm' (see section 8.2.3 below).

8.2.3 Cadaveric spasm

Under certain circumstances the stiffening of the hands or arms can take place immediately after death, this condition can be confused with rigor mortis. The condition is known as a cadaveric spasm and is often associated with violent death or where high emotion is involved. It is not uncommon for people who have held a weapon or such in their hands at the point of death to retain a tight grip on it immediately after death.

Where a suicide has been caused by shooting for example, the person can retain a very tight grip on the weapon. The observation of such tight gripping of weapons can be a useful indicator to an investigator that the deceased had been holding the weapon immediately prior to death. It would be extremely difficult, if not impossible, to replicate such a tight grip by someone placing the firearm in the hands of the deceased after death in order to give the impression of suicide. Care must be taken however not to confuse this with rigor mortis. Cadaveric spasm will remain until onset of putrefaction.

8.2.4 Lividity (liver mortis/hypostasis)

When the heart stops pumping, blood ceases to be circulated causing a gravitational pooling and settling of blood within the blood vessels in the lowermost areas of the body. This leads to a dark purplish discoloration observed at the lowermost unrestricted levels of the body.

For example, a body found lying on its back on the floor would not have any lividity discoloration on the parts of the body that have been in direct contact with the floor, therefore it would be expected that the buttocks, upper back and calves for instance would not be discoloured by lividity as illustrated in Figure 8.1. This is due to the pressure caused by the weight of the body on the small blood vessels which prevents them filling with blood.

Figure 8.1 Lividity development process

Blood settles into vessels in the lowermost point due to the effects of gravity

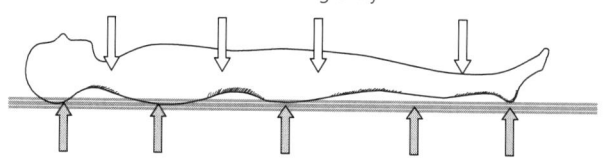

Areas in contact with a surface will restrict the blood vessels meaning that the blood cannot settle in these areas.

When the body is turned, the lividity would typically be present on the back in the shaded areas illustrated below.

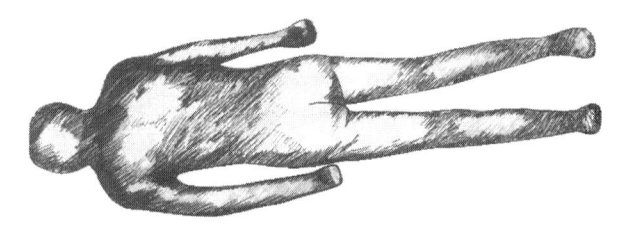

Note how the areas in contact with the surface the body was laid on, such as the shoulders, arms, buttocks, upper thighs, shins and heels are clear of, or display paler lividity.

Similar effects can occur where a person is wearing tight clothing which prevents blood pooling into the vessels in that particular area. Wrinkled bedding or items beneath the body such as coins for example, may lead to paler areas within the lividity. The observation and recording of such markings can assist the investigator in establishing whether the body has been moved in the time between death and the body being discovered. In cases of extensive blood loss, lividity may be very weak due to the lack of blood in the circulatory system.

The observation and interpretation of the status of the lividity markings should be undertaken and recorded by the pathologist if it is to be used evidentially.

Observation of the positions of discolouration can, in some circumstances, be indicative of whether a body has been moved since death. The settling of the blood to the lowest parts will begin as soon as the heart stops pumping and may be visible within 30 to 60 minutes after death. As the blood continues to settle, the intensity of the discoloration increases, becoming darker in appearance.

The settled blood will begin to clot and becomes 'fixed' in place. If an area of discoloration is pressed prior to it becoming 'fixed' it will lighten in colour; on removal of the pressure the discoloration will return. This is referred to as 'blanching'. When lividity is fully fixed and the blood has clotted, such blanching will no longer occur on the application of pressure.

The discoloration caused by lividity typically becomes fixed within six to 12 hours of death occurring, although this is subject to variables so can only be a general guide. Once fixed, the lividity will remain until discoloration from decomposition obscures it.

A body may be moved a number of times after death, prior to the discoloration becoming fixed and the blood will resettle to the lowest points in that new position. Once fixed however, the blood will remain in the original position, and not resettle to another position if the body is subsequently moved. Where lividity is not fully fixed when the body is moved, some blood may resettle to the lowermost areas of the subsequent position and some will remain in the original position, the intensity of the discoloration in this situation will depend on the extent to which the lividity was fixed before the body was repositioned.

Lividity colouration can differ as a result of poisoning, disease or environmental factors. In cases involving carbon monoxide or cyanide poisoning, hypothermia, refrigeration and aerosol inhalation for example, a bright red or pink colouration can be observed. Occasionally, lividity may appear as an unusual pattern or look like bruising. The pathologist will be able to clarify whether such marks are caused by lividity or bruising.

Case study—Lividity as an indicator for neglect of duty

A male living in shared accomodation was found dead in his bed at 10.00 in the morning.

It was reported by occupants at the house that the male had been out the previous night and had returned shortly before 11.00 at night and was reported to have been extremely intoxicated with alcohol. Due to the level of intoxication, the other occupants decided that the male should be checked at regular intervals during the night.

The CSI attended the scene with the investigating officers. The male was lying flat on his back, and on turning the body, the CSI noted that lividity was well established on the person's back and underside of his arms and legs. The areas of lividity were pressed and did not display any blanching, indicating that it was fixed.

The observation of the lividity indicated that the male had been deceased for some time as lividity was fixed, and that the body had not been moved during that time. This observation was confirmed by the findings of the pathologist during the post-mortem examination.

Due to these observations, it was found that the male had not been regularly roused during the night, as stated by the other occupants of the address.

> The observations made in this case were pertinent in refuting the version of events given by the occupants of the premises.
>
> Care must be exercised however, as such observations are subject to many variables. It is always worth recording any such observations, but only a qualified pathologist can reliably interpret such observations in conjunction with other factors which come to light during the post-mortem examination.

The numerous variables concerning the development of lividity make it an unreliable singular method of determining PMI.

8.2.5 Eyes

The examination of the eyes of the deceased can be a useful indicator in establishing the PMI. The following general observations can assist in establishing the time elapsed since death:

- The cornea becomes slightly milky/cloudy within eight to ten hours after death, however this process is dependant on variables such as whether the eyes are open or closed and the environmental conditions.
- Levels of potassium contained within the vitreous humour (the clear viscous substance behind the lens of the eye) will typically rise after death. A pathologist may take samples in order for the measurement and interpretation of potassium levels to be made.

The numerous variables concerning any changes in the eye make it an unreliable singular method of determining PMI.

8.3 Decomposition

Decomposition, or putrefaction, begins more or less immediately following death, although the observable appearance of such may not be apparent for a number of hours or possibly days, depending on the particular circumstances. The activities of bacteria and micro-organisms, resulting in the production of gases and enzymes within the body, lead to the breakdown of body tissues

The decomposition process advances through several observable stages. The sequence of observable changes for bodies on dry land will typically manifest as the development of a greenish colouration on the skin of the abdomen, due to the breakdown of the haemoglobin contained in the red blood cells. Gases produced as a by-product of decomposition activity can lead to a visible swelling that is particularly noticeable around the face, abdomen and genitals. A greenish or reddish 'marbling' pattern of the skin (subcutaneous marbling) will follow, due to the effect of decomposition on the veins close to the surface of the skin. Blisters filled with gases or fluid will begin to appear on the skin, which can later burst leaving large areas of skin detached from the body. The tongue will swell and as the internal organs begin to liquefy, fluid can leak from orifices.

Generally, the timing of the different stages of decomposition for a body on dry land is:

- A greenish discolouration of the abdomen and genitalia occurring between 36 to 48 hours after death.
- Blue or purplish subcutaneous marbling of veins may be apparent within 72 to 96 hours after death.
- Once bodily fluids have dried, a yellow parchment-like membrane forms.
- The swelling of the body due in part to the build up of decomposition gases will usually occur within five to six days.
- By three to four weeks following death, facial tissue degenerates making visual identification difficult. Skin slippage and detachment may occur.

Environmental temperature is a major factor in the onset of putrefaction; heat will accelerate the process and cold will retard it. The numerous variables that can affect decomposition rates make it an unreliable singular method for establishing the PMI.

8.3.1 Entomology

Entomology is the study of insects and in a forensic context it can be of value as certain insects will colonize dead and decomposing bodies in a fairly predictable manner under certain circumstances.

Entomology can offer the investigator some useful insights regarding the PMI and whether there is the possibility that the body has been moved from the site of death to the deposition site. The observation of insect activity may also provide information on the sites of wounds that may be obscured due to decomposition. The bluebottle (blowfly) is the most commonly encountered insect found colonizing on decomposing bodies above ground.

These flies will generally settle on a decomposing body within minutes after death to lay their eggs in orifices such as the mouth, nostrils and eyes and in the sites of open wounds. The blowfly will colonize a decomposing body more readily than other insects and in larger numbers, to be joined later by other insects such as houseflies.

By establishing the age of an insect sample, an entomologist can calculate a time-scale that can assist in establishing the time since death. In order to do this, the entomologist will have an indepth knowledge of the life and development cycles of particular insect groups and the variables that may affect the development.

Blowflies have a four-stage life cycle involving the egg, larval (maggot), pupal and adult stages. The larval stage consists of a further three sub-stages, referred to as instars. Between each of the instar stages the larva will shed its skin, allowing growth in the next stage. During the larval stage the maggot will feed on the dead tissue. The timing of the lifecycle from egg to adult fly can vary greatly with the most significant influence being that of environmental temperature. Generally the development from egg to adult fly can vary between seven to 18 days, dependant on circumstances including temperature, season and type of insect. Blowfly larvae are the most commonly utilized insect stage in the investigation of crime scenes. However, other developmental stages and other insect species should not be overlooked. Adult flies are perhaps the least useful as they can have come from anywhere and not necessarily have originated from the body in question.

In some cases, an entomologist may identify species that are not consistent with the body recovery site indicating the possibility that the body may have been moved from the original site. Larvae and insects can remain at the original site, and if located can contain DNA from the body to establish a link.

Some larvae will migrate away from the body. Migrating larvae may be left over from the first wave of flies which have matured and flown off and these can assist in establishing a more accurate PMI. Officers attending a scene where maggots are present should be mindful of where they walk and take actions to preserve the scene as outlined in Chapter 2.

The collection of insect samples should only be undertaken by an entomologist or a CSI.

The rate of decomposition is subject to many variables including environmental temperature, body mass, body temperature on death and insect activity. The estimation of the PMI can only reliably be made by a pathologist who will take into consideration all the indicators and associated variables before reaching a conclusion.

There are particular decomposition stages which can be observed under certain conditions.

8.3.2 Adipocere (saponification)

This is a decomposition stage which is observed as a greasy soaplike waxy substance which develops on bodies that have been subject to moist environments or submerged in water. Adipocere can develop over a period of a few weeks to several months, depending on the environmental conditions. Once developed, adipocere can retain the body and internal organs in a relatively well preserved condition for many months.

8.3.3 Mummification (dessication)

This is a condition of arrested decomposition caused by the absence of environmental moisture. For mummification to occur a warm atmosphere with a constant circulation of dry air is required and in optimum conditions mummification can occur in a matter of weeks. This process leads to body tissues becoming hard and dry as they dehydrate.

8.4 Cause of Death Indicators

Certain causes of death can lead to the display of particular conditions that can assist in establishing or confirming how a person died. Such circumstances include the following.

8.4.1 Asphyxiation

Asphyxiation can occur through a number of mechanisms, with the most common causes of death by asphyxiation being:

- compression of the neck—strangulation and hanging,
- inhalation of poisonous gases, and
- suffocation.

There are particular indicators as to the cause of asphyxiation which may be observed in the situations outlined below.

Strangulation

This is caused by the extended compression of the neck by hands or a ligature. There are different categories of strangulation which can display certain indicators. Manual strangulation is as a result of pressure on the neck which causes death by the blocking of blood vessels and/or airway. The indicators of manual strangulation are generally as follows.

- The presence of external abrasions/bruising of the neck (4–5 lbs of pressure is needed to block the veins on the side of the neck to cause asphyxiation).
- Internal damage to neck structures often involving fractures of larynx and hyoid bone.
- Petechiae are small pin-prick haemorrhages which appear as small spots. They are almost always present in the mucous membranes of the inner eyelids, on the eyeballs and/or on the face, particularly the forehead.
- Haemorrhage or trauma to the tongue is common.

Ligature strangulation/hanging

A body that has been subject to ligature strangulation presents with similar indicators as those observed in manual strangulation, with the following exceptions.

- Petechiae haemorrhages are not usually present in hanging where death has been rapid. Where petechiae are observed they should be above the ligature.
- Soft tissue damage within the neck is variable but generally will be less prominent than in manual strangulation.
- Fractures of the larynx occasionally occur, however fractures of the hyoid bone are unusual.

- Ligature strangulation will generally cause marks of a more horizontal appearance than in hangings, due to lack of extended suspension. The ligature marks in hangings tend to be an inverted 'V' shape.
- Hanging victims often have a swollen, protruding tongue which is red/red-black or black in colouration. The protrusion is due to the ligature pressure on the larynx which forces the tongue outward. The discoloration is due to environmental drying.

When dealing with deaths due to ligature strangulation or hangings, it is important that the ligature remains on the body. The only time a ligature must be removed is where there is the slightest chance the person may still be alive. Where possible, ligatures should be removed in a manner that will preserve any knots.

When the first officers attend the scene of a death by hanging, they should first establish that the body is deceased. Where it is apparent that the person is deceased, officers should ensure that the body remains in situ for the CSI examination and take steps to secure the scene to preserve potential evidence.

There may however be the need to cut down a suspended body. Such circumstances would include where the body cannot be satisfactorily shielded from public view or where there is a danger of collapse of the area the person is suspended from. The ligature should be cut at a point away from the knot; officers must inform the CSI of any cuts made by them. The ligature/noose must remain on the body. This also applies to any bindings on the hands or feet.

The potential evidence that can be gained from ligatures include intelligence information that can be gained from the type and characteristics of the knots, DNA from skin cells that may adhere to the ligature during the tying or fixing process, the type of ligature used which could be compared with similar material found at the victim's or suspect's home for example (depending on the case circumstances), fibres and other particulate material can potentially be present on the ligature.

Inhalation of poisonous gases (chemical asphyxia)

This will occur in an atmosphere where the oxygen has been displaced or depleted by a chemical agent or poisonous gas. This usually occurs in enclosed and poorly ventilated spaces. In such cases is it not uncommon to find multiple victims and there may be no immediate physical signs to indicate the cause of death.

The most commonly encountered deaths by chemical asphyxiation are those involving carbon monoxide (CO), which inhibits the absorption and transport of oxygen by the blood.

The most common causes of death due to carbon monoxide toxicity are:

- smoke inhalation during a structural fire;
- inhalation of vehicle exhaust fumes;
- malfunctioning of gas heating appliances.

Observations that may be made in cases of suspected carbon monoxide poisoning include the following.

- A distinct cherry red/pink colouration to any lividity, which is usually visible when a 30% concentration of carbon monoxide is reached in the haemoglobin of the blood. Such colouration can also be indicative of cyanide poisoning, which may be accompanied by an odour often described as being similar to bitter almonds.
- Where bodies are covered in soot, or in dark-skinned persons, the colouration may present in fingernail beds or the lining of the mouth.
- There may be areas on the body where the surface skin has separated from the deeper layers after death. The underlying tissue may be red or grey/tan in colour. Such areas of skin (epidermal) slippage can be misinterpreted as antemortem thermal burns/blistering. Such slippage is not specific for such poisoning.
- Carbon monoxide absorption ceases on death, therefore allowing for accurate post-mortem testing of the levels present.

Carbon monoxide is an odourless and colourless gas, which can be produced by faulty gas boilers/heating systems, solid fuel fires and vehicle exhaust fumes. Where first responding officers suspect carbon monoxide as being present at scenes of sudden death, the area must be *vacated immediately*, leaving doors open. The control room must be informed of the possible presence of carbon monoxide. The area must not be re-entered until it has been declared safe by the health and safety officer or appropriate specialist.

Inhalation of carbon monoxide will manifest as headaches, nausea, abdominal pain, dizziness, sore throat and dry cough, similar to symptoms of flu but without a rise in temperature. Extended inhalation of carbon monoxide can cause the development of symptoms including a fast and irregular heart rate, hyperventilation, confusion, and drowsiness and breathing difficulties. Seizures and loss of consciousness may also occur. The symptoms can occur days or months after exposure and in delayed cases can manifest as co-ordination problems, confusion and memory loss.

Suffocation

Suffocation is caused by the obstruction of the nose and mouth, resulting in the termination of the air supply. Observations that may indicate suffocation include the recovery of material from the item used to cover the nose and mouth from inside or around the nose or mouth and in the throat. The extent of injuries is variable and there may not be any visible trauma present. Where a violent struggle has occurred during the act of suffocation there may be petechiae present. However, this is not an exact indicator of any force used as the absence of petechiae does not necessarily mean there was no force used.

8.5 Drowning

Death by drowning is caused by suffocation due to the immersion in a liquid. It is not necessary for total submersion, providing that the nose and mouth are submerged in any type of liquid, drowning can occur. The cause of death is not necessarily due to the physical obstruction of the airway by the intake of water (classical wet drowning). In some cases death can be instantaneous, for example, caused by a cardiac arrest after entering water, particularly if the water is very cold.

A phenomenon referred to as 'dry drowning' can occur when the body reacts on immersion to water. Two instinctive defence mechanisms can occur which involve the swallowing of large amounts of water, combined with a simultaneous reflex spasm of the larynx preventing entry of water into lungs. This instinctive reaction can lead to unconsciousness and paralysis of the respiratory organs. The post-mortem examination can typically find that the lungs will be relatively free of water.

In general the observations that can be made of bodies that have been submerged in water include:

- a wrinkling of the skin on the hands and feet (where exposed) which will generally occur within 30 minutes;
- after several days the hands will begin to swell;
- the outer layer of skin will begin to separate from the body within five to six days, the skin and nails on hands and feet (where exposed) will be separated from the body within eight to ten days;
- possible vegetation growth on the body can occur within eight to ten days depending on the environment;
- in warm water, an unencumbered body will begin to float to the surface within eight to ten days, in cold water this can take two to three weeks. In very cold water, a body may not surface due to retardation of the development of decomposition gases;
- the greenish decomposition colouration is absent;
- lividity is typically most prominent on the face, chest and upper portions of the extremities, reflecting the position an unencumbered body will typically adopt when submerged (back bent at the waist with head and limbs dangling downwards).

A key question in cases of apparent drowning is whether the deceased was alive or dead prior to immersion. There are a number of observations that can be useful in establishing a possible sequence of events, which include the following.

- Petechiae are not usually present in drowning cases, however in cases of 'forced' drowning where a person has been held under water, petechiae may be observed, to be particularly noticeable in the lungs.

- The presence of froth in the nose and mouth is usually observed, this can be extruded by gentle pressure on the chest. The froth is formed from the active mixing of air and water. It can be a strong indication that the person was alive on submersion, but the absence of foam does not necessarily indicate death occurred prior to submersion. (Note too that the presence of froth is not specific for drowning and can occur in other circumstances.)
- The diagnostic value of silt, mud and water in the airways, lungs or stomach is of limited value in assessing whether a person was dead on submersion as such substances can passively enter a body after death.
- Diatom analysis (see section 8.5.1 below) can possibly indicate whether a person was alive or dead on submersion.

8.5.1 Diatoms

There are over 10,000 species of diatoms, which are microscopic aquatic organisms with exoskeletons of silica which can remain for a considerable amount of time after their death. They are ubiquitous in the environment and can be found in certain soils. Diatomaceous earth is used in some abrasive metal polishes and in the ballast of older safes. Diatoms can be found in areas of open water such as ponds, rivers, lakes, oceans and ditches and in mud, silt and similar damp conditions.

As a result of drowning, a person will take in some water into their lungs, which can enable any diatoms to enter the bloodstream to be transported into the major organs and bone marrow. Where a post-mortem examination recovers the same species of diatom in a deceased's bone marrow, for example, that are found in the water from where the body was recovered this can possibly provide some supportive evidence that the person was alive when initially submerged. The presence of diatoms in the organs such as the brain for example, may also provide supportive evidence, however it may be possible for diatoms to passively enter the organs where a body is submerged for a length of time. Diatoms in bone marrow can provide stronger evidence that the person was alive when entering the water.

The analysis to establish the presence or absence of diatoms, on its own cannot provide conclusive evidence of whether a person was alive or dead when they entered the water.

The analysis of diatoms can, in certain circumstances potentially distinguish between two separate bodies of water (for example, a garden pond and lake nearby) but may be less helpful in differentiating between two sites, separated by a mile, along a river or canal.

In cases involving submersion, it is worth considering that diatoms:

- may be present on the clothing, vehicle interior or home of an offender for example, and can remain until the area is washed;
- are not normally present in tap water or fresh rainwater, however may be present in water butts or similar;
- are particularly prevalent during spring and autumn.

Preservation of items for diatom analysis

Because of the potentially ubiquitous nature of diatoms in the environment, care needs to be exercised to avoid contamination between samples. In cases of death by drowning, the CSI should recover any such samples from the scene and the pathologist will recover the appropriate post-mortem samples. There may be occasions however where investigating officers are required to recover items from suspects, such as clothing, for potential diatom analysis and comparison.

Diatom samples from suspects

Where a person has been in contact with water containing diatoms, such as by running through a brook or in the commission of a 'forced' drowning, the clothing and other surfaces touched by the offender, for example the interior of a vehicle, may also contain diatoms. Diatoms recovered from these items can be compared with diatoms contained in the control samples from the scene/victim. Diatoms will remain on clothing and surfaces until they are washed.

The following considerations must be made when recovering items for diatom analysis.

- Recovered clothing or textiles ideally should by air dried in a darkened environment. Exhibits should be protected from light as this encourages algae growth which can denature the sample. It is possible, although not ideal, to recover diatoms from damp or mouldy garments.
- Exhibits need to be stored in a fridge, and should not be frozen.
- Items should be packaged in a plastic bag or a sealed rigid plastic container, which is then placed into a brown paper evidence sack.

8.6 Role of First Officers at Scenes of Sudden Death

When dealing with incidents involving sudden unexpected deaths, officers should consider whether the death has occurred due to a criminal act. There may be no apparent outward signs that a criminal act has occurred and officers must remain open minded. One example of such a scene involves deaths due to drug overdosing. Such scenes may be regarded initially as a tragic accidental death; however officers must consider whether the drugs were administered to the deceased by another person.

Case study—Rachael Whitear

Rachael was 21 years old when she was found dead in her bedsit in May 2000. She was discovered with a syringe in her hand and it was assumed that her death was due to an accidental overdose of heroin. These initial assumptions played a key role in the subsequent investigation into Rachael's death.

There was no post-mortem examination undertaken nor was a fingerprint examination of her bedsit undertaken for two weeks. There was speculation that Rachael's boyfriend had administered the drugs to her. Two arrests were made on suspicion of manslaughter but the Crown Prosecution Service (CPS) did not have enough evidence to pursue charges.

Failure to undertake a post-mortem and an examination of the scene in the initial investigation meant that any potential evidence to corroborate or refute such allegations was not secured.

Toxicology testing later revealed that the level of heroin in Rachael's blood was below the amount that would be fatal. Rachael's body was exhumed in March 2004 and a post-mortem examination undertaken as part of a second investigation. The inquest following this investigation returned an open verdict.

The handling of this case was referred to the Independent Police Complaint Commission (IPCC) who reported that there were organizational failures in the initial investigation, and recommended that any drug-related death should be treated as suspicious until proved otherwise.

Following a review of the case and a second investigation, it was concluded that Rachael's death was likely to have been caused by a heroin overdose and no evidence was found to implicate a third party involvement in her death. The protracted investigation into Rachael's death caused a great deal of distress for her family, and due to the initial failure to preserve and examine the scene any potential evidence to determine the cause and manner of death conclusively was lost.

This case highlights how the assumptions of what has occurred can have an impact on the subsequent investigation into such deaths.

It is advisable that all incidents that involve sudden, unexpected deaths be approached initially as if they were suspicious deaths, until it becomes absolutely clear that there are no suspicious circumstances surrounding the death. It is preferable to put scene preservation and management procedures in place unnecessarily, than to fail to preserve and manage a scene only to later discover that there may be suspicious circumstances surrounding the death. Chapter 2 outlines the procedures for the preservation and management of scenes. Where there is any doubt whatsoever that raises even the slightest possibility that the death may be due to suspicious circumstances, CID officers and CSIs must be informed immediately.

When dealing with sudden unexpected deaths whatever the circumstances, officers should be mindful that the deceased is a member of a family and should be treated with the same consideration and respect that officers would expect to be given to their own family members. The discovery of a deceased person can be a distressing event for the person finding the body and such persons should be shown sensitivity, tact and compassion.

The first responding officer attending a scene should take responsibility for the body and must ensure that the principles of continuity and integrity are established. The body should be tagged as soon as possible with details of name of deceased (where known), time, date and location found as a minimum. A sudden death report form must be completed for every case of sudden death.

8.6.1 Sudden death report form

The form required to report sudden deaths must be completed at the earliest opportunity as the information provided will enable the coroners' officer to establish the requirement for a post-mortem examination. The form must be completed as fully as possible. Where information is not available at the time, this should be recorded on the form. Officers must not delay the submission of the form until further information becomes available.

8.6.2 Identification of the deceased

A body can only be searched for identification purposes where it is clear there are no suspicious circumstances surrounding the death. Any property with the body must be exhibited by the first officers attending and retained for possible forensic analysis or safe-keeping where it is deemed the death is non-suspicious. If during such a search it is realized that there may be cause for suspicion, the search of the body must cease immediately and actions taken to preserve the scene, as outlined in Chapter 2. Officers should wear disposable gloves when handling the deceased and any associated property. All actions undertaken with regard to the deceased must be recorded and the CSI informed.

In cases where the identity of the deceased is unknown, a detailed description of the body including clothing worn, visible marks, tattoos and any other distinguishing features must be relayed to the control room as soon as possible. These details must also be recorded on the sudden death report form.

The first responding officer will be required to identify the body to the pathologist, for continuity purposes, prior to the post-mortem examination, as being the body found at the scene. This is referred to as police identification and is not the same as a personal identification which is made by a relative or someone who knew the deceased. There will be situations where a personal identification cannot be made due to the condition of the body or where relatives or those known by the deceased have not been located. Where a body is in an advanced state of decomposition or has been mutilated beyond recognition, identification may be possible by way of the following:

Checklist—Methods of identifying unknown deceased

- Fingerprints—These can be taken from the deceased and checked against Ident 1. Fingerprints may also be recovered from personal effects at a person's accommodation (where known) and compared with those of the deceased. Fingerprinting of the deceased will typically be undertaken by CSIs.

- DNA profiling—A DNA sample can be taken and searched against NDNAD. These samples are typically recovered by the pathologist during the course of a post-mortem examination.
- Marks such as tattoos, scars or evidence of medical procedures—Pathologists may discover the deceased has had an operation or a particular condition, and such information can be checked against medical records. Tattoos and other such permanent marks may aid identification and can be photographed by CSIs. Observation of any such visible scars or tattoos should be included on the report form.
- Descriptions of the person (where possible), any clothing worn and personal effects.
- Dental records—An odontologist or forensic dentist can compare the dentition of the deceased with appropriate dental records where available.
- Checking missing person reports for persons of a similar stature, age range and sex.
- Facial reconstruction techniques can be undertaken to produce an image of a probable likeness to the deceased.

Where identification cannot be made visually due to decomposition or mutilation, other techniques to establish and confirm identity will typically be arranged by the coroners' officer in consultation with the OIC. The roles and responsibilities of the different personnel that may be involved in the investigation of sudden deaths are outlined in Chapter 1.

8.6.3 Health and safety considerations

Officers should be mindful of the risk to health and safety when dealing with deceased persons, in particular the risk of infection from blood borne diseases such as HIV or hepatitis B for example. Disposable gloves must always be worn when handling or searching the deceased or associated property.

Where it is known that the deceased has an infectious disease, this information must be made available to all those who will have contact with the body or property containing body fluids. Initially this will typically be the CSI, undertakers, and pathologist. Details of any known infectious diseases must be recorded on the report form.

There may be occasions where officers are required to remove the suspended body of the deceased in cases involving hanging. This should not be undertaken where there is a risk that the body may sustain damage due to officers being unable to take the weight of the deceased. Such actions should not be taken unless absolutely necessary. The rationales for removing a suspended body must be recorded and CSIs informed.

Deaths occurring on the railway present particular hazards from high voltage electricity and moving trains. Officers must never approach railway lines until confirmation is received from the control room that it is safe to proceed. Be aware that the process to make the area safe can take time and so confirmation may not be immediate. Control rooms will generally inform British Transport Police of any incidents on the railways.

8.7 Chapter Summary

The changes that occur in a body after death can be useful to investigators, as the process will generally follow a predictable pattern according to the particular circumstances of the case. There is no one singular forensic method for establishing the time that has elapsed between the death and the discovery of the deceased, referred to as the post-mortem interval (PMI), due to the number of variables that can impact on the decomposition process. Only a pathologist can give a possible time and cause of death. This chapter outlines some of the processes to enable responding officers to gain a basic understanding of the processes that can be utilized.

Consideration should be given to the potential presence of forensic material at any scene of a sudden death. The deceased can contain potential forensic material such as fibres, glass, or DNA material upon them and it is vital that this potential evidence is not lost due to unnecessary handling of the deceased or any associated property. The location at which the body is discovered and any associated property may contain fingerprints, footwear marks, body fluids, fibres and other such material.

The preservation of life will always take precedence over forensic considerations. However when it is clear the person is deceased, officers must ensure that scene preservation actions are instigated where appropriate, as outlined in Chapter 2. The two main considerations initially will be to preserve life then preserve the scene, in that order. Any actions taken within the scene should be documented and the CSI informed. Where there is the risk of infection when dealing with the deceased and associated property, all personnel involved in such processes must wear disposable gloves and a disposable surgical type mask. Where it is known that the deceased is infected with HIV or hepatitis B, this fact must be made known to all those who will be in contact with the deceased or any property containing body fluids.

The sudden death report form should be completed as concisely and accurately as possible and submitted to the coroners' officer as soon as possible. The submission of the report form must not be delayed pending information becoming available, but the reasons for any missing information should be stated on the form. Where the identity of the deceased is unknown the form should contain the same details as the body tag, for example 'unknown female, exit ramp level 3, supermarket car park/date and time'. It can be useful for continuity purposes to include the log or incident number on the form and body tag.

It is preferable to treat any incident involving sudden death as a suspicious death until there is evidence provided to the contrary.

Chapter 8: Sudden Deaths

KNOWLEDGE CHECK—SUDDEN DEATH

1. How can establishing a PMI assist an investigation?

   The post-mortem interval (PMI) is the time that has elapsed between a death occurring and the body being discovered. It can be useful in an investigation in order to determine timelines of event, and possibly to corroborate or refute accounts.

2. State what information a pathologist can use to determine the PMI

   There is no singular scientific technique that can establish time since death; however a combination of factors can be used to ascertain an approximate time frame. These include observation of conditions such as rigor mortis, body cooling, lividity, condition of the eyes and the stages of decomposition.

3. What considerations should be made regarding a death by hanging?

   Ideally the body should remain in situ for the CSI to photograph. A suspended body should only be removed where there is the possibility the person is still alive, where there is a risk of collapse of the structure they are suspended from, or where the body cannot be adequately screened from public view.
   Ligatures must be cut at a point away from the knot, and the CSI informed of any cuts made by officers. The ligature must remain on the body, as must any bindings on hands and feet.

4. State the methods for establishing/confirming the identity of a deceased person where a personal identification cannot be undertaken.

   A personal identification, made visually by relatives or those who knew the deceased may not be appropriate due to advanced decomposition or mutilation. In such cases identification maybe made by way of fingerprints, DNA, marks such as scars or tattoos, facial reconstruction, dental records, medical records, checking against missing persons records and descriptions of the deceased's clothing and possessions where applicable.

5. What are the initial duties of the first responding officers attending the scene of a sudden death?

   Preservation of life and preservation of the scene. Preservation of life takes precedence over forensic considerations, but once this duty is fulfilled, officers must take action to preserve and manage the scene.
   Any actions taken must be recorded and the CSI and OIC informed of what was done.

8.7 Chapter Summary

Summary of the National Occupational Standards (NOS) for the Student Officer Learning Assessment Portfolio (SOLAP) relating to this chapter

The table below indicates where it may be possible to demonstrate the achievement of certain performance criteria.

NOS unit	Unit descriptor	Performance Criteria, Range, and Knowledge	Activity
2C1	Provide an initial police response to incidents	**2C1.1** pc 1, 2, 3, 4, 6 **Range** 1a–1g, 2a, 2b, 2c, 2d **2C1.2** pc 1, 2, 3, 8, 10, 11 **Range** 1a, 1b, 2a–2g **Knowledge** 8, 9, 12, 19, 21, 22, 23	Initial actions at a crime scene—identify nature of incident. Take action to establish the identity of the deceased and ensure that potential forensic evidence is preserved.
2G2	Conduct investigations	**2G2.1** pc 1, 3, 4, 5, 6, 12, 13, 15, 16 **Range** 2a, 2b, 3a, 3b, 4a–c, 5c, 7a, 7c, 7e, 7f **Knowledge** 1, 2, 3, 7, 9, 14, 15, 16, 17, 18, 19, 20, 23, 24, 25, 26	Undertake the initial assessment at the scene and take steps to preserve potential evidence. Liaison with CSI/CID and coroners' officer where applicable. Knowledge of the identification techniques available and methods to establish PMI.
2G4	Finalize investigations	**2G4.1** pc 3, 5, 8 **Range** 1c, 3a, 3b **Knowledge** 3, 10	Completion of appropriate documentation, dissemination of relevant information to others in the investigation.
4G2	Ensure your own actions reduce risks to health and safety	**4G2.1** pc 3, 4, 6, 7 **Range** 1e **4G2.2** pc 5, 6 **Range** 1a **Knowledge** 6, 7, 8, 9, 10, 13, 15	Demonstrate awareness of the particular risks involved with dealing with the deceased, and knowledge of the minimum requirements to reduce the risk. Report known risks to others who will be involved in the investigation.

Recommended Further Reading

Criminalistics, 8th edn, (2004) Saferstein, R.
Evidence & Procedure (2008) Johnston, D and Hutton, G.
Forensic Science (2004) Jackson, ARW and Jackson J.
Pathology for Death Investigators (2001) Dix, J.

9

Firearms and Ballistic Evidence

9.1	Introduction	172
9.2	Firearm Definition	173
9.3	Types of Firearm and Ammunition	173
9.4	Ballistic Examinations	178
9.5	Scenes of Shooting Incidents	179
9.6	Forensic Examination of Firearms and Ballistic Material	180
9.7	Examination to Establish Cause	183
9.8	Taser	184
9.9	Chapter Summary	185

Chapter 9: Firearms and Ballistic Evidence

9.1 **Introduction**

Firearm usage in the commission of criminal offences is being encountered increasingly and officers can be confronted with a variety of firearms and associated ballistic material such as cartridge casings and bullets, or the requirement to establish if a person has handled or discharged firearms. The health and safety of all personnel who deal with firearms is of paramount importance. Firearms should be considered as loaded until an authorized firearms officer (AFO) or equivalent has assessed the firearm and declared it as safe. Once a firearm has been made safe, any handling must be minimized to preserve the potential evidential material that may be present. Fingerprints, DNA from skin cells or body fluids, fibres and other trace material may be present on firearms and ballistic materials.

When dealing with firearm related incidents, the firearm and any related material such as cartridge cases, bullets, clothing and wound types can potentially provide an investigator with forensic evidence. Typically the questions to be addressed in any incident involving firearms include:

- identifying the type of weapon used;
- establishing the distance between the victim and the weapon;
- determining the direction of impact;
- identifying the type of ammunition used;
- establishing the sequence of shots, where multiple wounds exist; and
- whether the discharge was accidental or intentional.

Air weapons use a burst of high pressure air to force a projectile out of the barrel. The air pressure can be created by a mechanical system of a piston being pushed down a cylinder under the force of a compressed spring, between each shot the spring must be recompressed manually.

Pneumatic air weapons use a small tank of pressurized air which can be refilled by means of a hand pump or from a canister of pressurized air. Gas powered weapons utilize compressed or liquefied gas such as carbon dioxide in a replaceable sealed tank which is used to eject the projectile when the trigger is pulled.

Whilst air weapons do qualify as firearms, their use will rarely lead to fatalities, and for this reason, the firearms discussed in this chapter excludes air weapons.

The discipline of firearms and ballistics examination is a vast subject area and this chapter offers a brief overview of the most common types of weapon used, the basic composition of ammunition, ballistic examinations and how to preserve and recover the potential forensic evidence.

Due to the increasing use of firearms in criminal acts, the National Automated Ballistics Intelligence System (NABIS) was developed in order to gather and collate information on the criminal use of firearms. The system is essentially a national database that will hold a central registry of recovered weapons and ammunition and has the capability to undertake ballistics comparisons to link incidents, firearms and ammunition.

Police personnel dealing with firearm incidents should be aware of NABIS and ensure that they are familiar with force policies regarding its use.

9.2 Firearm Definition

The Firearms Act 1968 defines various offences relating to firearms, including air weapons, shotguns and related ammunition. Section 1 of the Firearms Act 1968 defines a firearm as being:

> A lethal barrelled weapon of any description from which any shot, bullet or other missile can be discharged and includes;
>
> Any prohibited weapon, whether it is such a lethal weapon as aforesaid or not; and
>
> Any component part of such a lethal or prohibited weapon; and
>
> Any accessory to such a weapon designed or adapted to diminish the noise or flash caused by firing the weapon

Prohibited weapons are defined by the Firearms Act 1968, s 5 and include CS spray, Tasers, grenades and air weapons with a gas cartridge system. The forensic recovery of Tasers and related material is briefly covered at the end of the chapter due to their increasing use by police firearm officers as a less lethal option for conflict management during appropriate incidents. The criminal use of such weapons is being encountered.

9.3 Types of Firearm and Ammunition

Firearms will generally fall into two main classifications of rifled and smoothbore weapons.

9.3.1 Rifled weapons

There are numerous styles of rifled weapons with a variety of ammunition available. This class of weapons consists of rifles or pistols, both of which are designed to fire bullets.

Definition—Pistols

Pistols can be defined as handguns, a firearm which is designed to be used in one hand. Pistols can be single-shot, self-loading or revolver.

Definition—Rifles

Rifles have longer barrels and are designed to be held with both hands.

Typically, the handguns encountered in an investigation will be either revolvers or self-loading pistols. Revolvers will retain the cartridge after firing until it is manually removed whereas the cartridge cases used in self-loading pistols are ejected from the weapon after firing. Therefore it is more likely to find spent (fired) cartridge cases at the scene of a shooting incident involving a self-loading pistol than a revolver.

The majority of pistols will have what are termed rifled barrels. The rifling in the barrel is a design structure incorporated in order to give some rotation or spin to the bullet, which in turn increases the stability and accuracy of the trajectory of a fired bullet.

Rifling consists of a series of lands and grooves that spiral down the length of the barrel, enabling the bullet to be gripped and rotated prior to leaving the weapon. The number of lands and grooves (see Figure 9.1) differs according to weapon type, as does the number of twists (rotations) along the barrel length.

Figure 9.1 Cross section of rifled barrel

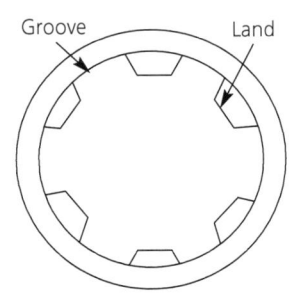

The rifling inside a barrel can leave microscopic scratch marks (striations) on a bullet which can be used to identify the weapon type and establish links between a piece of ammunition and the weapon that fired it. Each class of weapon will possess similar rifling marks to all those of the same make and model. The microscopic scratch marks left on cases and bullets as a result of the rifling and other internal mechanisms, such as firing pins, can be compared to establish if they were fired by the same weapon.

Where a weapon is recovered, marks left on the case and bullet of a test-fired round can be compared to the marks left on cases or bullets recovered from a crime scene.

As the number of lands and grooves and the widths between them, plus the direction and degree of twist of rifling marks on a fired bullet or case differ between makes and models of firearms, this information can enable a firearm examiner to check against a reference database containing technical information on weapons and determine the identity of the weapon to have fired the bullet.

Ammunition

The general design of the ammunition used in rifled weapons consists of four component parts—a cartridge case or shell, bullet (see Figure 9.2) propellant and primer which are generally referred to in their entirety as a 'round'.

9.3 Types of Firearm and Ammunition

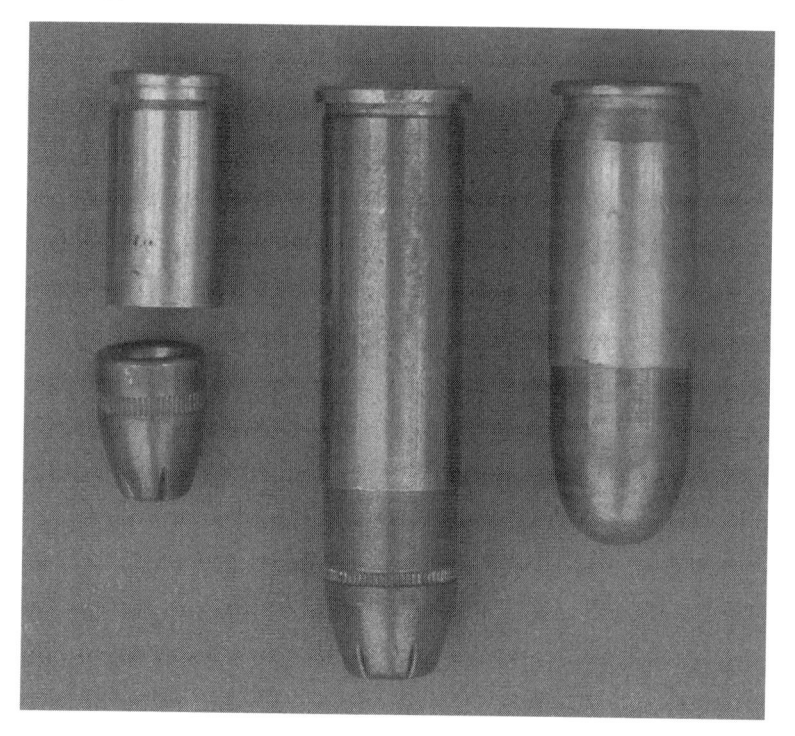

Figure 9.2 Typical round construction

The cartridge case contains a powdered explosive propellant with the bullet clamped into the top of the case. The bottom of the cartridge has a percussion detonator on the base; this is essentially a small metal cup which holds the primer. The detonator (see Figure 9.3) can be situated either centrally (centre fire) or around the edge of the base (rimfire), and contains the primer.

To fire the round, a firing pin strikes the percussion detonator (sometimes referred to as a percussion cap) containing the primer, which in turn ignites the propellant. This creates a relatively large volume of hot gas which causes the bullet and casing to separate, projecting the bullet forward down the barrel. The cartridge case will either remain in the firearm to be removed manually (revolvers and some shotguns) or be ejected from the weapon (self-loading), depending on the weapon type.

Figure 9.3 Cartridge base markings

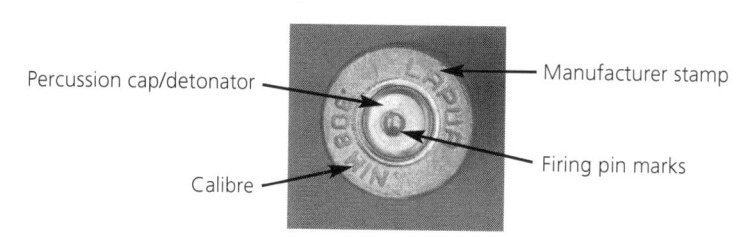

Bullets

Bullets are manufactured in a range of materials to cater for many different uses, far too numerous to cover in one chapter. The basic types of bullets typically encountered will fall into two categories: those which are jacketed or unjacketed. The most common material utilized to manufacture unjacketed bullets is lead, which may be alloyed with antimony or tin to increase the hardness. Jacketed bullets typically have a lead core which is coated in a harder metal such as copper, zinc or nickel alloy or with copper coated steel. Semi-jacketed bullets are not entirely encased but may have the tip exposed. This tip may be hollowed out.

9.3.2 Smoothbore weapons

Shotguns are typically classed as smoothbore weapons as the inside of the barrel is relatively smooth. Shotguns do not generally contain any rifling in the barrel. Shotguns can be single barrelled or double barrelled with two barrels either 'side by side' or 'over and under' (one barrel above the other).

Shotgun ammunition

Shotgun ammunition is quite variable, and can range from a single ball or cylinder to fit the diameter of the barrel down to numerous small pellets. The pellets are typically constructed of lead hardened with antimony, however due to concerns regarding the impact of lead accumulation in wild animals, substitutes for

Figure 9.4 Typical shotgun cartridge components

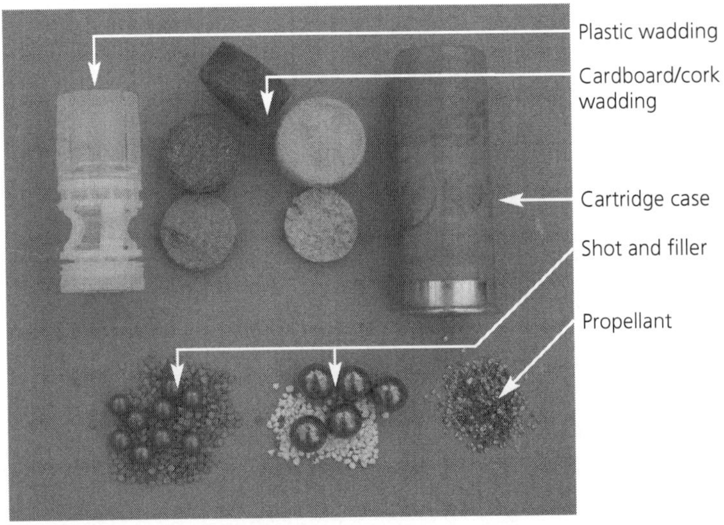

- Plastic wadding
- Cardboard/cork wadding
- Cartridge case
- Shot and filler
- Propellant

lead include pellets made of soft steel coated with copper or tungsten or bismuth alloyed with iron.

A shotgun cartridge may have a casing of plastic or card material, attached to a base similar to those of rifled rounds (see Figure 9.3 above). The base will contain the detonation cap holding the primer. The propellant is separated from the shot by wadding. The wadding can be a plastic cup type structure which will hold the pellet(s) or compressed discs of cardboard, cork or similar material as shown in Figure 9.4 above. The wadding keeps the components separated during storage. Figure 9.5 illustrates how the component parts of a cartridge case are structured.

When fired, the cartridge will remain in the barrel and the shot and wadding is discharged down the muzzle. It is typically the shot, any filler and wadding that will be found at a crime scene involving shotguns. However, cartridge cases may also be recovered where the firer has reloaded the weapon or if a self-loading weapon has been used.

Figure 9.5 Internal structure of a typical shotgun cartridge

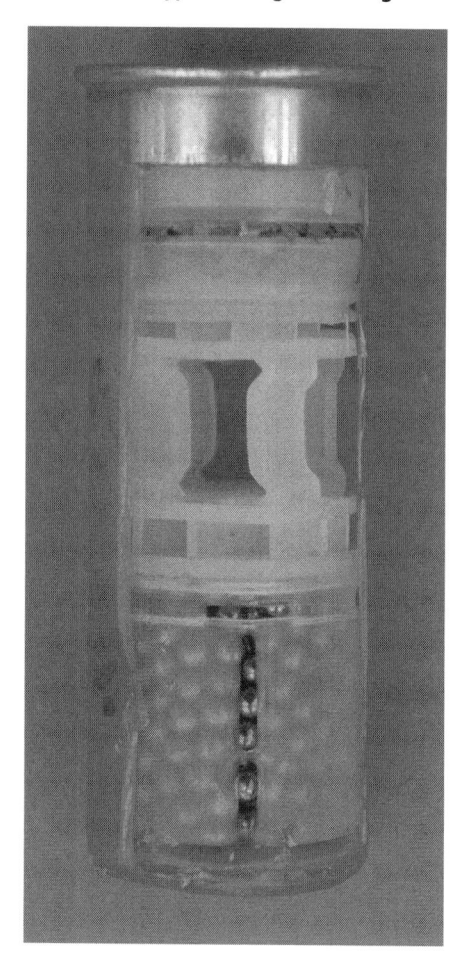

9.4 Ballistic Examinations

The forensic examination of firearms can be split into three general areas, referred to as the internal, external and terminal ballistics.

9.4.1 Internal ballistics

Internal ballistics deals with the mechanics of what happens inside the weapon from when the firing pin hits the primer to the moment a bullet exits the muzzle. It is at this stage that any imperfections inside the barrel can be transferred onto the bullet or wadding to enable an identification of the weapon used to fire the projectile. In addition to the identification and comparison of such striations (scratch marks), internal ballistic examinations can establish velocity, recoil and barrel pressures.

9.4.2 External ballistics

External ballistics is concerned with the behaviour of the projectile in flight, after it has been discharged from the weapon and before it reaches its target. The trajectory, maximum range and momentum of a bullet can be determined by the application of mathematical principles. This is of interest to investigators as it may aid a reconstruction of events and help to establish the relative positions of the firer and any victims.

9.4.3 Terminal ballistics

Terminal ballistics refers to the behaviour and effects a projectile has on its target. There are two aspects within terminal ballistics. One involves the penetration potential which is the ability of a projectile to penetrate various materials. The other aspect of terminal ballistics, typically used in the investigation of shooting incidents, is wound ballistics. This is concerned with the effect a projectile has on living tissue. Examination of shooting wounds can be useful in establishing the type of weapon used, the distance between a person and weapon when it was fired and the direction of fire.

Case study—Self-defence plea refuted by ballistics evidence

Anthony Edward Martin was the lone resident of an isolated and dilapidated farmhouse in Norfolk. On the night of 20 August 1999, Mr Martin alleges he was disturbed from his sleep by a noise downstairs. He took a loaded 12-bore pump action shotgun with him to investigate the noise. Mr Martin alleges he was blinded by torch light as he was halfway down the stairs, whereupon, fearing for his life he fired the shotgun towards the light.

Two males who had entered the house via a downstairs window were hit by the shots. It is believed the intent of the males was to commit burglary.

They both managed to get out of the house, one male sustained injuries to both his legs but made his way to neighbouring premises. The second male sustained injuries to his back and legs, and collapsed and died a short distance from the house.

The prosecution did not accept Mr Martin's assertion that he was in fear for his life and acted in self-defence, proposing instead that Mr Martin had lain in wait for the males having heard their approach to the house and had shot them with the intention of killing or seriously injuring them.

An aspect of the forensic firearm and ballistic evidence in this case was used to establish the relative positions of the parties involved. Mr Martin claimed he was midway on the stairs when he fired the shots.

The position of the cartridge cases and damage caused by the shots to the walls inside a downstairs room, out of the direct line of sight of the stairs showed that at least two of the shots had been fired inside that room and not from the stairway.

The examination of the wounds showed that the distance between the weapon and the males was inconsistent with Mr Martin's assertion that he was on the stairs.

It was possible that the first shot may have been fired from the stairway but the subsequent two shots, based on the forensic evidence, could not have been. They were fired at a closer range than could be achieved from the stairwell.

In April 2000 Mr Martin was sentenced to life imprisonment for murder, with ten years for wounding and one year for possession of an illegal firearm to run concurrently. This was reduced on appeal in October 2001, to manslaughter with three years for wounding, giving a total sentence of five years. Mr Martin was released in July 2003.

The evidence provided by the internal, external, and terminal (wound) ballistics in this case illustrates the way in which such evidence can be used to corroborate or refute different accounts of what has happened and aid a reconstruction of events to be determined.

A combination of the results from the internal, external and terminal ballistics examinations can provide investigators with a clearer picture of what occurred and enable the accounts given to be corroborated or refuted.

9.5 Scenes of Shooting Incidents

The preservation of life, both of any victims and personnel attending the scene, is paramount. The scene of a shooting incident, once it has been declared safe by authorized firearms officers (AFOs) or equivalent, must be preserved for the examination of the CSI or the forensic examiner. Where firearms are present at a scene, officers must not handle the firearm under any circumstances. Only an AFO or equivalently trained personnel should handle the firearm to make it safe. Where a firearm is left at the scene, officers should seek to preserve the scene ensuring that no one remains in the potential line of fire should the weapon discharge.

The evidence to be located and recovered is dependant on the weapon used. Generally the following material may be present:

- bullets/casings (entire or fragmented);
- the weapon itself;
- cartridge cases;
- wadding—card or plastic;
- shotgun pellets; and
- potential ricochet marks that can refute or corroborate claims of accidental discharge or unintentional targeting.

9.6 Forensic Examination of Firearms and Ballistic Material

It is crucial that the examination of a firearm is undertaken in a systematic manner in order to maximize the recovery of potential forensic material. In addition to the firearm and ballistic evidence that may be gained, consideration must also be given to the presence of other potential forensic material such as fingerprints, DNA, fibres and other particulate material.

It is common for firearms to be recovered that have had their identifying serial numbers erased by drilling or filing them off. Firearms examiners have techniques available to them to possibly recover such erased identifying marks.

9.6.1 Firearm recovery

Any firearm must be left in situ to be made safe by an AFO or equivalent, where appropriate. If in any doubt as to the nature of the weapon regarding whether it is real or imitation, it must be treated as a being real and fully loaded. Once the weapon has been declared safe, a CSI must ideally undertake the recording and recovery of the weapon. The CSI will photograph the firearm in situ, making a note as to the position of safety catches and in the case of revolvers mark the position of the chamber. Any magazine should be removed from the weapon.

The firearm should be secured into a box, preferably one with a transparent window (see Chapter 3 for guidance on securing items into a box) or purpose-specific firearm packaging if available. The box must be securely sealed and labelled and the 'made safe' certificate attached and clearly visible.

If wet, the firearm must not be packaged in plastic as rust will quickly develop and can change the striations created in any test firings. Wet firearms must be packaged into boxes sealed into paper evidence sacks. Firearms must be stored in secure dry locations; typically this will be in a secure purpose-built gun cabinet.

Firearms and ammunition must not be packaged, stored or submitted for forensic analysis together. The firearm and related material should be separated and kept away from other exhibits such as a suspect's or victim's clothing. At no time should anything such as fingers or pens be pushed into a barrel of a firearm. Gloves must be worn when handling a firearm and retained and exhibited after the weapon has been securely sealed.

Officers should avoid handling firearms where possible, taking action to preserve the scene and weapon for recovery by suitably trained personnel.

9.6.2 Casings and bullets or shot

Cartridge cases from rifled weapons or shotguns may be present at a shooting scene. Where the projectiles have not been fired, the recovery of DNA, fingerprints and other transferred material may be possible.

Once a round has been fired, the heat generated in the barrel can be detrimental to the recovery of DNA and fingerprint evidence. However, as techniques are always improving to recover such evidence, the presence of such must not be discounted. The evidence provided by a cartridge case that has been fired can include the identification of the weapon that fired it due to the marks made by the rifling and unique marks made by the firing pin and extractor (in self-loading pistols).

Recovered bullets or pellets can provide potential forensic evidence in addition to the determination of the weapon type that fired them. When a jacketed bullet hits a resistant surface the surface coating may peel apart, so all that can be observed is the metal casing. In some cases, the softer metal core of the bullet may be exposed and contain potential forensic material or information that can corroborate or refute versions of events. Trace evidence such as fibres, paint, glass or wood fragments may be embedded in the softer material of a bullet or shotgun pellet (see Figure 9.6).

Forensic recovery of bullets/cartridge cases

Disposable latex gloves must be worn at all times when handling any ballistic material. Cartridge cases should be handled to ensure the minimum amount of contact is made. The case should be placed into a rigid container such as a poly pot or, if it will fit, into a swab tube. The container should be padded out with polythene to stop the case moving about. The movement of the case in the container must be restricted to prevent any damage occurring to the fragile marks created by the firing pins, rifling and other mechanisms. The microscopic striations can be altered by movement or rough handling. The use of tissue paper or similar is to be avoided as this too may cause microscopic scratches to the casing. The same principles apply to shotgun wadding, whether plastic, card or cork.

Wet ammunition components must be packaged in paper evidence bags and stored in secure dry locations; typically this will be in a secure purpose built gun cabinet.

Once the items have been sealed and labelled, the gloves worn should also be exhibited.

Figure 9.6 Impact evidence from fired rounds

9.6.3 **Firearm discharge residue**

When a firearm is discharged the primer and propellant are expelled in a cloud from the muzzle and any gaps between the working parts of the weapon.

This cloud of particulate material is referred to as firearm discharge residue (FDR) and contains particles of partially burned and unburned propellant and combustion products of the primer, in addition to material from the barrel, casing and projectiles. The FDR will be deposited on the person firing the weapon, typically on the hands, clothes, hair and face, on surfaces in the vicinity including the target (if sufficiently close). The composition of any FDR can provide links between a crime scene and weapon.

Recovery of FDR from persons

It is vital that FDR residue is recovered from a suspect as soon as possible as it can be lost fairly quickly. The procedure for recovery of FDR is outlined in Chapter 4, however this process should only be undertaken by a CSI or equivalently trained person.

FDR particles can remain on clothing and other textile surfaces for considerably longer than they remain on skin. The swabbing of skin and hair combings to recover FDR must be done prior to the removal of a suspect's clothing. Recovered clothing should be packaged in paper evidence sacks as per guidance given in Chapter 3.

The presence of FDR can provide supportive information that a weapon has been fired or handled, although on its own it is not possible to say definitively when the weapon was fired.

The issue of contamination and transfer of FDR material is a very real risk. The location, victim and suspect should each be treated as a crime scene in their own right and steps taken to avoid transfer and contamination of material between them. Officers dealing with one aspect of the incident, such as the location, must not then have contact with the suspect or victim. Any personnel involved with the scene must not have had contact with firearms in the seven days prior to dealing with the incident where the recovery of FDR is likely to be a requirement.

9.7 Examination to Establish Cause

There may be a requirement to corroborate or refute allegations or versions of events. It is rare for someone to admit that they have deliberately shot someone; it is quite possible that they will claim that a person was shot due to a deflection or ricochet of the bullet, or that the weapon discharged accidentally. Forensic firearm examiners can establish the likelihood of such actions occurring.

9.7.1 Ricochet

A ricochet occurs when a projectile is deviated from its original course due to impact with a surface. Evidence of ricochet at a scene may be in the form of damage at the impact site or on the bullet or pellet which may have evidence of the surface it has hit embedded upon it. (See Figure 9.6 showing fibres and fabric imprints.) When a projectile bounces or ricochets off a surface it will lose a lot of its velocity and as a consequence, its stability. This will cause the bullet to wobble or tumble. Bullets ricocheting off smooth surfaces such as glass, steel, concrete or wood will typically have a flat spot where they have made contact with the surface, and this area may have particles of the surface adhering to it.

Wounds caused by a ricocheting bullet will have a distinctive pattern due to the tumbling action of the deflected missile, which will typically result in a ragged entry wound.

9.7.2 Accidental discharge

A forensic firearms examiner can provide valuable information as to whether a particular weapon could accidentally discharge and the circumstances required for this to occur by undertaking a thorough examination of the mechanics of the weapon.

The pressure required to pull the trigger and the condition of any safety catch and firing mechanisms can be established to ascertain the likelihood of any such discharge occurring.

9.8 Taser

A Taser is classed as a s 5 firearm under the Firearms Act 1968 and is increasingly being used by police firearms officers as a less lethal option for conflict management, during incidents that may previously have required a conventional firearms response. The word Taser stands for 'Thomas A Swift's Electronic Rifle'. The Taser is regarded as a less lethal option to a conventional firearm, to be employed in order to gain compliance without the substantial risk of serious, permanent or fatal injury. The Taser is a hand-held electronic device which can discharge a pair of probes that can attach to a target up to 6.4 m (21 ft) away. At the end of the probes are sharp barbs which can penetrate clothing or skin. When both barbs are connected via attaching to clothing or skin, an electrical circuit is completed which conducts 50,000 volts down the wires and into the subject. Fatalities occur very rarely with the use of Taser; however the risk is considerably lower than that associated with the use of conventional firearms.

The criminal use of such devices has been encountered by investigators. The following section deals with the procedures and evidence that can be recovered following a police Taser discharge, but the same principles regarding potential evidential material can be applied to criminal discharges. Note that the same considerations as apply to firearm recovery apply to Tasers and similar, that is, they should only be handled and made safe by appropriately trained personnel.

Following a Taser discharge certain materials must be collected for evidential purposes. Please refer to the checklist below for more information.

Checklist—Materials to collect for evidence following Taser discharge

- Probes embedded in clothing may be carefully removed by an officer. Probes embedded in skin must only be removed by medical personnel. In such circumstances, the wire close to the probe can be broken to detach the Taser unit from the subject. Probes that have pierced skin must be treated as biohazards as they will contain body fluids.

- Forensic information can be gathered from a discharged Taser unit; data regarding the discharge can be downloaded.

- On discharge a Taser will emit numerous confetti type data tags known as AFID (anti-felon identification). These contain unique serial numbers which enables the identification and auditing of the unit.

- The wires can be forensically examined to determine distances between a subject and the unit when fired. Under no circumstances should the wires be recovered by wrapping the wires around the cartridge or similar.

Where serious injury or death occurs following the use of Taser, the scene must be secured and preserved as a crime scene.

9.9 Chapter Summary

Firearms and ammunition can contain potential forensic evidence to link projectiles with the weapon that fired it, to identify a firearm from a fired projectile, and to determine a sequence of events which can corroborate or refute allegations.

In addition to the risks to health and safety, there is a very real risk of the inadvertent transfer of FDR. The only personnel who should enter the scene of a shooting incident where a firearm is present in the first instance, must be authorized firearm officers (AFOs) to make the weapon safe and a forensic examiner or a CSI.

The role of the first officers attending the scene should be to preserve and manage the scene (see Chapter 2 for scene management guidance) once the duty for the preservation of life has been undertaken. Where a weapon is at the scene do not allow anyone to stand in the area that is within the line of sight of the weapon. Where any doubt exists regarding whether a weapon is a real or imitation weapon, the assumption must be that it is real and it is fully loaded.

In addition to the potential firearm related evidence that can be available, consideration must also be given to the presence of other potential evidence such as DNA, fingerprints and traces of material such as fibres, glass or paint for example. Be mindful that the minute striations on a cartridge case or bullet can be easily destroyed by rough handling. Such items must be packaged in a rigid container padded with polythene (piece of clean plastic bag) to prevent movement of the item. Wet items must not be packaged in plastic; with firearms this will encourage rust which can render any forensic analysis invalid.

KNOWLEDGE CHECK—FIREARMS AND BALLISTICS

1. State the definition of a s 1 firearm under the Firearms Act 1968.

    A lethal barrelled weapon of any description from which any shot, bullet or other missile can be discharged and includes:
    (a) any prohibited weapon, whether it is such a lethal weapon as aforesaid or not; and
    (b) any component part of such a lethal or prohibited weapon; and
    (c) any accessory to such a weapon designed or adapted to diminish the noise or flash caused by firing the weapon.

2. What potential forensic evidence can be gained from a fired metal cartridge?

    The make and model and calibre can be indicated on the base.

Rifling and other mechanically created marks (from firing pin and extractors for example) can help to determine the make and model of the weapon that fired it. Such marks can be compared with other recovered cases to establish a link between scenes. Where the firearm is also recovered, a test firing will establish if the marks are the same as those on a recovered case.

Firearm discharge residue (FDR) can potentially link the case to the firearm, scene, victim, and suspect.

3. What is NABIS?

NABIS is the recently developed National Automated Ballistics Intelligence System, which is a national database containing information from recovered firearms and ballistic material. It has been developed in order to provide a central registry of criminal firearm usage and it can compare material from scenes across the country to establish links between incidents, weapons and ammunition.

4. What is a Taser?

Taser stands for 'Thomas A Swift's Electronic Rifle'. It is a s 5 firearm as defined by the Firearms Act 1968. It is a hand-held device that is a less lethal option than conventional firearms. It can be deployed by authorized firearms officers (AFOs) for conflict management and its use is directed and controlled by force firearms policies.

The Tasers can deliver 50,000 volts of electricity when both probes are discharged into a subject's skin or clothing to form a complete electrical circuit.

Tasers and similar devices may also be used by criminals.

5. State the forensic evidence that is available following discharge (firing) of a Taser.

When a Taser is discharged, two wires with probes attached at the end are discharged, up to a maximum distance of 6.4 m or 21 ft. The probes have barbs which can penetrate skin or clothing. Numerous identification tags called AFIDs are also expelled. These have unique serial numbers which can provide an identification of the unit they came from as well as an audit trail and these must be collected from the scene.

Following a discharge, the data held in the device can be downloaded to give technical information regarding the discharge.

The wires must not be wrapped around anything to package them as they can provide evidence of the distance from the unit and subject.

The probes can be carefully removed from clothing by an officer, however where they have penetrated skin, they must be removed by a medical practitioner and treated as containing biohazard material. Wires can be broken close to the probes in skin in order to detach the Taser from the subject.

Consideration must also be given to fingerprints, DNA, and other potential forensic evidence that may be available.

9.9 Chapter Summary

Summary of the National Occupational Standards (NOS) for the Student Officer Learning Assessment Portfolio (SOLAP) relating to this chapter

The table below indicates where it may be possible to demonstrate the achievement of certain performance criteria.

NOS unit	Unit descriptor	Performance Criteria, Range, and Knowledge	Activity
2C1	Provide an initial police response to incidents	**2C1.1** pc 1, 2, 3, 4, 6 **Range** 1a–1g, 2a, 2b, 2c, 2d, **2C1.2** pc 1, 2, 3, 5, 7, 8, 9, 10, 11 **Range** 1a, 1b, 2a–2g, 3a, e **Knowledge** 6, 8, 9, 12, 13, 16, 19, 21, 22	Initial actions at a crime scene—identify nature of incident. Take action to ensure that potential forensic evidence is preserved and the relevant personnel are tasked to deal with the scene.
2G2	Conduct investigations	**2G2.1** pc 1, 3, 4, 5, 6, 12, 13, 15, 16 **Range** 2a–2c, 3a, 3b, 4a–c, 5a–e **Knowledge** 3, 9, 10, 13, 14, 15, 16, 17, 18, 19, 23, 24, 25, 26	Demonstrate the initial assessment at the scene and take steps to preserve potential evidence. Liaison with AFO/CSI/CID and where applicable, knowledge of the forensic value of firearms and ballistic material.
2G4	Finalize investigations	**2G4.1** pc 3, 5, 8 **Range** 1a–e, 2a–b, 3a–b **Knowledge** 3, 10, 16	The identification and dissemination of relevant information to others in the investigation.
4G2	Ensure your own actions reduce risks to health and safety	**4G2.1** pc 3, 4, 5 **Range** 1c, e **4G2.2** pc 2, 5, 6, 8 **Range** 1a **Knowledge** 3, 4, 6, 7, 8, 9, 10, 13, 15	Demonstrate awareness of the particular risks involved with dealing with firearm incidents and related material and requirements to reduce the risk. Ensure the appropriate personnel deal with firearms. Report known risks to others who will be involved in the investigation.

Recommended Further Reading

Blackstone's Police Operational Handbook, 2nd edn (2007) Police National Legal Database.
Forensic Science (2004) Jackson, ARW and Jackson J.
Handbook of Firearms and Ballistics: Examining and Interpreting Forensic Evidence (1997) Heard, BJ.
R v Anthony Edward Martin [2001] EWCA Crim 2245.
Understanding Firearm Ballistics, 6th edn (2006) Rinker, RA.

10

Footwear, Tyre and Tool Marks

10.1	Introduction	190
10.2	Footwear	190
10.3	Tyre Marks	195
10.4	Tool Marks	196
10.5	Chapter Summary	197

10.1 Introduction

The marks and impressions left by footwear, tyres and tools at crime scenes can provide evidence to potentially link scenes and provide intelligence that may lead to the identification of an offender. Marks recovered from crime scenes can then be compared with the actual item recovered to establish if it was the one that made the mark at a scene. These comparisons and potential links can be made by initially looking at the overall shapes of the marks which can indicate a make and model in the case of footwear and tyres. In the case of a tool mark it may be possible to establish the size and generic type of the implement used, for example a ten millimetre flat-bladed tool.

To link marks from different scenes or marks to items, an examiner will look at the general characteristics such as the type and size of the marks. The unique individualizing marks created during manufacture, and then through subsequent wear and tear will then be microscopically examined. Links between a mark and the tyre, footwear or tool can be made by the comparison of such details.

This chapter gives a brief overview into the forensic potential of such marks and guidance on the preservation and recovery of potential evidence.

10.2 Footwear

Impressions left by footwear will be present at every crime scene as offenders will have walked in and out of the scene. The marks may not always be visible, but they will be there. They can be in the form of impressed marks such as those left in soil or on pieces of paper that have been walked over. The other types of marks frequently encountered at scenes of crime are those which are left in substances such as dust, paint or blood for example, that are transferred from the sole of the footwear onto surfaces walked on.

Officers need to be aware of where they are stepping when entering a crime scene as it is easy to obliterate footwear marks left by offenders. Avoiding offender footwear marks at crime scenes can be difficult; assessment of the most likely routes an offender would have used is required and actions should be taken to avoid such routes.

Where life is at risk, the most direct route to the victim should be taken. At scenes of serious incidents, a common approach path should be established as outlined in Chapter 2. The CSI should be informed of the routes taken by officers into and out of a crime scene.

Although there may be many pairs of the same shoes in circulation, wear patterns differ with each individual. Footwear impressions can provide evidence linking a suspect to a scene, or a series of scenes and can possibly provide an idea of the number of people involved and their movements around the scene. Impressions recovered from a crime scene are typically loaded onto a database such as SICAR (Shoeprint Image Capture and Retrieval) or equivalent system. The footwear of suspects can also be loaded onto SICAR or equivalent, where available in custody units. A footwear analyst can then classify the characteristics of the sole patterns of the footwear marks from crime scenes and those of recovered suspects' footwear. A large reference database containing images of the sole patterns and images of the uppers for footwear can be searched to potentially establish the identity of the make and model of the footwear. An examination and comparison of the unique individual damage and wear characteristics present can establish a match between the shoe and a scene mark. To be used evidentially, such matches can only be made by appropriately trained scientists. A CSI or footwear analyst can provide information for intelligence purposes only.

10.2.1 Recovery of footwear marks at scenes

Where possible it is preferable for the whole item bearing the footwear mark to be recovered. Where this is not appropriate, several methods are available for the recovery of footwear impressions from non-portable items and the one utilized by the CSI will be dependent on the type of the impression and the surface it is on.

There are two broad categories of footwear marks found at crime scenes:

- **Two-dimensional transfer marks.** These are marks which are left on a hard, flat surface such as a laminated floor, glass or counter top for example. Mud, dust and other substances that are present on the sole are transferred onto the surface to leave a two-dimensional impression.
- **Three-dimensional impressed marks.** These occur as marks that leave indentations on soft surfaces such as in mud, snow, sand, paper or on some carpets.

It is important to note that footwear marks may not always be apparent to the naked eye. A CSI will use lighting techniques to search an area of interest, and a variety of options that are available for the recovery of the marks.

Many of the techniques for the recovery of fingerprints can be utilized for the recovery of footwear. In summary, once a mark has been located, the process is as follows.

- The mark should be photographed with a measurement scale. This enables the photograph of the mark to be reproduced to accurately reflect the size of the mark, thus giving the footwear analyst further points of comparison between scenes and suspect marks.
- The use of powders and chemical techniques can be used to enhance the mark. Marks in dust-type materials can be lifted straight from the surface using gel lifters or an electrostatic lifting apparatus (ESLA). The ESLA method involves laying a Mylar foil material over the mark, an electrostatic charge is applied to the foil which attracts the fine dust material onto the foil to give an impression of the sole pattern. ESLA can also be used on vertical surfaces such as walls and doors. Chemical development techniques can also be utilized to recover footwear marks

- For indented or impressed marks in soil or sand, for example, a casting material is poured into the mark to give a 'life size' three-dimensional copy of the sole. Electrostatic Document Apparatus (ESDA) is an excellent method for recovering indented marks left on paper (see Chapter 14 for details on this technique) which is typically used to recover indented writing from paper. On some types of close pile carpets that bear an impression, photography and possibly ESLA can be used to recover the mark.

10.2.2 Footwear marks from suspects

The footwear of detained suspects can be taken by virtue of of the Police and Criminal Evidence Act (PACE), s 61A(3). The procedures and techniques for the recovery of footwear from persons are detailed in Chapter 4. Footwear from suspects can also be recovered during a search under warrant.

The footwear of suspects can be electronically scanned onto the SICAR or equivalent database, where available. The scanner plate must be cleaned prior to and following the scanning of footwear, to avoid any potential transfer of material occurring between unrelated items of footwear. Footwear pads can be used to make an impression of the sole of the footwear where electronic scanning is not available. Photocopying of footwear is not appropriate for comparison purposes as the quality can be variable.

Officers must be mindful of the potential presence of other types of forensic evidence that may be on footwear. Where body fluids or trace evidence are believed to be present, footwear marks must not be taken by scanning or printing. The footwear must be photographed first by a CSI, who can then recover any other potential forensic material such as blood, glass or soil for example. This will ensure the integrity of any potential evidence by avoiding contamination or transfer of material and ensures the appropriate health and safety precautions are observed with regard to body fluids.

> **POINT TO NOTE—HANDLING FOOTWEAR**
>
> Disposable gloves must be worn when handling items of footwear.

10.2.3 Searching and comparison of scene and suspect footwear marks

The analyst will search a reference database of footwear sole patterns in order to identify the brand and model of the shoe. Many shoes have very similar patterns, so if the analyst only has a small area of a crime scene mark to work with, it can be very difficult to give a definitive answer as to what type of shoe made the mark. The marks recovered from scenes are searched against other crime scene marks in order to identify any linked offences. Footwear impressions taken from suspects are then searched against the scene marks database.

The initial comparison focuses initially on the patterns of the sole; the analyst will then look for any obvious unique wear and damage characteristics before making any provisional links between scenes or suspects. However, any such links have to be confirmed by a qualified forensic scientist footwear examiner before it can be used evidentially.

A scientist can compare footwear items to marks recovered from crime scenes according to a number of criteria, outlined in the checklist below.

> **Checklist—Criteria for comparing footwear items to marks recovered from crime scenes**
>
> - Pattern types on the sole to determine make and model.
> - The particular arrangement of the pattern types, which can be useful where partial footwear marks are present.
> - The size of the footwear. This is not a simple task of measuring the length of the mark. The size of footwear is determined by the internal length; therefore different sizes of shoes can have the same external sole length. As shoe sizing can vary between manufacturers it is not a reliable singular comparison point. Marks from scenes are generally compared to test marks made with the same brand and model of footwear in varying sizes. The relative size and positioning of elements in the sole pattern can enable a size to be established. This technique enables the size of footwear to be determined for partial footwear marks.
> - The amount and position of wear patterns and areas of damage are compared between the suspect footwear and the crime scene mark. These can be unique and individualizing.

A conclusive match between a suspect's footwear and marks recovered from crime scenes is possible if sufficient detail is present from the crime scene marks.

The wear and damage patterns on the soles of footwear will change with continued wear, therefore comparisons between scene marks and suspects' shoes may not be valid after a month. However, such potential evidence should not be discounted. The offender may have stored in their wardrobe the shoes worn to commit an offence and not subsequently worn them. In such circumstances comparison between the recovered shoes and a crime scene mark may provide valuable evidence. The circumstances of each case should be considered individually rather than dismissing potential evidence because of the time that has elapsed since the incident.

10.2.4 Considerations regarding footwear evidence

Two common defences that are often put forward where footwear evidence has been established are for the suspect to state that the shoes were worn by someone else on the day in question, or that the suspect acquired the footwear after the offence from the original (usually unknown) previous owner. There are forensic examinations that may corroborate or refute such accounts. A 'feet–in–shoes' or

'Cinderella' examination may be able to establish the regular wearer of footwear items. It is not effective if someone has only worn the shoes for a short period of time. However, if two people have worn the shoes for a period of time it may be possible to detect this through the impressions inside the shoes. This type of examination requires footwear of a similar type and construction as the questioned shoes, along with the barefoot or stocking foot impressions from the persons linked to wearing the shoes. Ideally barefoot impressions should include standing and walking impressions and a three-dimensional impression made in a material such as biofoam.

10.2.5 Preservation of footwear evidence

The techniques required to preserve footwear will depend on the type of mark and the surface it has been deposited upon. The following checklist indicates the most appropriate method for the preservation of the different types of footwear marks often encountered at crime scenes.

> **Checklist for the recovery of footwear marks**
>
> - Impressed marks such as those in mud or soil can be covered by a rigid cover such as an old-style dustbin lid. Care must be taken to avoid pushing any further soil or debris into the impressed mark.
>
> - Where paper has been walked over by offenders, impressed marks may be recovered using ESDA. The item bearing the mark should be placed in a rigid card folder or box to prevent further indentations occurring. Do not lean on the item to write exhibit labels. Chapter 3 details packaging techniques.
>
> - Transfer marks in dust on hard surfaces such as laminate flooring, window sills, and worktops for example can be recovered by a CSI utilizing ESLA; care must be taken not to disturb these areas.
>
> - Marks on non-porous surfaces can be recovered by the CSI who can employ a variety of techniques to locate and recover footwear marks similar to those used to recover fingerprints. Marks on porous surfaces can be recovered utilizing chemical development techniques. (See Chapter 5 for details of these techniques.)
>
> - In areas where public access may be a problem, investigators should establish when the floor or surface was last cleaned. For example, an area in a shop can reasonably be expected to contain a lot of footwear marks, however if the incident occurred prior to the shop opening and the floor was cleaned after closing the previous day, the footwear recovered is likely to be of better quality and forensic value.
>
> Footwear evidence can be best preserved by employing the scene preservation techniques as outlined in Chapter 2.

10.3 Tyre Marks

The same basic principles regarding footwear marks can be applied to tyre marks located at a crime scene. Tyre marks can be impressed into soil or cardboard or can be transferred marks in contaminants such as mud, for example. Tyre marks may also be present on the clothing of a hit and run victim for instance. Tyre marks are only of forensic use for comparison purposes where a pattern is discernible, skid marks and scuffs with no apparent detail cannot be linked to a particular tyre by comparison of the patterning.

A CSI will initially photograph the tyre mark to show its relative position in the crime scene, followed by close-up shots to record the detail within the mark.

Where a tyre mark has been transferred to a portable surface, such as a piece of board or a victim's clothing, the entire item should be recovered. Where a tyre mark has been wet and then subsequently dried onto a surface such as glass, board, hard-coated floorings or plastic for example, fingerprint powders or chemical enhancement techniques may be utilized to develop any marks.

10.3.1 Suspect tyres

A CSI or forensic vehicle examiner will be responsible for taking any impression from a suspect tyre for comparison purposes. The tyres must not be removed from the vehicle. They will be photographed and then one of two methods will be employed. Either the vehicle will be driven through a similar soft surface to that at the crime scene to replicate impressed marks which will be photographed. A cast will be made of the test mark which can be compared with a cast of the impression from the crime scene.

Alternatively, the tyre could be inked in a manner similar to that of taking a fingerprint. The vehicle is then rolled along a roll of paper for at least one full revolution of the tyre to produce an image of the tread of the tyre.

10.3.2 Tyre marks at scenes

Tyre marks located at a crime scene can potentially lead to an identification of the brand of tyre, provided that enough detail is present in the mark. Marks that do not contain detail, such as skid marks, are of little use for this purpose.

The information on the side wall of tyres, such as brand name and model details, can sometimes be impressed into the side of the mud where a mark is deep enough. A cast of the tyre mark in these circumstances can record such details. Where a number of tyre marks have been left by the same vehicle, it may be possible to establish the width of the wheelbase. The information from the identification of a tyre brand and the width of the wheelbase can be of use to the investigation to establish the types of vehicle that may have been used.

When examining tyre marks to establish links between scenes and suspect tyres, the patterning specific to the brand and the unique wear and damage are compared, similar to the process used for footwear comparison.

10.4 Tool Marks

Tool marks, such as those left by an implement that has been used to force open a window for example, are regularly found at crime scenes. The CSI should photograph and take a cast of the mark where appropriate. Such marks can provide evidence that can occasionally lead to the identification of the tool or implement responsible, and by association possibly lead to an offender. Tool marks are also useful for identifying possible linked scenes. Typically, tool marks found at scenes fall into two general categories, lever marks and cutting marks.

10.4.1 Lever marks

Lever marks are created in surfaces where a jemmy, crowbar, screwdriver or such has been used to force entry. It may be possible to establish an indication as to the size and shape of an implement used. Lever marks are typically found in the frames of windows and doors. A CSI should photograph such marks with a scale (ruler) so that the image of the mark can be reproduced at actual size, and a three-dimensional cast of the mark should be taken.

Irregularities on the edges of tools, caused by the manufacturing process and the subsequent damage caused by use are uniquely identifiable to a particular tool. This can enable scientists to make a positive match between a tool mark and the instrument that made it. The minute striations and imperfections present in the mark have the most value, and ideally the item bearing the tool mark should be submitted for examination. Where this is not appropriate, a cast of the mark will contain the fine detail required for a comparison. Recording a mark by photography alone may not be sufficient for comparison purposes as the microscopic details may not be captured.

Where lever marks exist in a painted surface for instance, the CSI will also take a sample of the paint from the area. When a levering tool is used, it will pick up some of the paint onto the blade; if such an instrument is recovered, comparison of the paint located on the tool with the paint recovered from the crime scene can provide further evidence to support a link between a tool and a scene.

10.4.2 Cutting marks

Cutting marks will be left when, for example, wire cutters or bolt croppers have been used to cut through padlocks, chains or metal link fencing. Where cutting tools have been used, the unique, microscopic imperfections from manufacture and damage due to use will be present on the cutting blades. When a cut is made, these imperfections will impart microscopic scratches (striations) on to the cut surface. The cut item such as a padlock, chain or part of a wire fence should be recovered and submitted for examination. The marks can be compared to establish potential links between scenes and where the cutting tool is recovered, comparisons can be made to establish a link between the tool and the cut items recovered from crime scenes.

As with lever marks, where a painted or coated surface has been cut it may be possible to establish links between scenes and the recovered tool through the examination of the paint or other coating material.

As with footwear and tyres, the microscopic details present on a tool will be changed with continued use so may not be capable of providing any comparative value if not recovered soon after the incident under investigation. However, if the tool has not been subsequently used following the incident, the characteristics for comparison may be present indefinitely.

10.5 Chapter Summary

Marks made by footwear, tyres and tools can, in the absence of the item that made them, potentially provide valuable intelligence to an investigator regarding the possible make and model of the footwear or tyre, or the generic type and size of a tool, such as establishing that the tool that made the mark is a 25-millimeter flat-bladed or bevel-edged implement for example. In the absence of an item to compare the marks to, the information provided is of intelligence value. However, when an item such as the suspect vehicle, footwear or tool is recovered, comparison between the marks at crime scenes and the item can provide strong evidence of contact.

There are different techniques available for the recovery of such marks from crime scenes, and by far the best evidence is to seize the item bearing the mark, however this is not always possible. Marks should be photographed to place them in context of the wider scene and then close up, with a scale (ruler) to record the detail in the mark. The next best recovery method for impressed marks, such as footwear in soil or a tool mark on a window frame, is for the CSI to take a three-dimensional cast of the mark. There are methods available for the CSI to recover footwear or tyre marks from snow and from soil submerged in water.

Impressed marks in paper can be recovered by the use of electrostatic document apparatus (ESDA). Surface transfer marks in dust can be recovered from hard surfaces such as laminated or tiled flooring or from kitchen worktops for example, by the CSI utilizing an electrostatic lifting apparatus (ESLA), which can also be used to recover marks in dust on vertical surfaces such as walls or doors. Conventional fingerprint recovery techniques can also be used to recover such marks.

Footwear marks will be present at every crime scene as offenders will have to have walked into and out of the scene, therefore officers should be careful where they walk as such marks may not be immediately visible. It is important that CSIs are informed of the routes taken by officers, and where the incident is of a serious nature, a common approach path should be identified as outlined in Chapter 2.

Impressed marks in soil for example, should be protected by covering them with a rigid container such as a box, the cover should not be in contact with the marks and care must be taken to avoid pushing further soil into the marks.

Footwear, tyres and tools can also provide evidence of contact with a crime scene due to transferred material such as body fluids, paint, glass or soil that may be present on them. The comparison of such materials between the scene samples and the item can provide strong evidence of contact. Officers must be aware of the other potential evidence that may be available on recovered suspect footwear, tyres or tools and must wear gloves when handling such items.

The scanning or taking of inked type impressions should be avoided if body fluids and other such material may be present on shoes. A CSI should photograph the footwear and will take the appropriate recovery methods for any other potential evidence that is present.

KNOWLEDGE CHECK—FOOTWEAR, TYRE AND TOOL MARKS

1. What potential information can footwear marks at crime scenes initially provide to investigators?

   The make and model of the footwear can be determined by searching a reference database of footwear sole patterns. The size can be established, and if such information is not present in the mark (some footwear will have a size stamped on the sole) the size can be determined by a scientist.

   Footwear marks can indicate the number of people present and their movements around a scene.

   The marks can be searched on a database to establish if similar marks have been recovered from other scenes.

   Searches of footwear marks taken from suspects can be searched to establish the possibility of a link with crime scene marks.

   Where links are made between a suspect's footwear and crime scene marks, a scientist will undertake comparisons of the microscopic detail present on the footwear and in the crime scene marks to determine if the footwear made a particular mark.

2. Tyre marks are located in mud at a scene. What information can this provide to an investigator?

   The brand and model of the tyre can possibly be determined if enough detail is present in the mark. The information on the side wall of the tyre can leave impressions in the side of the mud trench.

   Where several tyre tracks are present from the same vehicle, the wheelbase of the suspect vehicle can potentially be established; this can narrow down the possible identity of the vehicle and eliminate some types of vehicle from an enquiry.

3. How can a recovered crowbar be forensically linked to a crime scene(s)?

   The size and shape of the crowbar will initially be compared with the marks recovered at crime scenes to establish if they are similar. Examination of the unique marks left on the crowbar from manufacture and wear and tear will be compared with the scene marks to establish whether they share common characteristics, which could determine if a particular implement could have made a particular mark.

4. Where tyre or footwear marks in mud or soil are located at a crime scene, how should they be protected from adverse weather conditions?

    Such marks should be protected with a rigid cover such as a box. The cover must not be in contact with the mark and care must be taken to ensure that soil is not pushed into the impression.

5. What is ESLA?

    ESLA is an electrostatic lifting apparatus which can be used on compact surfaces such as laminate or tiled flooring, window sills, counter tops and even walls and doors to recover marks in dust.
    A sheet of Mylar film that is black on one side is laid onto the surface and an electrostatic charge is applied to it. This charge attracts the fine dust particles to the sheet, to recover any marks present.

Summary of the National Occupational Standards (NOS) for the Student Officer Learning Assessment Portfolio (SOLAP) relating to this chapter

The table below indicates where it may be possible to demonstrate the achievement of certain performance criteria.

NOS unit	Unit descriptor	Performance Criteria, Range, and Knowledge	Activity
2C1	Provide an initial police response to incidents	**2C1.1** pc 1, 2, 6 **Range** 1a–1g, 2a–2d, **2C1.2** pc 1, 2, 7, 8, 9, 10, 11 **Range** 1a–1b, 2a–2g, 3a, 3d **Knowledge** 6, 8, 9, 16, 19, 21	Initial actions at a crime scene—identify nature of incident. Take action to ensure that potential forensic evidence is preserved and the relevant personnel are tasked to deal with the scene.
2G2	Conduct investigations	**2G2.1** pc 1, 3, 4, 5, 6, 7, 12, 13, 16 **Range** 2a–2c, 3a–c, 4a–c, 5a–e **Knowledge** 3, 9, 10, 13, 14, 15, 16, 17, 18, 19, 23, 24	Demonstrate the initial assessment at the scene and take steps to recognize and preserve potential evidence. Knowledge of the forensic and intelligence value of footwear, tyre and tool marks.
2I1	Search individuals	**2I1.1** pc 10, 11 **Range** 1b **Knowledge** 5, 8, 16	Recovery of footwear for comparison with crime scene marks and the potential for other potential forensic material to be present.

Recommended Further Reading

Criminalistics, 8th edn (2004) Saferstein, R.
Footwear Impression Evidence, Detection, Recovery and Examination, 2nd edn (2000) Bodziak, WJ.
Footwear Marks Recovery Manual (2007) NPIA.
Forensic Science (2004) Jackson, ARW and Jackson J.
<http://www.forensic.gov.uk> For case studies and fact sheets.

11

Glass, Paint, and Soils

11.1	Introduction	202
11.2	Glass	202
11.3	Paint	210
11.4	Soils	212
11.5	Chapter Summary	213

11.1 Introduction

Glass, paint and soils are capable of providing intelligence and potential forensic evidence to link persons to crime scenes. Such material may be present in microscopic amounts and as such can be easily lost over time, as it will tend to fall off any surface it initially adheres to.

The issue of inadvertent secondary transfer is a very real risk where microscopic amounts of material are concerned. Different officers must recover potential evidence from different scenes, for example clothing from a suspect must not be seized by the same person seizing clothing from a victim. A key area for potential secondary transfer is via police vehicles. Victims, suspects and witnesses should not be transported in the same vehicle where possible; it is advisable for officers to keep a note of the fleet number of the vehicle they use to transport such persons. Alternatively, paper covers should be placed on the seats and backrests to capture any material that may drop from transported persons, this paper can then be retained and exhibited.

This chapter gives a basic overview of the evidential value of glass, paint and soils and the considerations an officer will need to make regarding the forensic viability of glass, including the effects of the time elapsed between the commission of the offence and the recovery of items from a suspect.

11.2 Glass

Glass can be a valuable source of forensic evidence as microscopic fragments can potentially adhere to the clothing and hair of any person who breaks any sort of glass. The glass fragments present on a person's clothing can be compared with the glass samples taken from the crime scene to establish if there are links between the crime scene and the person.

All glass contains traces of other elements due to impurities from the raw materials which contaminate the glass during manufacture. In addition, some elements may be deliberately added to create different colours in the glass. As glass is often broken in the commission of offences, particularly burglaries, theft of and theft from vehicles, it is possible to compare the glass at the scene with that recovered from a suspect's clothing.

The value of glass analysis is not restricted to these types of offences however, and can be employed for incidents such as assault scenes where glass objects such as bottles or drinking vessels have been broken, or to determine if a person was in a vehicle when it crashed, or to provide links between a broken window and the object used.

In addition to the comparison of samples, glass will bear unique breakage features, so a physical fit between two samples may be possible. The way in which glass breaks can also provide information concerning the direction of the force and indicate the number of blows used.

11.2.1 Glass types

The most frequently encountered types of glass in our environment are:

- soda-lime glass which is used for the manufacture of windows and bottles;
- specialized glass such as Pyrex glass, which contains higher levels of certain constituents (boron oxides);
- 'lead crystal' glass, which contains lead (II) oxides;
- toughened or tempered glass which has been heat treated so when it breaks it creates cuboid fragments, rather than sharp-edged shards. Typically this type of glass is found in the side and rear windows of vehicles;
- laminated glass which is produced by creating a 'sandwich' of plastic film in between two sheets of glass, and is typically used for vehicle windscreens and 'bullet-proof' glass.

The determination of the type of glass is often the first step in the analytical process.

11.2.2 Fracture patterns

Figure 11.1 Side view of breaking glass

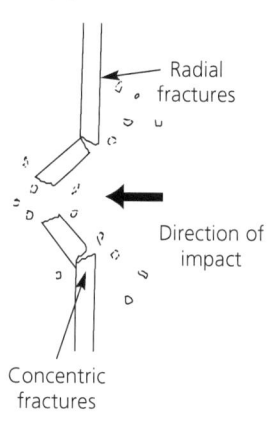

It can often be helpful to know from which side a piece of glass was broken. When a small projectile travelling at speed, such as a stone or bullet, breaks a window, a small crater-type hole will be evident which will be narrower on the side of impact. As the size of a projectile increases and velocity of impact decreases, the shape of the hole will be less likely to be representative of what caused it.

When non-toughened glass is broken by an impact, it will bend slightly under the force. This causes the glass on the side opposite the impact to stretch before breaking. This produces a series of 'radial' fractures which radiate out from the point of impact like spider legs. Figure 11.1 above shows a side view of what happens to glass on impact.

Chapter 11: Glass, Paint, and Soils

Where the impact is sufficient, the stretching effect causes the glass on the side of the impact to crack again, these cracks occur between the 'radial' fractures, in effect joining the 'spider legs' to form a web type pattern, as illustrated in Figure 11.2.

Figure 11.2 Fracture pattern to determine sequence of blows

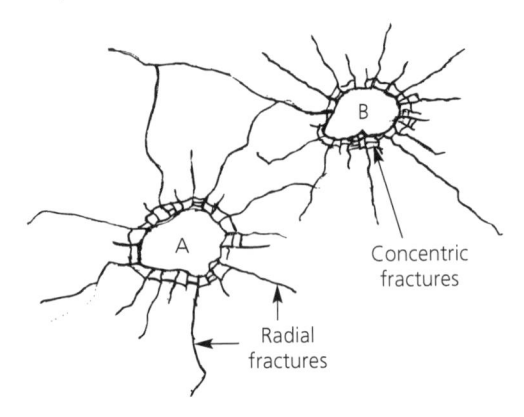

When a pane of glass undergoes successive impacts which do not break it, it is possible to see which impact came first as the radial fractures of secondary impacts will always terminate at the previous fracture. In Figure 11.2, the fracture pattern of (A) terminates when it meets the radial fracture of (B).

The bending and stretching of non-toughened glass during breakage also leaves distinct curved markings on the edges of the break, called chonchoidal lines, or hackle marks, as illustrated in Figure 11.3. At one end of the curve the mark will form an approximate right angle with the surface; the other end will run almost parallel with the opposite surface. The position of the mark can indicate from which side the glass was broken.

Figure 11.3 Chonchoidal lines on broken edge of glass

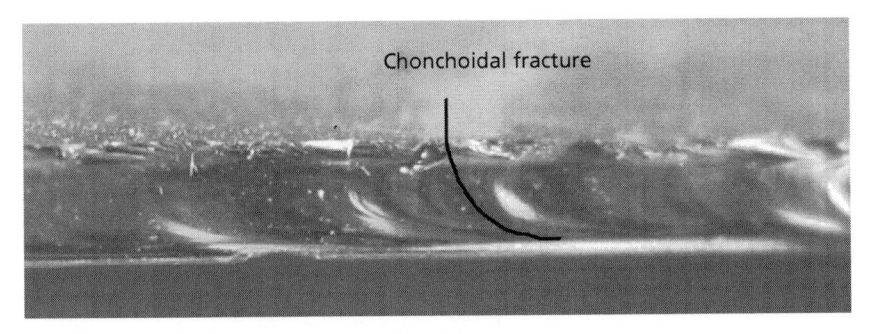

- On the edge of a radial crack the perpendicular side (1) will always be on the *opposite side* of the impact.
- On the edge of a concentric crack (1) will be on the side of impact.

A simple way of remembering this principle is to consider the 4Cs: 'Concentric Cracks Curve on side of Collision (impact)' or the 3Rs: 'Radial cracks make Right angles on Reverse side of impact'.

There are a number of factors a scientist can consider when analysing glass, and the more points of comparison there are between a questioned sample and a control sample the stronger the evidential value.

- **Physical fit.** No two pieces of glass will break in exactly the same way, therefore it is sometimes possible to fit pieces of glass together to see if they originated from the same source. It is vital where this type of analysis is to be considered that the glass samples are packaged so as not to break further in transit.
- **Glass Refractive Index Measurement (GRIM).** This analysis enables a scientist to make a comparison between the recovered scene sample and the questioned sample from a suspect, to ascertain if they share a common source. It is imperative that several samples from the crime scene are provided, as the refractive index can display slight variations within the same piece.
- The colour, thickness and density of the glass can be examined.
- The impurities present in the glass can also be analysed to give further support in a comparison of samples.

It is also important to bear in mind the potential presence of other evidence on glass, such as fingerprints, blood, fibres, and footwear marks, for example.

11.2.3 The persistency of glass

There may be occasions however, when despite contact with broken glass, very little if any material will be transferred. The degree of transfer is dependant on the nature of the receptor materials. Close woven materials will not retain much material, whereas a fleecy type fabric will retain much more.

Transferred material such as glass fragments will be gradually lost from the surface retaining it; this factor is referred to as the 'persistency' of a material and is a factor that will affect particulate materials such as glass, paint and fibres for example. The rate of loss for glass fragments is dependant on the size of the fragments, the nature of retaining surface combined with the subsequent use of the item. The amount of glass fragments will reduce where an item has been washed or continually worn following the commission of an offence. However, if an offender removes clothing following the act of breaking glass, and subsequently does not wear the item again, the glass fragments will be retained indefinitely until it is worn or washed.

Chapter 11: Glass, Paint, and Soils

> **POINT TO NOTE—GLASS SAMPLING**
>
> The key points to remember when considering sampling for glass are:
>
> - The greater the distance from a breaking window a person is stood, the less likely they are to have glass on them (see Figure 11.4).
> - After one hour following the commission of the offence, almost all of the glass will have been lost.

Factors to consider regarding the retention of glass on clothing include the texture of the fabric as glass will adhere more readily to textured fabrics like wool or fleeces for example, as opposed to smoother fabrics such as nylon or leather. However, it will settle into creases, seams and pockets where it can remain for longer.

11.2.4 Glass on suspects

When a pane of glass is broken, it will bend slightly under the impact causing fragments to fall both in the direction of the impact and backwards in an outward direction. This is referred to as backward fragmentation.

Glass fragments will fall onto anyone standing in the immediate vicinity with the number of fragments decreasing the further away a person is stood from the breaking glass, as illustrated in Figure 11.4.

Figure 11.4 Backward fragmentation of breaking glass

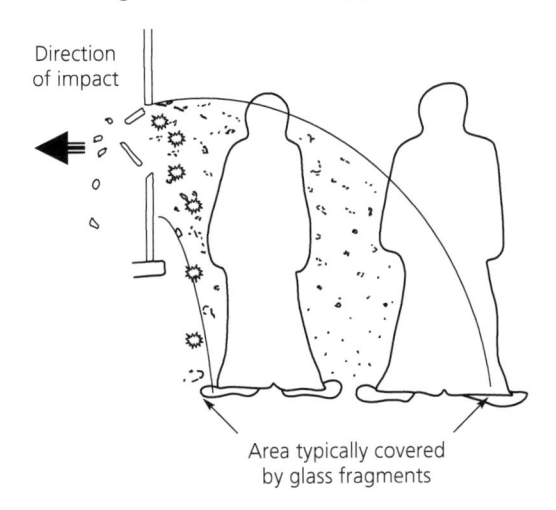

The distance travelled by glass fragments will vary according to their size and the force of any impact, with smaller fragments travelling further. Therefore, a person standing close to a window when it breaks can be expected to have glass fragments trapped in their hair, upper clothing, lower clothing, uppers and soles of shoes. A person standing further away may only have glass fragments on the lower half of their clothing.

- A person standing within a few feet of a window when it is broken is likely to be showered with hundreds of glass fragments.
- The number of glass fragments decreases as the distance from the impact increases.
- Very few glass fragments will travel as far as 3 m from the window, and those that do will generally be very small (less than 0.5 mm in size).

The fragments can be microscopic and may also be trapped in areas such as pockets, turn-ups and the seams of clothing and footwear for example. The location of glass fragments on a person or their clothing may help a scientist to indicate how close a person was standing to the breaking glass. If such information is required, officers must ensure that clothing is not shaken or handled too much during recovery as this will dislodge glass fragments. Figure 11.5 illustrates the typical potential evidential value that may be ascertained from the location of glass fragments recovered from a person or their clothing.

Officers should discuss the individual requirements of a case with the forensic service provider or the CSI where the location of recovered glass fragments may be an important factor in the investigation.

Figure 11.5 Decreasing evidential value of glass fragments

- Hair combings and shoe uppers
- Upper clothing
- Lower clothing
- Pockets/turn-ups
- Soles of shoes

Note:
- If a window was broken by being kicked for example, it would be stronger evidence if glass were found in the soles. Always bear in mind the individual requirements of a particular investigation.
- Glass can remain in pockets and turn-ups for some time; it can be possible to distinguish between fresh and old glass fragments as sharp edges of fragments will become blunted over time to become more rounded in appearance.
- Glass can come from any number of sources. Drinking glasses, ornaments, mirrors, and crockery for example can also be sources of glass fragments.

The techniques for recovering glass samples from the hair and clothing of persons is outlined in Chapter 4. Consider the possibility of glass being on the clothing of witnesses if they were standing sufficiently close when the incident occurred, as this can serve to corroborate or refute the allegations and versions of events being given. The requirement to consider witness clothing will be dependent on the case and such options should be discussed with the OIC or SIO and forensic service provider as to the value of such an examination.

11.2.5 Recovery of glass from scenes

There is a misconception that most window glass is all the same, due to the few sources of manufacture. This is not so. For example, the windows in any given vehicle or premises can differ greatly from each other forensically, due to windows being replaced or some being tinted, for instance. Each piece of glass will have microscopic characteristics that can be examined by a forensic scientist and can have variations across each individual pane; these variations can enable a scientist to link glass from a scene to that recovered from a suspect.

The recovery of glass from crime scenes is required in order to compare with any samples recovered from suspects. Ideally any samples required for forensic analysis should be recovered by a CSI. However there will be occasions where officers must recover items from crime scenes. Gloves must always be worn when recovering glass samples, and the glass handled carefully by the edges, so as not to disturb any potential evidence.

Pieces of glass recovered from the scene of a burglary may contain 'pick out' marks (finger or glove marks), where offenders have removed pieces of glass from the frame to enable a safe entry into a premises. These marks are usually not visible and can easily be lost by improper handling and packaging.

Glass must never be placed straight into plastic bags as it can puncture the bag, allowing material to be lost, contamination of the sample to potentially occur and it can also cause injury to anyone who handles the exhibit.

> **POINT TO NOTE—TAKING GLASS SAMPLES FOR COMPARISON**
>
> Glass samples taken for comparison purposes must always be recovered from the frame for integrity purposes. Samples must never be taken from the ground or from seats of vehicles under any circumstances.

Chapter 3 outlines the techniques for packaging exhibits, however the key points regarding the recovery of glass are listed below.

Checklist—Samples required from a broken window of a premises

- Larger pieces of glass found on the floor at scenes can contain footwear marks, fingerprints, fibres and potential DNA material. These should remain in situ where possible and be preserved for recovery by a CSI. To protect such pieces from further damage they should be covered to protect them. The cover must not touch the surface of the glass. If the pieces cannot be covered in situ, they can be carefully moved to a safe area. Officers should mark the original position of the glass and inform the CSI. If the glass cannot be protected then officers should consider recovering and exhibiting the glass.

- Larger pieces of glass should be secured into a rigid box to ensure further breakage is avoided and that any fingerprints, footwear marks, DNA material and other potential evidence is not rubbed off by friction. Secure the glass in place with string or cable ties. Adhesive tapes should not be used to secure glass into a box, as this can damage other potential evidence types.

- When secured into a rigid container such as a box, the glass should then be sealed into a tamper-evident bag or, if the glass is wet or damp a paper evidence bag. It is important that the glass is packaged in such a way as to prevent movement of the pieces which will cause further breakage and damage.

- At least six pieces of glass are required from different parts of each frame. All pieces from one frame can be one exhibit, labelled as 'Glass samples from frame of kitchen window' for example. For double-glazed panes, at least six pieces from each pane are required.

- One piece of the glass should ideally contain a mark denoting the interior or exterior surface.

- It is useful to take a measurement of the distance between the ground level and the sill of the broken window if possible. A sketch plan of the broken window in relation to other fixed points may be useful.

- Any pieces of glass recovered that contain stains that may be blood must have the exterior of the packaging clearly labelled 'biohazard'.

- This process should be undertaken for each broken window. Samples from several windows must be exhibited separately.

Checklist—Samples of glass required from the broken windows of vehicles

- The windscreen of a vehicle will be made of laminated glass and the side and rear windows are typically toughened glass.

- About 50 'pebbles' from each window frame, where possible, should be taken.

- Laminated glass from the windscreen should contain both layers, with a piece marked to denote the interior or exterior surface; this piece should ideally be packed separately in order for the scientist to be able to quickly identify it from the rest. This can be achieved by wrapping the marked piece in paper or placing it into a small bag which can then be packaged with the remainder of the sample.

- The sample should then be packaged either in a paper envelope that is tightly rolled/wrapped to secure the glass, or into a rigid container such as a poly pot, which are then sealed into a tamper-evident bag.

- Samples from different window frames are separate exhibits and the location of where recovered from should be stated, for example 'Glass sample from R/O/S (rear off side) window frame'.

- Glass from mirrors and headlamps will contain variations even within vehicles of the same make and model. This can be analysed to provide potential links between a vehicle and a scene.

- Generally, vehicle glass breaks in a manner that is too small for the recovery of fingerprints; however fibres and possible blood may be present.

11.3 Paint

Paint is a material that is almost everywhere in our environment in various forms. Although it is mass produced, it displays wide variation as the manufacturing process uses over a thousand differing types of raw materials including pigments, additives, binders, solvents, oils and anti-mildew agents, all in numerous variations and quantities according to the paint type. The commonly encountered paint samples submitted for analysis are architectural and vehicle paints. Where an implement such as a crowbar has been used to force open a painted window frame, there is the potential for a two-way transfer. Paint from the window frame can adhere to the tip of the crowbar, and any paint already on the crowbar can also be transferred to the window frame.

For example, an offender who has forced open a painted window or door may have fragments of paint on their clothing. Where force occurs, such as when a tool is used to force a window or a person is hit by a vehicle, paint fragments will be embedded onto the tool or in the victim's clothing. This impacted paint will bear a distinctive appearance and can provide evidence of impact as opposed to a casual light contact.

Where paint has been used in criminal damage or hate crime graffiti cases for example, samples from the scene can be analysed and may provide intelligence information regarding the make and type of paint. Paint may be present on a suspect's clothing, hair or footwear that can be compared to samples recovered at the scene. Where paint cans are recovered from a scene, these should be submitted to the laboratory as whole items rather than taking a sample from the can, in order to preserve the integrity of the sample and avoid any potential contamination of the sample.

11.3.1 Vehicle paint

Where vehicles collide with another surface, paint may be transferred between the vehicle and the surface upon which it impacts. These samples may be present as smears or as flakes or chips which can be forensically analysed to potentially provide links between scenes and persons.

Vehicle paints generally consist of at least four coatings:

- the pre-treatment coating, typically a zinc electroplating designed to inhibit the development of rust;
- the primer, an epoxy resin containing corrosion resistant pigments;
- the top coat, which can be a single, multi or metallic colour layer; and
- the clear coat which is an unpigmented coating added for gloss and durability.

It can be possible, in certain circumstances for a scientist to determine the make, model and age range of a vehicle from paint samples left at the scene of an incident. This will be difficult where a vehicle has been resprayed as the reference databases contain information of paint coatings utilized at the time of the vehicle manufacture.

The analysis of paint samples, whether from vehicles or architectural or decorative sources, can include the following, outlined in the Checklist below:

> **Checklist—Analysis of paint samples**
>
> - Physical fit of larger paint flakes recovered from a scene to a suspect's vehicle for example, in a hit and run incident.
> - Colour analysis—the multitude and combinations of colours and shades that exist provide paint with its most distinctive forensic viability. The information can provide valuable intelligence to an investigation.
> - The number of layers can be microscopically examined—architectural and vehicle paint will most likely display layers of different colours in various combinations. The structure and sequence of these layers can provide good points for comparison to link two or more samples.
> - Chemical composition of additives or pigments can be identified.
> - Environmental contaminants may be sealed within the paint sample which can possibly be identified and give further points for comparison and intelligence information.

Very often however, paint samples from scenes are not present in good-sized flakes with distinct layering. It is fairly commonplace to find paint as smears, for which physical fit and layer sequences may not be viable options for analysis. However the colour, type and chemical composition can be analysed to provide useful information for investigators and determine whether two samples have a common origin.

11.3.2 Recovery of paint samples

Paint samples required for forensic analysis should ideally be recovered by a CSI, as the recovery process requires the use of clean scalpel blades to scrape an area of paint down to the bare surface from the window frame, vehicle or surface in question. Where visible paint flakes are found at a scene or adhering to clothing of a victim or suspect, these can be collected in paper envelopes and sealed into tamper-evident bags. If physical fit will be required, it is vital the paint flake does not receive further damage so it must be packaged in a rigid container. Paint samples should not be recovered on adhesive tape as this can interfere with some analytical results.

Clothing required for the examination of paint must not be shaken or unduly handled as material can be lost. Guidance on the recovery and packaging of potential forensic evidence from persons and clothing is outlined in Chapter 4.

The persistency of paint fragments on clothing, hair or implements such as crowbars will depend on the factors as outlined above for glass fragments.

11.4 Soils

Soils are made up of organic matter, minerals and manmade materials such as fragments of brick, glass, concrete or water. Soils can readily adhere to surfaces that are in contact with it and are easily transferred to other sites such as inside vehicles and premises. Soil samples recovered from shoes, clothing, vehicle tyres and wheel arches for example, may be examined and compared to samples recovered from crime scenes. It can be possible for samples recovered from suspects or their vehicles to be identified as originating from a particular location, which can open up further lines of enquiry for investigators.

Forensically, soils can provide information to an investigation regarding the potential source of a soil sample and may provide evidential links between scenes and suspects. The composition of soil will differ greatly between locations; even neighbouring gardens can have differing soil types due to the variations in what individuals grow or use as fertilizers for instance. At any location soil will also differ in its composition at various depths. The differences observable at varying depths is referred to as the soil profile and will appear as horizontal bands or layers each bearing different characteristics. The checklist below outlines what the forensic analysis of soil samples will typically include.

> **Checklist—forensic analysis of soil samples**
>
> The forensic analysis of soil samples will typically include the following:
>
> - Visual observations of the colour and texture
> - Microscopic examination of the structure of the soil which may also reveal the presence of man-made, plant or animal material
> - The determination of any minerals and rock fragments
> - Determination of the soil particle sizes and distribution

One difficulty with establishing the evidential significance of soil samples arises due to the natural variation of soil in any given location and between differing areas. The comparison of a sample recovered from a scene with a sample from suspect's footwear for instance, relies on the determination of as many features as possible that are present in both samples. The more points of comparison the samples have in common, the stronger the link. However, unless there is something unique in both samples, that can be shown to only occur in the location of the scene, such a link will not be conclusive evidence.

Soil analysis is not routinely used in the investigation of volume crimes but should be a consideration for more serious cases where appropriate. The samples required from a scene should be recovered by a CSI or forensic scientist. Investigating officers are more likely to be recovering clothing from suspects or victims for the examination for potential forensic evidence which may include glass, paint and soil. The techniques for clothing recovery are outlined in Chapter 4.

11.5 Chapter Summary

Transferred material such as glass, paint and soil can provide evidence of contact. When recovered from crime scenes and compared with samples recovered from a suspect or victim, links can be established between them.

The analysis of vehicle paint, in the absence of a sample for comparison, can provide potentially valuable intelligence to an investigator regarding the possible make, model and age range of vehicle.

Glass can provide information that can include establishing the number and sequence of blows and the direction of the impact which caused it to break.

The analysis of soil can, in certain circumstances, indicate the possible geographical location of its origin.

The retention of glass, paint and soil on surfaces is dependant on factors such as the nature of the receptor surface, the amount of material transferred, the pressure and duration of the contact and whether the receptor surface is subject to subsequent wear, activity, or washing following the incident.

Chapter 11: Glass, Paint, and Soils

Trace amounts of glass, paint or soils which are not readily visible can be present on the hair, clothing and shoes of victims and suspects. As such small amounts of material are easily transferable, this makes them extremely susceptible to inadvertent cross-transfer. Where evidence of contact is required, it is vital that there can be no allegation or suggestion that any evidence found on one item is as a result of cross-transfer from another item. Officers must not recover such potential evidence from more than one person involved with the incident. Victims, suspects and witnesses should not be transported in the same vehicle; it is advisable for officers to keep a note of the fleet number of the vehicle they use to transport such persons. Alternatively, paper covers should be placed on the seats and seat backs to capture any material that may fall from transported persons, this paper can then be retained and exhibited.

KNOWLEDGE CHECK—GLASS, PAINT AND SOIL

1. A vehicle has had all its windows smashed, what samples would be required for analysis?

   Samples are required from each broken window and should consist of about 50 'pebbles' of glass taken from the frames.
   Each sample from different windows will be a separate exhibit.
   The exhibit label should denote which window the sample came from.
   Laminated glass from the windscreen should contain both layers and one piece marked to indicate internal or external surface.
   The samples should be either securely wrapped in a paper envelope or placed into a rigid container such as a poly pot, and then sealed into a tamper-evident bag.

2. State the factors that determine the presence and retention rates of glass fragments on a person.

   Glass fragments will adhere more readily to textured surfaces such as wool or fleecy material. Close woven fabrics such as nylon or leathers will not generally retain glass fragments readily; fragments that have been impacted into the fabric by use of force may be retained for relatively longer periods.
   The distance of a person from breaking glass will determine how many glass fragments will be present on hair and clothing.
   The activity following the breaking of the glass will impact on how much can be recovered from hair or clothing, but in general most fragments will be lost after an hour of normal wear. However, if clothing is removed and not worn or washed following the incident, glass can still be present.
   Fragments can settle into pockets, turn-ups and seams and will be retained for longer; it can be possible to distinguish between fresh and old glass fragments as sharp edges of fragments will become blunted over time to become more rounded in appearance.

3. What considerations should be made regarding the evidential value of the positioning of glass fragments on a person?

The position of glass fragments on a person can provide information to corroborate or refute versions of events. Where a person has stood by a window and smashed it, glass fragments would be expected to be recovered from the following:

- hair and shoe uppers;
- upper clothing;
- lower clothing;
- pockets/turn-ups; and/or
- soles of shoes.

The evidential value will be determined according to where the fragments are found. Thus, if they are only found in the soles of the shoes, this would not be strongly supportive of a person standing next to the window, as they could have merely walked through the fragments on the floor.

However, if a window was broken by being kicked for example, it would be stronger evidence if glass were found in the soles of the shoes. The individual requirements of a particular investigation must be considered when assessing the evidential value of glass.

4. A smear of paint is left on a gatepost as a result of an impact with a vehicle being driven away from the scene of a dwelling burglary. What can forensic analysis of the paint provide to investigators?

Vehicle paint can be analysed to determine colour and the chemical composition of the sample. This can then be checked against a reference database which contains most of the paint compositions used during manufacture of the vehicle.

It may be possible to determine a particular make, model and age range of an unknown vehicle from the sample.

This becomes increasingly difficult to determine where a vehicle has been resprayed with paint other than that used for the factory finishes.

Such information can provide investigators with lines of enquiry to follow up.

Chapter 11: Glass, Paint, and Soils

Summary of the National Occupational Standards (NOS) for the Student Officer Learning Assessment Portfolio (SOLAP) relating to this chapter

The below table indicates where it may be possible to demonstrate the achievement of certain performance criteria.

NOS unit	Unit descriptor	Performance Criteria, Range, and Knowledge	Activity
2C1	Provide an initial police response to incidents	**2C1.1** pc 1, 2, 6 **Range** 1a–1g, 2a–2d, **2C1.2** pc 1, 2, 7, 8, 9, 10,11 **Range** 1a–1b, 2a–2g, 3a, 3d **Knowledge** 6, 8, 9, 16, 19, 21	Initial actions at a crime scene—identify nature of incident. Take action to ensure that potential forensic evidence is preserved and the relevant personnel are tasked to deal with the scene.
2G2	Conduct investigations	**2G2.1** pc 1, 3, 4, 5, 6, 7, 12, 13, 16 **Range** 2a–2c, 3a–c, 4a–c, 5a–e **Knowledge** 3, 9, 10, 13, 14, 15, 16, 17, 18, 19, 23, 24	Demonstrate the initial assessment at the scene and take steps to recognize and preserve potential evidence. Knowledge of the forensic and intelligence value of glass, paint and soils.
2I1	Search individuals	**2I1.1** pc 10, 11 **Range** 1b **Knowledge** 5, 8, 16	Recovery of clothing for comparison with crime scene samples and the potentials for other potential forensic material to be present.

Recommended Further Reading

Criminalistics, 8th edn (2004) Saferstein, R.
Forensic Science (2004) Jackson, ARW and Jackson J.
<http://www.forensic.gov.uk> For case studies and fact sheets.

12

Hair and Fibres

12.1	Introduction	218
12.2	Hairs	219
12.3	Fibres	222
12.4	Transfer and Retention of Hairs and Fibres	224
12.5	Chapter Summary	225

Chapter 12: Hair and Fibres

12.1 **Introduction**

The human body contains millions of hairs which can be shed naturally or pulled out during a struggle. In a forensic capacity, head and pubic hair are the most commonly encountered hair at crime scenes and can be a valuable source of evidence.

Hair that has a root with a sheath containing cellular material from the skin can potentially provide DNA that can be profiled and searched on the national DNA database (NDNAD). Where no root is present, there is the possibility that mitochondrial DNA (MtDNA) could be recovered. Chapter 6 covers the DNA potentials of hair. In addition to possible DNA evidence, the length and colour of hair can be of some use for intelligence purposes and a microscopic examination can, in some cases, provide investigators with the racial origin of the donor.

A scientist can establish whether the recovered hair is human or animal in origin by examination of the physical characteristics. Hair can also provide information on drug usage to establish whether a person has regularly ingested a particular substance over a period of time.

Fibres can provide evidence of contact between people and textile items. For example in cases of assaults involving close contact, fibres from the offender's clothing will be transferred onto the victim's clothing and vice versa. Scientific analysis of fibres can determine the type of fibre, the colour, and in some cases may also be able to extract pigments which can be analysed to establish a possible origin: for example, a dye that may have be used by a particular manufacturer to produce certain items. However, due to the mass production and distribution of textiles, this is not always possible. Each case must be assessed on the particular circumstances.

Hairs and fibres are capable of providing intelligence and potential forensic evidence to link persons to crime scenes. The presence of hairs and fibres may not be readily visible and such material can be easily lost over time as it will tend to fall off the surfaces it initially adheres to. As such material may not be readily visible to the naked eye, inadvertent secondary transfer of material is a real risk. Different officers must recover potential evidence from different scenes; clothing from a suspect must not be seized by the same person seizing clothing from a victim for example.

A key area for potential secondary transfer is via police vehicles. Victims, suspects and witnesses should not be transported in the same vehicle where possible; it is advisable for officers to keep a note of the fleet number of the vehicle they use to transport such persons. Alternatively, paper covers should be placed on the seats and backrests to capture any material that may fall from transported persons, this paper can then be retained and exhibited.

This chapter gives a basic overview of the evidential value of hairs and fibres and outlines the considerations an officer will need to make regarding effects of the time elapsed between the commission of the offence and the recovery of items from a suspect.

12.2 Hairs

Hair can be recovered from crime scenes and examined to provide intelligence information to investigators. Hair can be compared with the hair of suspects and victims.

Hair grows from follicles in the skin and has three distinct growth stages.

- The active 'anagen' phase, where hair is growing at the maximum rate. During the anagen phase, the hair has a good root and it requires some force to remove the hair. If a root sheath is present and the hair is in the anagen growth phase, a scientist may be able to conclude that the hair has been subject to forcible removal, which can include vigorous brushing or combing and inadvertent snagging as well as being pulled out during a struggle.
- The 'catogen' phase where growth is slowing and the root begins to reduce in size.
- The 'telogen' phase where the hair has ceased growing and the root has reduced to a size that will no longer anchor the hair in the follicle. It is during the 'telogen' phase that hair falls out naturally. At this stage the hair has no root sheath and is not viable for obtaining material that can be searched on the NDNAD; however, mitochondrial DNA may be obtained (see Chapter 6 for more details on the DNA potential of hair). A root without a sheath indicates that the hair fell out naturally. If the root is not present, an even break with regular edges indicates that it was cut off, and an irregular break generally means that the hair was broken off.

Hairs recovered from crime scenes will typically be in the first or third stage of growth, where they have been naturally shed or pulled out by force. Consider the potential for hairs to be present on weapons that have been used; for example, where someone has been hit over the head with a baseball bat, their hair may be transferred onto the bat to offer corroborative evidence of the assault.

12.2.1 Analysis and evidential potentials of hair

The physical characteristics of hair and the chemical isotopes that can be found in hair can provide valuable information to an investigator, which can serve to open up lines of enquiry, eliminate or implicate suspects, lead to identification of a person and provide links between suspects, victims and scenes.

Physical analysis of hair

A scientist will examine the hair microscopically to determine whether the hair is human or animal in origin. The microscopic examination of the physical characteristics of hair will determine the colour(s), the width of the hair, the structure of the central core (medulla), and the structure of the scales on the outer surface of the hair, which make it possible to determine whether the hair is human or animal in origin. In the case of human hair, examination can also potentially determine the following.

Chapter 12: Hair and Fibres

- The possible location on the body that the hair has come from, for example, pubic hair has different characteristics from the hair from the scalp.
- Hair can display characteristics which can indicate the racial origin of the donor.
- Animal hair will display variations according to species, making it possible to identify which species a sample originates from.
- A scientist can examine the shape of the root, which can indicate whether force was used to remove the hair.

The examination of hairs recovered from crime scenes can provide intelligence information to investigators, by indicating the colour(s) and length of the hair; however this can be of limited value as hair can be cut or dyed different colours. It is worth noting that the analysis of hair can provide evidence that varies in its strength: good evidence may be provided from hair that has been dyed and has an area of undyed regrowth available, whereas undyed hair of a mid-brown colour for example, may provide less evidential strength. Each case must be assessed on the particular requirements.

Chemical analysis of hair

Hair will generally grow about a centimetre a month, and as hair growth is essentially fed by the bloodstream, the hair can store traces of substances that flow through the blood, including the chemicals that are present in water, food, the air we breathe and drugs ingested. The hair therefore can act as a record of the diet of a person through analysis of the isotopes in the hair.

Case study—Hair

In November 2002 a female was murdered. In each hand she had strands of hair approximately 9 cm long. This hair did not belong to the female. The hair was analysed and it was determined from the isotopes present in the hair that the donor of the hair sample had visited Eastern Spain and Southern France in the 11 weeks prior to the hair being cut, and had also visited Florida in the eight to 17 days prior to the hair being cut.

This analysis provided investigators with valuable information that opened up the lines of enquiry. It is believed that the hair in the victim's hands may belong to a missing Italian girl. This potentially links the two females to the same offender, and information from both enquiries can provide investigators with more material to work with to track down the killer.

The physical and chemical analysis of hairs can provide investigators with valuable information. However, if the donor of the sample is unknown and there is no DNA material present, identification of the donor is not possible. It also must be borne in mind that whilst hair can differ from person to person, wide variation can also be observed in the hairs from one individual.

12.2 Hairs

Recovery of hair samples

An offender's hair may be snagged on a window frame at a burglary, caught in jewellery or pulled out during an assault, or found in a hat that has been dropped at a crime scene for example. It will be necessary for officers to recover hair from a suspect if a comparison with hair recovered from the scene is required. To recover a sample for comparison purposes with hair recovered from a scene (whether a victim's or suspect's hair) or for drugs analysis, a hair collection kit should be used, as illustrated in Chapter 4 which details the recovery of forensic evidence from persons. In summary, an officer taking a hair sample from a person must consider the following, outlined in the checklist below:

> **Checklist—Considerations when taking hair samples**
>
> - Hair combings for glass, paint or other such evidence, if required should be done first.
> - Hair samples taken from a person should be from the same area of the body as the hair at the scene. Comparison of head hair cannot be undertaken with pubic hair, for example. (Head hair samples are classed as non-intimate whereas pubic hair is intimate and can only be taken by a medical practitioner. See Chapter 4 for details of intimate and non-intimate samples and the relevant legislation.)
> - A representative sample of at least 25 hairs is required, cut from as close to the scalp as possible.
> - Do not use tweezers to remove the hair as this may cause crushing to the surface of the hair.
> - Cut hair from various sites around the head to obtain a representative sample of lengths and colours.
> - Place the hair onto the paper cover provided in the hair collection kit. Carefully fold the paper containing the hair sample and place in tamper-evident bag. The exhibit should be stored in a dry store.

Where hair is observed at a crime scene, such as snagged on a broken window, on a weapon or on the broken window of a vehicle involved in a hit and run for instance, it may be necessary for officers to recover such samples to prevent their being lost. This can be done by carefully removing the hair with clean tweezers or with gloved fingers. Care must be taken with this method of recovery as the sample could be lost. The hair should then be placed into a piece of folded paper or an envelope and then sealed into a tamper-evident bag and exhibited. Another method for recovering such samples is to use an adhesive tape, pressed onto the hair. The tape should then ideally be placed onto an acetate sheet, but a piece of clean transparent plastic bag, or paper would suffice. This should then be sealed into a tamper-evident bag and exhibited.

12.3 **Fibres**

Fibre evidence is potentially present at virtually any type of crime scene, although it may not be readily seen with the naked eye. A CSI or forensic examiner can utilize high intensity light sources to search for and locate fibres. This technique is non-destructive and can enable otherwise non-visible fibres to be easily located due to the fluorescent properties in many fibres.

Fibres are everywhere in the environment and can provide good evidence of contact. Fibres in clothing, from vehicle seats, carpets and bedding for instance will potentially transfer onto items that come into contact with them. This two-way transfer can provide some very strong links between a person's clothing, the crime scene and other associated areas.

....

Case study—Fibre links to murderer

Sarah Payne was eight years old when she went missing on 1 July 2000. A suspect was identified and his van was seized for forensic examination. Seventeen days after Sarah went missing, her body was recovered.

A shoe was recovered near to the body's deposition site and identified as belonging to Sarah. This was the only item of Sarah's clothing to be recovered. The shoe had a Velcro strap which had trapped 350 fibres. Fibres from the shoe matched fibres from a red sweatshirt recovered from the suspect's van. This evidence was further strengthened by the presence of a multi-coloured cotton fibre on the shoe; this was found to have come from fabric that had been produced for Boots the Chemist as curtains for their baby changing rooms. It was established that only 1,500 m of this fabric had been produced, meaning that such fabric was fairly unusual and unlikely to be found in general use. This matched fibres from a clown curtain recovered from the back of the van. In addition other fibre links were established between Sarah's clothing, the suspect's clothing and seats in the van, and at the site at which Sarah was found.

The defence put forward the argument that the number of fibres present was not enough to provide conclusive links. However, the scientist explained that although the fibres may not be unusual in their composition, this did not reduce the value of the links and that the combination of fibres could provide extremely strong evidence of contact between Sarah, the van and the suspect. Due to the evidence provided by one hair and the fibres, Roy Whiting was found guilty of the kidnap and subsequent murder of Sarah and sentenced to life imprisonment in December 2001.

....

The mass production and wide distribution of many textiles can limit the evidential value of fibres, and only in exceptional circumstances can fibres produce a conclusive identification of an unknown item. However, as illustrated in the above case study, the combination of fibres, even commonly encountered ones, can provide strong evidence of contact.

12.3.1 Analysis and evidential potential of fibres

Fibres will fall into two broad categories: natural fibres such as wool, silk or cotton and manufactured synthetic fibres such as nylon and polyester. The analysis of fibres can establish the fibre type in the first instance. With regard to fibres that originate from animals such as wool, the examination will follow the procedures as outlined for hair, in that the physical characteristics of the fibre can determine its origin.

Synthetically produced fibres can also be identified by the microscopic examination of the physical characteristics such as colour and diameter and the shape of the cross-section of a fibre. In addition, synthetic fibres may contain a delusterant that is added during manufacture to reduce shine.

Fibres that have been dyed may be chemically analysed to establish the composition of the dyes. The more points for comparison that can be achieved between a sample from a crime scene and a suspect sample, the better the evidential value. The significance and evidential value of fibre evidence will depend on the circumstances of the case, and the number, combinations and nature of the fibres recovered.

12.3.2 Recovery of fibres

Fibres may be snagged on a window frame at a burglary, caught in items of jewellery during an assault, or on a vehicle that has hit someone, for example. Fibres in some form will be available at almost all crime scenes where contact is made with textile surfaces. Ideally fibres at a crime scene should be recovered by a CSI; however there may be occasions when it will be necessary for officers to recover such potential evidence from the suspect, victim, or scene.

The technique for recovering potential forensic evidence from persons is outlined in Chapter 4. In summary, an officer recovering potential fibre evidence from a person must consider what is outlined in the checklist below:

Checklist—Considerations when recovering potential fibre evidence from a person

- Hair combings should be done prior to the removal of clothing using a hair collection module.
- Visible clumps of fibres should be recovered with tweezers or gloved fingers if there is a danger they will be lost.
- Place the fibres onto a piece paper (provided in the hair collection kit). Carefully fold the paper containing the fibres and place in tamper-evident bag. The exhibit should be stored in a dry store.

> - Fibres can easily be transferred; officers must not recover the clothing of more than one individual relating to the incident. Different officers must recover clothing from suspects and victims and different locations must be used to avoid inadvertent transfer of fibres.
> - Clothing required for the examination of fibres must not be shaken or unduly handled as material can be lost. Guidance on the recovery and packaging of potential forensic evidence from persons and clothing is outlined in Chapter 4.

Where fibres are readily observed at a crime scene, such as when they are snagged on a broken window, a weapon or on the broken window of a vehicle involved in a hit and run, it may be necessary for officers to recover such samples to prevent them being lost. Fibres are fragile evidence and can easily be dislodged. Recover fibres by carefully removing them with clean tweezers or with gloved fingers. Care must be taken with this method of recovery as the sample could be lost. The fibres should then be placed into a piece of folded paper an envelope or poly pot and then sealed into a tamper-evident bag and exhibited.

Another method for recovering such samples is to use adhesive tape, pressed onto the fibres. The tape should then ideally be placed onto an acetate sheet, but a piece of clean transparent plastic bag, or paper would suffice, although not ideal it is better than losing potential evidence. This should then be sealed into a tamper-evident bag and exhibited.

12.4 Transfer and Retention of Hairs and Fibres

Many common fibres are used in manufacture of clothing, household textiles, carpets, rugs, cushions and vehicle seats. In most environmental conditions fibres are resistant to environmental factors such as biological, physical and chemical degradation and can persist intact for long periods of time. However there may be occasions when despite contact, very little—if any—material will be transferred. The degree of transfer depends on various factors, which include:

- the nature of the materials—closely woven materials will not generally retain or shed fibres whereas a fleecy type fabric will retain and shed much more readily, and
- the extent of the contact—a brief brush past two people will generally provide less transferred material than where close prolonged contact has been made. The length of time and strength or pressure of contact will affect the availability of transferred material.

The amount of transferred hairs or fibres will be reduced where an item has been washed or continually worn following the commission of an offence. However, if clothing for example, is removed soon after the incident, and is subsequently not worn, the hairs and fibres will be retained indefinitely until such items are worn or washed.

12.5 Chapter Summary

Transferred material such as hair and fibres can provide evidence of contact. When recovered from crime scenes and compared with hairs and fibres recovered from a suspect or victim, links can be established between them. The analysis of hairs and fibres, in the absence of a sample to compare them with, can provide potentially valuable intelligence to an investigator regarding the possible origin of the material.

Hair acts as a trap for certain substances transported by the bloodstream and can in certain circumstances, determine aspects of lifestyle such as the use of drugs and diet, which can be of value to investigators. Where hair has a root with a sheath attached, it can be possible to obtain a DNA profile suitable for loading onto the national DNA database (NDNAD). Where a root is not present, mitochondrial DNA may be extracted from the hair shaft.

The transferability and retention of hairs and fibres is dependant on factors such as the nature of the receptor surface, the amount of material transferred, the pressure and duration of the contact and whether the receptor surface is subject to any subsequent wear, activity, or washing following the incident.

Fibres can be searched for and located by the use of high intensity light sources, which cause many fibres to fluoresce brightly against the background. Screening areas for fibres with such a light source should only be undertaken by an appropriately trained CSI or forensic examiner. It is a non-destructive method for the search and recovery of potential fibre evidence. Fibres can be present on the hair and clothing of victims and suspects which are not readily visible. As fibres are easily transferable this makes them extremely susceptible to inadvertent cross-transfer. Where evidence of contact is required it is vital that there can be no allegation or suggestion that any evidence found on one item is as a result of cross-transfer from another item. Officers must not recover such potential evidence from more than one person involved with the incident. Victims, suspects and witnesses should not be transported in the same vehicle; it is advisable for officers to keep a note of the fleet number of the vehicle they use to transport such persons. Alternatively, paper covers should be placed on the seats and backrests to capture any material that may fall from transported persons, this paper can then be retained and exhibited.

Chapter 12: Hair and Fibres

> **KNOWLEDGE CHECK—HAIR AND FIBRES**
>
> 1. What information can be provided by the analysis of hair?
>
>   The analysis of hair can determine:
>
>   - whether the hair is human or animal in origin (if animal hair, a scientist may be able to determine the species);
>   - possibly the racial origin of the donor;
>   - information regarding colour, length, and any dyes present, although this is of limited value as hair can be cut and dyed;
>   - whether it is head hair or pubic hair;
>   - various lifestyle factors such as drugs taken and possible diet;
>   - a potential identification of an individual if a root with a sheath is present and DNA can be extracted; and
>   - whether hair has been removed by force or has fallen out naturally.
>
> 2. Describe the procedure for recovering hair from a person for comparison or drug analysis purposes.
>
>   - A hair collection kit must be used.
>   - Hair combings for glass, paint, fibres or other such evidence, if required should be done first.
>   - Wearing gloves, a representative sample of at least 25 hairs is required, cut from as close to the scalp as possible. Hair should be cut from different areas around the head to obtain a representative sample of length and colours.
>   - Tweezers should not be used to remove the hair as they can damage the surface of the hair.
>   - Place the hair onto the paper cover provided in the hair collection kit. Carefully fold the paper containing the hair sample and place in tamper-evident bag. The exhibit should be stored in a dry store.
>   - It is important that hair samples taken from a person should be from the same area of the body as the hair at the scene. Comparison cannot be undertaken of head hair with pubic hair. Pubic hair is classed as an intimate sample and can only be taken by a medical practitioner.
>
> 3. How can officers demonstrate the integrity of potential hair and fibre evidence?
>
>   The transferability of hairs and fibres means that inadvertent transfer can occur which may render any potential evidence inadmissible.
>
>   In order to avoid such transfer, officers must not deal with more than one person involved in the incident. For example, the same officer must not deal with different suspects and victims as the defence may argue that the fibres on a suspect came from the officer who had just dealt with the victim.
>
>   Officers must be mindful that a key area for the transfer of such material is in police vehicles, thus suspects and victims must be transported in different

vehicles where possible. It is advisable to place a paper cover on the seat which will also cover the backrest for the person to sit on. This paper cover must then be retained and exhibited as it will potentially contain material that has fallen from the person during transportation.

Be mindful that this may be upsetting to victims, and ensure that an explanation of why this action is necessary is provided (to preserve the maximum amount of potential evidence in the investigation of the incident).

4. State the factors that influence the transferability and retention of hairs and fibres.

The transferability and retention of fibres is affected by:

- The nature of the receptor surface, for example close woven nylon will not shed or retain fibres readily, whereas a mohair jumper would both shed and retain other transferred fibres for a lot longer.
- The pressure of contact, since more fibres will be transferred during prolonged close contact than when two people swiftly brush past each other.
- The subsequent activity following the contact. Continued wear and washing will reduce the quantity of any transferred hairs and fibres. However, if clothing is removed and stored soon after the incident the transferred material can remain indefinitely.

Summary of the National Occupational Standards (NOS) for the Student Officer Learning Assessment Portfolio (SOLAP) relating to this chapter

The table below indicates where it may be possible to demonstrate the achievement of certain performance criteria.

NOS unit	Unit descriptor	Performance Criteria, Range, and Knowledge	Activity
2C1	Provide an initial police response to incidents	**2C1.1** pc 1, 2, 6 **Range** 1a–1g, 2a–2d, **2C1.2** pc 1, 2, 7, 8, 9, 10, 11 **Range** 1a–1b, 2a–2g, 3a, 3d **Knowledge** 6, 8, 9, 16, 19, 21	Initial actions at a crime scene—identify nature of incident. Take action to ensure that potential forensic evidence is preserved and the relevant personnel are tasked to deal with the scene.
2G2	Conduct investigations	**2G2.1** pc 1, 3, 4, 5, 6, 7, 12, 13, 16 **Range** 2a–2c, 3a–c, 4a–c, 5a–e **Knowledge** 3, 9, 10, 13, 14, 15, 16, 17, 18, 19, 23, 24	Demonstrate the initial assessment at the scene and take steps to recognize and preserve potential evidence. Knowledge of the forensic and intelligence value of hairs and fibres.

Chapter 12: Hair and Fibres

NOS unit	Unit descriptor	Performance Criteria, Range, and Knowledge	Activity
2I1	Search individuals	**2I1.1** pc 10, 11 **Range** 1b **Knowledge** 5, 8, 16	Recovery of clothing for comparison with crime scene samples and the potentials for other potential forensic material to be present.

Recommended Further Reading

Criminalistics, 8th edn (2004) Saferstein, R.
Forensic Science (2004) Jackson, ARW and Jackson J.
<http://www.forensic.gov.uk> For case studies and fact sheets.

13

Drugs of Abuse

13.1	Introduction	230
13.2	Types of Drugs	230
13.3	Illicit Laboratories	236
13.4	Forensic Potentials from Drugs Packaging	237
13.5	Bulk and Trace Analysis of Drugs	238
13.6	Chapter Summary	239

Chapter 13: Drugs of Abuse

13.1 Introduction

There are many types of drugs taken by people for recreational purposes because of the mood enhancing or altering qualities they possess. These can be illegally produced or diverted from lawful sources. The main legislation regarding the control of drugs is the Misuse of Drugs Act 1971, which defines and classifies what are referred to as controlled drugs.

Controlled drugs are categorized in accordance with the harm they can cause to health:

- **Category A** are the most harmful to health and include cocaine, crack, heroin, ecstasy, LSD (lysergic acid diethylamide) and amphetamines prepared for injection;
- **Category B** includes amphetamine in powdered form, barbiturates;
- **Category C** drugs are regarded as the least harmful of the controlled drugs and include anabolic steroids, some mild amphetamines and cannabis leaf and resin.

There are several key questions that need to be addressed when investigating drug offences. Depending on the case, these will typically include the identification of the substance in question, the quantities of any controlled drug, whether the sample can be linked to other samples to establish a location of origin of the drugs and whether any drugs in body fluid or tissue samples are of a concentration sufficient to have caused intoxication or death.

This chapter will provide a basic overview of the most commonly encountered controlled drugs and the production methods, scene handling and the forensic potentials available.

13.2 Types of Drugs

The types of controlled recreational drugs commonly encountered include cannabis, heroin, ecstasy and amphetamines. The investigation into the supply and production of controlled drugs can provide evidence which can potentially link scenes, link batches of drugs from different scenes and possibly establish their origin. Forensic examination of the packaging and drug-related paraphernalia and equipment used in the sale and production of controlled drugs can also bear other potential forensic evidence such as fingerprints and DNA which may identify persons.

13.2.1 Cannabis

Cannabis is perhaps the most widely used drug worldwide and is increasingly being grown in the UK rather than being imported as a supply option. The active components in cannabis are present in the leaves and flowering tops of the plant, and are known as THCs (tetrahydrocannabinols). The concentration of THC is dependant on the physical form of the processed cannabis.

Typically these forms are as follows.

- Leaves/herbal—The dried crushed leaves can be mixed with the dried stems, flowers and seeds of the plant. This will typically have the lowest concentration of THCs.
- Resin—This is gained from extracting the resin from the plant, usually the seeds and leaves. It is usually supplied in slab or block form. The THC concentration is typically between that of the herbal and oil forms.
- Cannabis oil—This is typically a dark coloured oil or sticky tar like substance obtained by using solvent extraction techniques on resins or the plant material. It can be potent, with the highest levels of THC of all the forms.

A form of herbal cannabis known as Skunk is produced from specific varieties of the plant which contains higher levels of THC than normal plants. It is typified by its strong odour. However a strong odour on its own does not necessarily mean high THC content.

Cannabis cultivation

Cannabis can be cultivated indoors and officers may encounter the cultivation of a few plants in pots, or larger scale production. When investigating cannabis cultivation incidents, the key questions that need to be addressed include establishing the identity of the plants being cultivated, the actual and possible yield from the plants, the quality of the plants by analysing the THC levels, whether the scene can be linked to other cultivation scenes or supplied drugs, and to establish the identity of those involved in the cultivation.

The growth cycle of the cannabis plant will develop through five growth stages, namely:

- Germination—The germination period for cannabis seeds is generally three to ten days.
- Seedling— Following germination, the seedling stage will typically last for four to six weeks.
- Vegetative—This is the period of maximum growth with normal growth rates of one to two inches per day, although reports of four to six inches of growth per day have been reported.
- Pre-flowering—This is a transition phase where growth rates slow down but the flowers have not blossomed.
- Flowering—This phase, as the name suggests, is when the plants display flowers for a period of about six weeks. Whilst both the male and female plants produce flowers, only the unfertilized female flowers are retained as these are a good source of THC. It is common for male plants to be removed from the crop.

Like any plant, the growth cycle of the cannabis plant is regulated by the amount of daylight it receives. In natural circumstances the plant will undergo its maximum growth phase during the summer when daylight lasts longer. As the daylight reduces, as in autumn, the plants will flower. Indoor cultivation artificially reproduces the effects of daylight by the use of powerful timed lighting systems. This means that the flowering phase can be regulated; reducing the life cycle of the plant enables successive crops to be grown, so that the number of plants grown in any given period can be increased to maximize the crop.

The plants cultivated in this manner can be grown in pots of compost or by a technique known as hydroponics. Hydroponics is a growing technique that does not use soil. The plants are grown in circulating water which contains added nutrients. The plants may be supported by a material such as vermiculite or rockwool.

Cultivation scenes

There is no one singular method adopted by all growers. In addition to the number of plants being grown, which will indicate the scale of cultivation, the following may typically be present.

- Lighting systems that utilize high powered lamps which are usually operated by a timer system. It is not uncommon for the set up to be replicated in different rooms to produce plants at different growing stages.
- White coated or reflective coverings on walls to maximize the effects of the lighting. Windows and skylights for instance will be covered in order to exclude any natural daylight which can disrupt the timed growing stages.
- Air circulation systems are required to prevent fungal growth on the plants. The air circulation system can include extraction fans to ensure a circulation of fresh air is maintained. Carbon dioxide may be introduced into the circulated air to promote growth.
- Mother plants are specimens of the female plants which are used to supply cuttings for future crops. These are normally kept separately from the main crop.
- Seedling nursery areas where new plants are grown from cuttings or seeds. Typically the number of these young plants will be greater than the number that will be subsequently grown to maturity. A forensic scientist is able to establish whether a plant has been grown from a cutting or a seed.
- There may be documentation detailing growing schedules kept in paper form or on computer.
- Water tanks or trays and pump systems may be present. These would be used in a hydroponics system. The plants grow by immersing their roots into the nutrient-enriched water in the tank, the pump circulates and aerates this fluid, which may be free flowing or filtered through a medium such as clay pebbles or vermiculite.
- There may be stocks of plant nutrients, insecticides, dehumidifiers, temperature measurement and control devices, scales and packaging materials for instance. All these can provide an investigator with potential forensic evidence and intelligence.

Each cultivation scene will differ according to the sophistication of the operation, however there is a wealth of potential evidence to be gained from such scenes.

Recovery of plants

The process required for the recovery of the plants is dependant on the scale and complexity of the cultivation operation and the evidence required for the charge in question.

For instance, a scene where cannabis is being cultivated on a small scale, and production-only offences are being considered, will require a different approach to a more sophisticated commercial operation where supply and production offences are being considered.

In larger scale operations investigating officers should establish whether there are plants at different growth stages, and whether there are separate growing rooms with timers set for the different growth stages. In addition, note should be taken as to the appearance of the plants, which can indicate whether they are of the same species. Differences in leaf shape and colour may indicate different types of plant.

Table 13.1 below outlines general guidance for the recovery of cannabis plants for analysis. It is advisable for officers to seek advice and guidance from the forensic service provider regarding each case and the particular requirements of an investigation.

Table 13.1 Sampling guidelines for cannabis cultivation scenes

Evidential requirement	Samples required
Identification only (no yield information required)	Up to three plants (whole plant or top only). The roots of soil-grown plants are not required unless a determination of the cultivation method is needed (see below).
Identification and yield	At least two whole plants (with roots attached if hydroponically grown). Ideally the plants should represent a mid-range height from each room or area. Rooted seedlings or cuttings in propagators—a single plant from each propagator. Mature female plants of similar heights—two whole plants. Mature female plants of differing heights—one plant of each representative size (small, medium and large). Large immature plants which appear to have pieces cut from them—these may be mother plants and must be photographed to show any cut areas. These do not necessarily need to be submitted for forensic analysis unless examination is required to link cuttings with the mother plant.
Cultivation method	Plants with roots need to be submitted to the forensic service provider. This can establish whether plants have been grown from seed or from cuttings. Most of the growing medium should be carefully removed.

All plants and related vegetable matter should be packaged individually, in paper evidence sacks and submitted to the forensic laboratory as soon as possible. Such material must never be packaged in plastic bags. See Chapter 3 for appropriate packaging techniques.

The cultivation equipment does not necessarily require to be submitted to the forensic laboratory. Officers should consider the potential forensic evidence that may be present on the equipment such as fingerprints, footwear, and DNA.

The CSI will photograph the scene and must take photographs of plants with a scale (ruler) in order to show the actual size of the plant. Photographs taken that do not include a scale (ruler) are of no use evidentially as the size of the plant cannot be determined.

It is advisable for a forensic scientist to visit the scene of large scale complex cultivation sites, as they can indicate the best samples to be recovered.

For imported cannabis material, the scientist may be able to offer information regarding the country of origin of the material.

Health and safety at cannabis cultivation scenes

Such scenes must be approached with care as there are particular risks associated with cannabis cultivation sites. It is not uncommon for cultivation scenes to contain booby traps designed to injure any uninvited person entering the premises.

The following are general health and safety considerations to be made at cultivation sites. The list is not exhaustive and officers must be mindful of the risks at particular scenes and undertake a risk assessment at each stage.

- The risk of booby traps. Investigating officers should make themselves familiar with intelligence reports on known systems. Officers must approach such scenes with caution.
- Electrical risks. Often the electrical systems employed are of a poor standard of construction. Be mindful that the mains electrical supply may have been bypassed; therefore turning off the mains will not make the scene safe. If in any doubt, the electricity service provider can be contacted for advice and guidance. The combination of electricity and water from irrigation systems is potentially hazardous.
- Trip hazards may be plentiful as the wiring and cables supplying the equipment can be draped all over the premises. In addition lighting rigs and temporary partition walls can be hazardous as they may not be securely fixed in place.
- The lamps create a lot of heat sufficient to cause burns to unexposed skin.
- Chemicals used in the growing process may be corrosive or they may present a risk by skin contact or inhalation. Cannabis plants and rockwool can cause skin irritation.
- The odour from the plants can become overwhelming and cause breathing difficulties. A disposable mask must always be worn if officers are required to enter such scenes.
- Legionnaire's disease may be present due to the water and humid conditions.

- Canisters of CO_2 may be present—ensure these are switched off. This gas is heavier than air and can fill cavities below the floor level, avoid entering small spaces where the gas may accumulate.

When dealing with cultivation scenes all personnel must wear a disposable oversuit, disposable gloves and a disposable face mask as a minimum requirement.

13.2.2 Heroin

Heroin is derived from morphine extracted from the opium formed in the unripe pod of certain poppies. Opium is typically brown coloured and contains between 4–21% morphine. Morphine can be readily extracted from the opium and a further process is required to derive heroin, which involves the morphine reacting with acetic anhydride or acetyl chloride. This produces a powdered substance that is highly soluble in water enabling it to be administered by intravenous injection.

When the drug is sold, it will typically contain other substances such as starch, lactose, milk powder, sugars, caffeine and other drugs to increase the apparent amount offered for sale. These are referred to as cutting agents and may be present in other forms of drugs. The presence of cutting agents will impact on the purity of the sample.

13.2.3 Cocaine

Cocaine is derived from the leaves of the coca leaf. Cocaine is typically administered by sniffing the powder which is absorbed through the mucous membranes in the nose. Crack cocaine is created by mixing cocaine with baking soda and water; this is then dried and can be broken into lumps known as rocks. Crack is normally smoked.

13.2.4 Amphetamines

This class of drugs provide the user with a stimulant effect on the central nervous system, and are taken to increase alertness and activity. Amphetamines are typically encountered in powder form and are usually inhaled by sniffing.

Methamphetamine is a chemical derivative of amphetamine capable of being administered by intravenous injection. A form of methamphetamine that can be smoked has recently been encountered. This is known as 'Ice' and is reported to be highly addictive. Ice is produced by slowly evaporating a solution of methamphetamine to produce clear glass like pieces or 'rocks' which are then smoked.

13.2.5 Club drugs

These are synthetically produced and include ecstasy (MDMA), GHB (gamma hydroxybutyrate), Rohypnol, ketamine and methamphetamines for example. These are typically encountered in tablet form.

Chapter 13: Drugs of Abuse

GHB and Rohypnol act as depressants on the central nervous system and have been connected with drug facilitated crimes such as sexual assaults. Alcohol can increase the potency of the effect of these substances.

13.2.6 Hallucinogens

LSD (lysergic acid diethyl amide) is derived from certain types of grain fungus. A small amount of LSD can cause auditory and visual hallucinations, and is typically ingested on a small piece of blotting paper which has been soaked in a solvent containing the dissolved LSD. The paper is then dried and the solvent evaporates to leave the absorbed LSD. The paper is then cut into small squares for consumption. LSD can also be ingested on small tablets known as microdots or on pieces of dried gelatine. LSD has been found supplied on the back of postage stamps (non-self adhesive types). LSD may also be absorbed via the skin.

Psilocybin is similar to LSD but is a naturally occurring substance in a particular variety of mushrooms, commonly referred to a 'magic mushrooms'.

13.3 Illicit Laboratories

Whilst undertaking unrelated enquiries, officers may encounter such scenes where an illicit laboratory is suspected. In this instance, officers should leave the scene immediately. Under no circumstances should officers search such scenes unless critical factors such as the preservation of life are necessary. Officers must be aware that such set ups can also be used for the manufacture of explosives. Much of the information regarding illicit laboratories is restricted; however police personnel should be able to access information concerning the indications of such premises through their own force.

In the event that officers inadvertently discover what is believed to be an illicit laboratory, the following actions should be undertaken.

> **Checklist—Actions to take on discovery of illicit laboratories**
>
> - Due to the high level of risk involved to health and safety in such circumstances, officers and others in the vicinity, must retreat to a safe distance from the scene due to the risk of fire, explosion and chemical contamination.
>
> - Mobile phones and radios must not be used in the immediate vicinity. Officers must inform the control room when at a safe distance of the observations made at the premises.
>
> - Officers must not switch lights or electrical appliances, or power supplies any equipment on or off.

- Under no circumstances should officers touch or open any bottles or containers.

- The premises should be kept under observation from a safe distance.

- Management of the scene should be instigated by the use of cordons and a scene log established where appropriate. A sketch plan of the layout observed will be of great benefit to the scene personnel who will be required to enter the scene. See Chapter 2 for guidance regarding scene management and preservation.

- Only those who are appropriately trained and equipped to deal with such incidents can re-enter the scene.

First responding investigators must ensure the preservation and management of the scene is established as a priority. Officers who have inadvertently entered an illicit laboratory will be considered to be contaminated by drugs residue or chemical traces, and should ensure that this factor is highlighted to the control room, the SIO and CSI. Avoid close contact with other personnel arriving at the scene.

13.4 Forensic Potentials from Drugs Packaging

The wrappings of drugs can provide valuable evidence, such as a physical fit between pieces of foil and the roll it came from. Plastic wrapping and bags can potentially be linked to a single source (batch match) by examining and comparing microscopic manufacturing marks. Adhesive tapes can be linked to a source roll and may contain fingerprints or fibres. Depending on the type of packaging, there may be the opportunity to recover fingerprints. Chapter 5 outlines the different techniques available to recover fingerprints. Officers should consider the following with regard to drug packaging:

Checklist—Considerations for officers dealing with drug packaging

- The initial analysis must be one of identification of the substance before any examination for fingerprints or other potential evidence. The substance must not be decanted into other packaging. The drugs, in the original packaging, should be submitted to the forensic service provider to undertake identification analysis. If the packaging is required for the recovery of fingerprints, requests should be made to the forensic scientist to preserve the packaging for fingerprints.

- Where a physical fit or batch match examination is required to match a piece of packaging to its source, this must be undertaken before any chemical fingerprint development techniques are employed.

- Fingerprints may be developed on plastic bags and cling film using the superglue technique. Where fingerprint ridge detail is developed, it may be possible to also recover DNA material from beneath the superglue deposit. This can be of use where there is not sufficient detail in any fingerprints to make identification.

  If DNA analysis is required then the item must be submitted to the forensic service provider as soon as possible.

- Where wrappings such as cling film or tin foil are badly crumpled, it can be very difficult to recover fingerprints. Officers should consider the surface area available to hold a fingerprint deposit; sometimes the surface area of the wrapping may be too small to hold sufficient ridge detail to make fingerprint identification possible.

  If in doubt, submit the item and the fingerprint development officer can assess the suitability for fingerprint development techniques.

- Some packages containing drugs may have been secreted in bodily orifices. These will most likely contain bodily fluids and must be handled as biohazards with a high risk of transmitting infectious diseases.

- Gloves must always be worn when searching for and recovering drug packages.

13.5 Bulk and Trace Analysis of Drugs

Bulk material is defined as that which can be measured. Trace samples are those that are not readily visible but can be present in minute amounts.

Bulk samples are typically analysed to establish the identity of the sample and to determine the composition and ratios of different constituents. Comparison between samples from different scenes can be undertaken to establish if the samples have a common origin.

Trace analysis can be undertaken on a variety of items such as potential packaging materials, banknotes and mobile phones for instance.

13.5.1 Bulk analysis

Analysis of bulk samples will typically begin with initial observations regarding the appearance of the sample, followed by presumptive testing. There are several different presumptive tests that can be indicative of a sample's identity. Although such tests cannot provide a conclusive identification, they do serve to reduce the range of possibilities and enable the scientist to undertake appropriate analysis to identify and quantify the substance. The techniques utilized can provide the identity of a substance and information on the combinations and ratios of substances present in a sample. This may enable links to be made with other samples recovered from different scenes.

13.5.2 Trace samples

Trace samples are typically required when attempting to establish the presence or absence of drugs, for example:

- Biological samples. These are analysed to determine if a person had drugs in their system. The samples that may be examined are blood, saliva, breath samples, urine, stomach contents, hair, nails, sweat and other tissues and body fluids available during a post-mortem examination. The biological samples required for analysis will depend on the individual circumstances of the case.
- Suspected drug related items such as scales, blades, wrappings and other surfaces that may contain small amounts of a drug. Food and drink and relevant containers that may have been adulterated with drugs can also be analysed.
- Mobile telephones, banknotes, vehicle steering wheels and other such items may contain trace amounts of material if they are handled by those who have had contact with drugs. The evidential value of trace samples recovered from such items must be considered in the context of each case, due to the transferability of such trace material.

Due to the microscopic amounts and transferability of material, the inadvertent transfer and contamination of samples are very real risks. Different items recovered from distinct separate locations (for example from different rooms) that may require trace analysis must be handled by different officers. Gloves must be worn and retained and exhibited after each distinct area has been searched.

Exhibits that potentially contain trace amounts of a substance need to be analysed as soon as possible, ideally in a matter of weeks rather than months. Heroin and cannabis for instance, can degrade over time, especially in warm temperatures.

Exhibits containing drugs or potential drug residues must be stored in cool temperatures away from other potential sources of drug contamination.

It is important that officers keep exhibits for bulk and trace analysis separated. It can be argued that a bulk sample has interfered with the trace sample, but it is unlikely that a trace sample can sufficiently contaminate a bulk sample.

13.6 Chapter Summary

The analysis of drugs can provide investigators with an identification of a substance, the quantity and purity of the sample, and determination of any links between substances recovered from different scenes. The cultivation of cannabis and the production of synthetic drugs are increasingly being encountered. The forensic examination of such scenes can provide potential evidence to identify persons involved and link scenes and possibly identify supply networks.

The recovery of potential forensic evidence from such scenes should only be undertaken by a CSI or forensic scientist. Officers should only recover items under the direction of a CSI or forensic scientist. The scenes of controlled drug production can be extremely dangerous, booby traps are often set to cause injury to uninvited visitors, the set up of equipment and electrical wiring is most likely to be below safe standards and hazards exist in the form of chemicals that may be present. Where such scenes are inadvertently discovered by investigators, the immediate response should be to secure the scene for CSIs or other specialist personnel. Investigating officers must not attempt to undertake a search of the scene unless preservation of life is an issue.

There will be other potential forensic evidence available, such as DNA, fingerprint and fibres present on wrappings, paraphernalia and equipment used. The presence of other evidence must be considered, whether dealing with a production scene or recovering smaller amounts from an individual. Care must be taken to ensure that cross-transfer of drug material does not occur. Gloves must be worn when handling any items potentially bearing drugs, and these gloves should be retained and exhibited. Exhibits for trace analysis must be kept separate from bulk samples, as a bulk sample can contaminate a trace sample, but it is unlikely that a trace sample can sufficiently contaminate a bulk sample.

> **KNOWLEDGE CHECK—DRUGS**
>
> 1. How should cannabis plants be submitted to a forensic service provider?
>
>   Cannabis plants should be packaged in paper evidence sacks and stored in a cool, dry store.
>   The roots of the plant are not required unless they are grown hydroponically or if there is a need to establish if the plants were grown from seed or cutting (as much soil as possible must be removed from the roots in such cases).
>
> 2. What is meant by the term hydroponics?
>
>   Hydroponics is the term used for a method of plant cultivation which does not use soil or compost. The plants have the roots immersed tanks of nutrient enriched water, which is circulated and aerated, either free flowing or through clay pebbles or vermiculite, by a pump.
>
> 3. What information can a scientist provide to an investigator regarding a sample of white powder?
>
>   A scientist can identify the substance, determine the quantity and ratios of different constituents, establish the purity (or otherwise) of the sample, and potentially provide links with the sample to other samples submitted. This can potentially lead to links between crime scenes and possibly determine a supply chain.

13.6 Chapter Summary

> 4. What are the possible health and safety risks at a cannabis cultivation scene?
>
> There is the risk of:
>
> - booby traps;
> - unsafe electrical wiring;
> - hazards associated with electricity and water from irrigation systems;
> - trip hazards due to wiring and cables which can be draped all over the premises;
> - lighting rigs and temporary partition walls can be hazardous as they may not be securely fixed in place;
> - the lamps can cause burns to unexposed skin;
> - chemicals used in the growing process may be harmful;
> - cannabis plants and rockwool can cause skin irritation;
> - the odour from the plants can cause breathing difficulties;
> - Legionnaire's disease may be present due to the water and humid conditions;
> - CO_2 may be present in canisters.
>
> When dealing with cultivation scenes all personnel must wear a disposable over-suit, disposable gloves and a disposable face mask as a minimum requirement.

Summary of the National Occupational Standards (NOS) for the Student Officer Learning Assessment Portfolio (SOLAP) relating to this chapter

The table below indicates where it may be possible to demonstrate the achievement of certain performance criteria.

NOS unit	Unit descriptor	Performance Criteria, Range, and Knowledge	Activity
2C1	Provide an initial police response to incidents	**2C1.1** pc 1, 2, 6 **Range** 1a–1g, 2a–2d, **2C1.2** pc 1, 2, 7, 8, 9, 10, 11 **Range** 1a–1b, 2a–2g, 3a, 3d **Knowledge** 6, 8, 9, 16, 19, 21	Initial actions at a crime scene—identify nature of incident. Take action to ensure that potential forensic evidence is preserved and the relevant personnel are tasked to deal with the scene.
2G2	Conduct investigations	**2G2.1** pc 1, 3, 4, 5, 6, 7, 12, 13, 16 **Range** 2a–2c, 3a–c, 4a–c, 5a–e **Knowledge** 3, 9, 10, 13, 14, 15, 16, 17, 18, 19, 23, 24	Demonstrate the initial assessment at the scene and take steps to recognize and preserve potential evidence. Knowledge of the forensic and intelligence value of potential evidence from drugs and associated material.

Recommended Further Reading

Criminalistics, 8th edn (2004) Saferstein, R.
Forensic Science (2004) Jackson, ARW and Jackson J.
The Examination of Cannabis Cultivation Scenes—Guidance for Police Officers (2006) Forensic Science Service.
<http://www.forensic.gov.uk> For case studies and fact sheets.

14

Document Examination

14.1	Introduction	244
14.2	Handwriting Analysis	244
14.3	Forged Handwriting	246
14.4	Indented Impressions	248
14.5	Other Document Examinations Available	249
14.6	Recovery and Preservation of Documents	251
14.7	Chapter Summary	252

14.1 Introduction

A document is any piece of paper bearing written, printed or pictorial forms of communication. However, blank sheets of paper can also be examined to provide potential evidential material. The types of document that can be encountered in the investigation of a crime typically include forged or altered cheques and vehicle documents, ransom notes, malicious mail and suicide notes.

Document examination can provide evidence in the form of fingerprints, footwear marks, indented writing, handwriting analysis and physical fit of a piece of paper to a pad from which it has been torn for example. There are a number of facets involved in document examination and the aspects utilized will depend on the circumstances of the case. The following examinations are those typically employed in document analysis:

- Handwriting analysis
- Forged/altered document examination
- Recovery of indented writing
- Recovery of fingerprints
- Physical fit
- Comparison of a printed document to printer

Most paper materials recovered during the investigation of volume crime incidents are generally submitted for fingerprint analysis, for example when an offender has rifled through paperwork during a burglary. Chemical development techniques can be utilized, generally within force chemical enhancement laboratories or equivalent, for the recovery of fingerprints. The techniques for the chemical development of fingerprints are outlined in Chapter 5.

Where an offender has walked over paper items it can be possible to recover indented impressions of footwear using an electrostatic document analysis apparatus (ESDA). This technique is more commonly used for the recovery of indented writing impressions from apparently blank writing paper (see section 14.4 below). This process is typically carried out in force by the chemical development laboratory (or equivalent).

This chapter will outline the analytical techniques available for the examination of documents and the considerations that an investigator should make regarding the evidential potentials of documents typically encountered and the recovery techniques required to maximize any potential evidence.

14.2 Handwriting Analysis

Handwriting analysis enables the comparison of handwriting between items of malicious mail for example, and the suspect's handwriting. The analysis should be undertaken by a forensic scientist who can potentially:

- establish the author of questioned (crime scene) samples by comparison of the samples provided by suspects;

- determine whether a signature is genuine or forged; and
- determine common authorship between different handwritten documents to establish links.

The basis of this analysis relies on the fact that generally, the writing style of adults tends to be stylized and unique to the author, displaying an individualistic style.

14.2.1 Handwriting types

There are four general categories of handwriting that can enable the analyst to classify the style of writing to potentially identify points for comparison:

- **Capitals**—All the letters are written in upper case. This can potentially individualize an author, as the shape of letters and the way they are formed will vary from person to person. An analyst will examine the number of pen strokes and the directions of pen movements.
- **Cursive**—This is 'joined up' writing with no breaks between the letters in words and is the most common form of adult handwriting. There is vast variation in individual styles.
- **Disconnected**—This is a variation on the cursive style where breaks between some of the letters in some of the words exist. The breaks vary from person to person and can be dependant on the word being written. Some people will write certain words with the breaks always in particular places. This style is another common form of handwriting.
- **Signatures**—These are highly stylized and most often illegible. This type of handwriting is frequently examined by scientists due to attempt forgeries. Signatures display enormous variation due to their highly stylized nature. They are often very different from the normal writing style of a person which means it can generally be difficult to link signatures to normal handwriting.

A person's handwriting will display natural variation and will never be identical on two separate occasions. Such variations can be due to simple random variation, the physical state of author, different writing tools being used or different writing surfaces. The natural variations can however be characteristic of a particular person. The extent of these variations can potentially be determined by analysis; therefore the more samples provided by a suspect for comparison will increase the reliability of the results.

The examination of handwriting is a systematic and painstaking task which will typically include the following, outlined in the checklist below:

> **Checklist—Examining handwriting**
>
> - The observation of the overall characteristics of the writing, including spelling and grammatical structure.

- Detailed examination of individual words and letters.

- Direction of pen movements determined by observation of changes in ink density and striation marks in the ink lines. Striations are caused by the imperfections in ball point pens due to manufacture, damage or wear through use. Such defects are common. When the damaged tip rotates ink will be unevenly distributed.

- The direction of the striations present in the writing can be indicative of the handedness of the author, as left or right handed people tend to form letters differently.

- The density of ink will tend to be thinner when a pen makes contact with, and leaves, the surface of the paper.

14.3 Forged Handwriting

People may attempt to disguise their handwriting in order to later deny authorship, such as when attempting to forge someone else's handwriting or signature. A person producing handwriting that is disguised will typically attempt to alter the overall appearance of their own natural writing style. Changing the slope, spacing between letters and words, using cursive rather than disconnected writing styles and vice versa are the most common methods used to disguise handwriting.

It is very difficult to disguise handwriting consistently as letter formation tends to be performed subconsciously. There will typically be many changes in style, most commonly between the slope and size of letters, throughout a piece of writing, and as a result altered handwriting is very often untidy, especially where it has to be produced in large amounts and rapidly.

The most frequent form of disguised handwriting encountered by forensic examiners are signatures. These are perhaps the most difficult type of handwriting to analyse due to the small amount of writing available for examination and comparison. The forgery of a signature requires a person to produce a basically correctly-reproduced and smoothly-written signature. The reproduction of signatures will fall into two general categories, depending on the circumstances in which they are made.

- **Rapidly-made disguised signatures.** Such signatures may be made when being watched, such as credit card or cheque transactions in a shop for example. These signatures will generally be fluently written, and may be of a sufficiently good reproduction to satisfy a shop assistant that it is genuine. When forensically examined however, such rapidly-made forgeries will typically display incorrect proportions.

- **Slowly-produced disguised signatures.** The accuracy of slowly-made disguised signatures, produced where a person has more time to copy the genuine signature will typically be a good reproduction on general observation. A lack of fluency will become apparent however, when examined by a scientist. Writing that has been produced slowly and deliberately tends to be angular and shaky in appearance, rather than flowing smoothly. The density of ink will typically be more even when writing slowly.

Another form of slowly-produced forged signatures that may be encountered are those produced using tracing paper to copy over the original, or by writing heavily over an original signature onto a document beneath and then inking in the impression made. Signatures copied in this way can bear good overall similarity to the original signatures, but will display the characteristics of a slowly-written signature.

The forensic examination and comparison of signatures requires as many samples of the genuine and the suspect samples as possible. Signatures are never written exactly the same; a large number of samples enable a more accurate assessment of the natural variations that can occur.

14.3.1 Signature samples

The types of signature required for comparison with samples recovered from the crime scene fall into two categories. Unrequested signatures are the most reliable source for comparisons as these are produced under normal circumstances and will give indication of the natural variations that occur. These can be from a range of documents that have been previously signed by the suspect.

Requested signatures should be obtained where unrequested signatures are unavailable or are limited in number. These are produced by the suspect after the event and may be affected by the circumstances of the case. These are not ideal for comparison purposes but their use may be unavoidable.

When requesting samples from a suspect, an investigator should consider the following.

- The sample should be representative of the person's usual handwriting.
- The sample should contain enough writing to make an effective comparison with the scene samples. Be mindful that letter formation is a subconscious act and it is very difficult to consistently disguise natural writing style.
- If the sample from the scene is written in capital letters, then officers should request the suspect provide a sample in capital letters. The document examiner can only compare like with like.
- Avoid directing suspects to produce a certain style of writing, for example cursive (joined-up) or disconnected writing, as this will lead to unnatural variations in the sample.

- Where possible the same sort of pen used to produce the scene sample should be used to produce the suspect sample. Avoid using new pens for sample collection.
- Ensure the suspect has a suitable writing surface to produce the samples.

Ideally, take as many samples as possible; the minimum requirements will depend on the case. Typically the following are required:

- for signature comparison, at least 12 samples;
- for cheque fraud, at least 12 signature samples and a further six handwriting samples.

For handwritten document comparison such as in malicious mail cases, it is advisable to discuss the requirements with a document examiner who will offer guidance on the sampling process required for the particular case. The sample required will be dependant on the size of the handwriting sample that has been recovered from the crime scene. Once the size of a suspect sample has been established, officers should consider the following.

- Where possible, take samples from the suspect at different times.
- The suspect must never be shown the questioned (scene) sample.
- Officers should dictate what they require the suspect to write at a reasonable pace in order to ensure the suspect produces their natural handwriting style.
- The suspect should sign and date each sample as it is completed.
- As each sample is completed, it must be removed from the sight of the suspect (to avoid any copying of characters or style).
- Each sample must be numbered sequentially as they are produced. The time of each sample must be recorded.

The potential evidence provided by the analysis of handwriting will depend on the amount of handwriting available, the number of distinctive features present, the degree of disguise and the suitability of the suspect samples obtained.

14.4 **Indented Impressions**

When a person writes on a piece of paper that forms part of a pad or notebook for example, the indentations caused by the pressure of writing can be revealed from sheets several pages below the original. Such information can be used to link a series of malicious mailings or provide intelligence information.

The indentations caused by the pressure created by writing or by footwear when standing on paper, will not always be readily observed. A technique which is utilized in many in force chemical development laboratories (or equivalent) to recover such impressions is the Electrostatic Document Apparatus (ESDA). This technique can potentially recover valuable information from apparently blank notebooks or sheets of paper. ESDA is a simple and effective examination technique and, as it is non-destructive to the sample, it can be undertaken prior to other examination techniques. The ESDA technique for recovery of indented impressions involves placing the piece of paper onto a porous bronze plate; a thin transparent film is then placed on the top of the paper. Air is drawn through the plate essentially pulling the paper and film flat. Following the application of an electrostatic charge to the film, a powdered toner is gently tipped onto the film. The indented areas will be fractionally lower than the surrounding area, so when the toner is applied to the statically-charged film, it will settle into the areas of indentations. Any indentations will be revealed by the toner on the film which is lifted from the paper and secured to a clear acetate sheet. Figure 14.1 shows an ESDA lift taken from a page of seemingly blank pad, which revealed writing that was linked to two malicious communications. The technique can also reveal footwear marks and in some cases fingerprints.

This technique can also be useful to gather intelligence. For example, the pages of a map book from a recovered stolen vehicle which was believed to have been used in a series of burglaries were examined with ESDA. The examination revealed telephone numbers and other valuable information that was not visible. The offender had probably leaned on the pages to write notes on pieces of paper. This provided investigators with information that opened up lines of enquiry.

Consideration of whether indented writing or footwear could be present and useful in a particular investigation is important, as CSIs (if they have recovered the item) and the chemical development laboratories (or equivalent) need to be made aware of this requirement.

> **POINT TO NOTE**
>
> ESDA may not be undertaken as a matter of course and if the document is treated with chemical techniques to recover potential fingerprints first it will render ESDA examination useless. If the item has been wet, this can dramatically reduce the presence of any indentations.

14.5 Other Document Examinations Available

14.5.1 Printed documents

A document examiner may be able to establish whether a photocopied or printed document has been produced on a particular machine, by examining defects that are reproduced by a particular machine. Computer printed documents can be examined in order to establish links between a document and the printer that produced it. Some printers will produce a mark on documents that is not visible to the naked eye, referred to as a bitmap. When examined, these bitmaps can potentially provide information on the make and model of certain printers.

Chapter 14: Document Examination

Figure 14.1 Example of ESDA lift

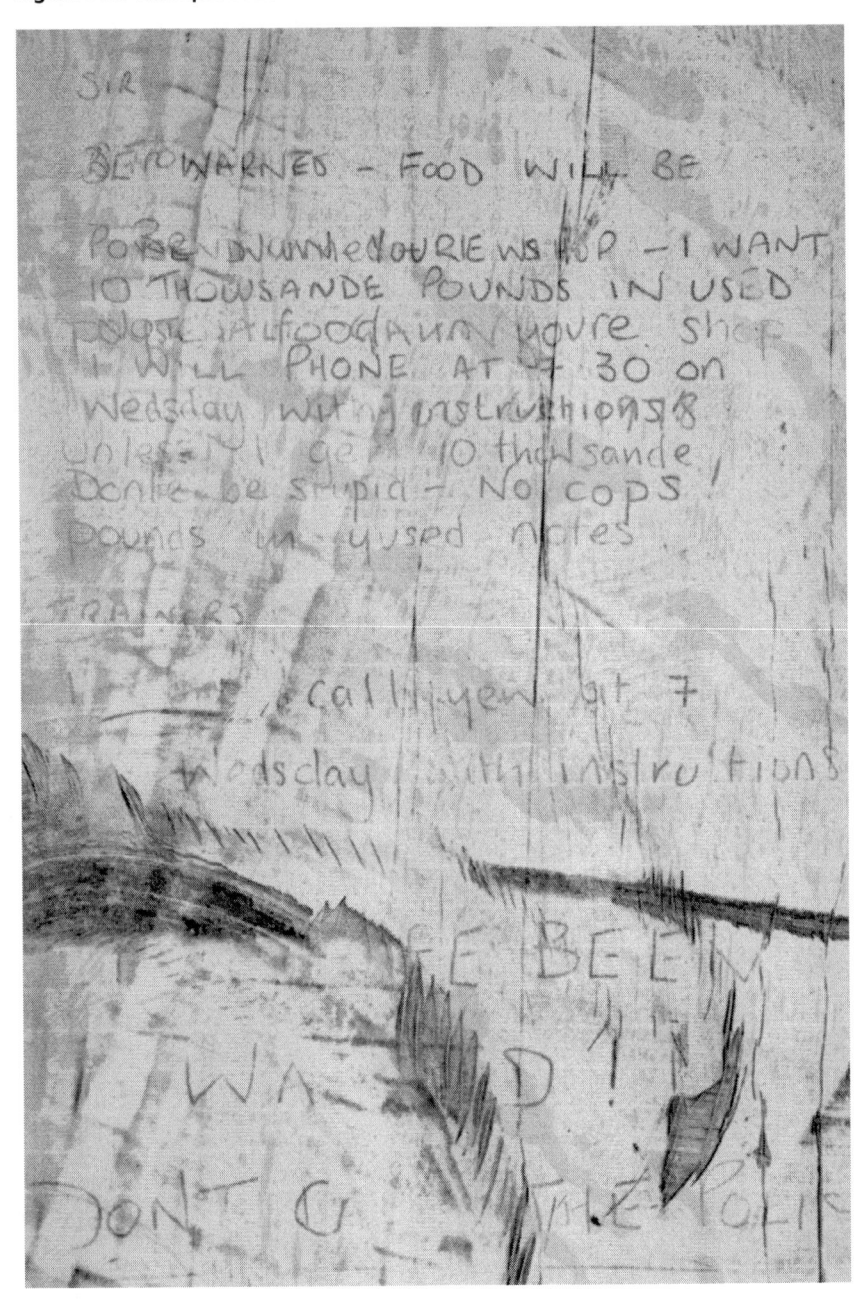

For guidance on samples required for such comparisons, seek advice from the forensic service provider who can offer guidance in line with the particular circumstances of each case.

14.5.2 Analysis of inks

A scientist can provide information on the type of ink used and indicate the type of writing instrument used. Ink analysis can provide information regarding the presence of any alterations on a document, such as when a cheque or vehicle excise licence (tax disc) for example, has been altered. The video spectral comparator (VSC) technique may be provided by some in-force chemical development laboratories (or equivalent). This technique involves observing the fluorescent properties of the ink on the document. Different inks, although appearing to be the same colour in natural daylight, will react differently when fluoresced. This makes it possible to distinguish between ink used for the original document and ink used to alter the document.

The chemical composition of inks can be analysed to potentially provide links between written documents and a particular pen.

14.5.3 Paper analysis

The examination and analysis of paper can be undertaken to compare two or more pieces of paper to determine if they have a common origin. The manufacture of paper involves differing materials, pigments and bleaching agents. A document examiner can utilize these variable properties of paper production to establish whether the pieces can have come from a common source.

14.5.4. Physical fit

It may be possible to determine whether two pieces of paper were originally part of a larger sheet by matching pieces together. This type of examination may be able to establish links between pieces of paper torn from a pad, or between a document that has been torn up or shredded.

14.6 Recovery and Preservation of Documents

In order to maximize the potential evidence available from documents, the considerations outlined in the following checklist should be made.

Chapter 14: Document Examination

> **Checklist—Considerations for recovering/preserving documents**
>
> - Always wear gloves when handling items of potential forensic evidence.
>
> - A photograph or photocopy of the original document should be made and exhibited, depending on the requirements of the case.
>
> - To preserve a document for the examination of indented writing or footwear, the item must be placed in a cardboard box or card folder, the lids from photocopier paper boxes are ideal. These can then be placed into a paper or plastic evidence bag.
>
> - Never lean on a document exhibit to complete the label, the writing will transfer onto the document to be revealed by the ESDA examination. This may jeopordize any useful indented evidence recovered.
>
> - If indented impressions are not required, a paper or plastic evidence bag is suitable for exhibiting documents.
>
> - Documents should be stored in cool dry conditions, dampness and heat can alter or destroy potential evidence.
>
> - Do not stick, staple or clip anything to the document.
>
> - Submit original documents for handwriting analysis and not photocopies.
>
> - Chemical development techniques to recover potential evidence will prevent ESDA examinations, the detection of alterations, and ink or paper comparisons. Chemical development techniques should be undertaken last if other forensic examinations are required.

14.7 Chapter Summary

The examination of documents can provide investigators with intelligence information or forensic evidence.

Handwritten documents, such as malicious mail or forged cheques can provide evidence of authorship. The comparison of the handwriting from a crime scene sample with that produced by a suspect will be more reliable where officers can supply the scientist with numerous samples of a suspect's handwriting. Ideally this should be in the form of unrequested samples, but where this is not feasible, requested samples produced under supervision of officers are acceptable.

ESDA can recover indented impressions such as writing or footwear that may not be visible. It is important that the CSI or chemical laboratory technician (or equivalent) is informed of the requirement for ESDA, as it may not be undertaken automatically. The use of chemical fingerprint development techniques will render any ESDA examination invalid, as will be the case where the document has been wet.

Printed documents can be linked to the printer or copier that produced them, and the analysis of inks can determine where different writing implements have been used to alter documents. Physical fit examinations can determine if a piece of paper has originated from a certain pad for example. It can also be possible for shredded documents to be reconstructed.

The chemical fingerprint development techniques are the most destructive form of examination regarding documents; officers should consider the potential evidence that may be available in the context of the particular requirements of the investigation. Where other aspects of document examination may be beneficial, these should be undertaken before chemical development for fingerprint recovery.

KNOWLEDGE CHECK—DOCUMENTS

1. What can an ESDA examination provide to an investigator?

   Electrostatic Document Apparatus (ESDA) is a technique that can potentially recover valuable information from notebooks or sheets of paper, even where they appear to be apparently blank.

   It is a non-destructive technique that can reveal the indentations caused by the pressure created by writing, or by footwear when standing on paper. The impressions can be recovered from several sheets beneath the original surface and can reveal information that can be of intelligence value. Where impressions are recovered, this can provide a link to the original piece of paper bearing the writing, for example a piece of malicious mail recovered from a victim can potentially be linked to a writing pad recovered from the suspect.

2. How can indented impressions be best preserved for examination?

   Any items bearing possible indented writing or footwear marks must be packaged in a manner that will prevent any further indentations occurring. A shallow bow, such as a lid from copier paper boxes, or a card folder sealed into a paper or plastic bag are suitable for this purpose.

   The exhibit must not be leaned on to write notes or labels as this can be revealed by the ESDA and can destroy potential evidence.

3. What handwriting samples are required to compare a suspect's writing with that of a questioned (crime scene) document?

   The minimum requirements will depend on the case. Typically the following are required:

   - for signature comparison at least 12 samples, and
   - for cheque fraud, at least 12 signature samples and a further six handwriting samples.

For handwritten document comparison such as in malicious mail cases, it is advisable to discuss the requirements with a document examiner who will offer guidance on the sampling process required for the particular case. The sample required will be dependant on the size of the handwriting sample that has been recovered from the crime scene.

4. State the considerations that should be made regarding the recovery of suspect samples.

- The sample should be representative of the person's usual handwriting and should contain enough writing to make an effective comparison with the scene samples.
- If the sample from the scene is written in capital letters, request that the suspect provide a sample in capital letters.
- Avoid directing suspects to produce a certain style of writing, for example cursive or disconnected writing.
- Where possible the same sort of pen used to produce the scene sample should be used to produce the suspect sample.
- Avoid using new pens for sample collection.
- Ensure the suspect has a suitable writing surface to produce the samples.
- Where possible, take samples from the suspect at different times.
- The suspect must never be shown the questioned (scene) sample.
- Dictate the words required at a reasonable pace in order to ensure the suspect produces their natural handwriting style.
- The suspect should sign and date each sample as it is completed.
- As each sample is completed, it must be removed from the sight of the suspect (to avoid any copying of characters or style).
- Each sample must be numbered sequentially as it is produced.
- The time of each sample must be recorded.

Summary of the National Occupational Standards (NOS) for the Student Officer Learning Assessment Portfolio (SOLAP) relating to this chapter

The table below indicates where it may be possible to demonstrate the achievement of certain performance criteria.

NOS unit	Unit descriptor	Performance Criteria, Range, and Knowledge	Activity
2C1	Provide an initial police response to incidents	**2C1.1** pc 1, 2, 6 **Range** 1a–1g, 2a–2d, **2C1.2** pc 1, 2, 7, 8, 9, 10, 11 **Range** 1a–1b, 2a–2g, 3a, 3d **Knowledge** 6, 8, 9, 16, 19, 21	Initial actions at a crime scene—identify nature of incident. Take action to ensure that potential forensic evidence is preserved and the relevant personnel are tasked to deal with the scene.
2G2	Conduct investigations	**2G2.1** pc 1, 3, 4, 5, 6, 7, 12, 13, 16 **Range** 2a–2c, 3a–c, 4a–c, 5a–e **Knowledge** 3, 9, 10, 13, 14, 15, 16, 17, 18, 19, 23, 24	Demonstrate the initial assessment at the scene and take steps to recognize and preserve potential evidence. Knowledge of the forensic and intelligence value of potential evidence from documents.

> **Recommended Further Reading**
>
> *Criminalistics*, 8th edn (2004) Saferstein, R.
> *Forensic Science* (2004) Jackson, ARW and Jackson J.

Bibliography

Association of Chief Police Officers (ACPO) (2005) *DNA Good Practice Manual*, London.
—— (2007) *Investigation of Volume Crime Manual*, < http://www.acpo.police.uk/asp/policies/Data/volume_crime_manual.doc >.
—— /Centrex (2007) *National Crime Scene Investigation Manual*, London.
—— /Crime Committee/National Crime and Operations Faculty (2003) *ACPO Family Liaison Strategy Manual*, London.
—— /Forensic Science Service (FSS) (1996) *Using Forensic Science Effectively*, London.
—— /National Centre for Policing Excellence (NCPE) (2006) *Murder Investigation Manual*, London.
—— /National Policing Improvement Agency (NPIA) (2005) *The Core Investigative Doctrine*, London.
Bevel, T and Gardner, RM (2001) *Bloodstain Pattern Analysis with an Introduction to Crime Scene Reconstruction* (2nd edn), CRC Press: London.
Bodziak, WJ (2000) *Footwear Impression Evidence, Detection, Recovery and Examination* (2nd edn), CRC Press: London.
Dix, J (2001) *Pathology for Death Investigators*, Academic Information Systems: USA.
Forensic Science Service (2004) *The Scenes of Crime Handbook*, Chorley.
—— (2005) *Safety at Scenes of Crime Handbook*, London.
—— (2006) *The Examination of Cannabis Cultivation Scenes – Guidance for Police Officers*, London.
—— <http://www.forensic.gov.uk>. (For case studies and fact sheets.)
Fortunato, SL (1998) 'Development of latent fingerprints from skin' Journal of Forensic Identification 48 (6) pp 704–17.
Heard, BJ (1997) *Handbook of Firearms and Ballistics: Examining and Interpreting Forensic Evidence*, John Wiley and Sons Ltd: Sussex.
Home Office Circular No 30 (1999) *Post Mortem Examinations and the Early Release of Bodies*, London.
Home Office Scientific Development Branch (HOSDB) (2004) *Manual of Guidance for Fingerprint Development*, St Albans.
Hutton, G and McKinnon, G (2008) *Blackstone's Police Manuals Vol. 4 General Police Duties*, Oxford University Press: Oxford.
Jackson, ARW and Jackson, J (2004) *Forensic Science*, Pearson Education Limited: Essex.
James, SH and Eckert, WG (1998) *Interpretation of Bloodstain Evidence at Crime Scenes* (2nd edn), CRC Press: London.
Johnston, D and Hutton, G (2008) *Blackstone's Police Manuals Vol. 2 Evidence & Procedure*, Oxford University Press: Oxford.
Lee, HC and Gaensslen, RE (2001) *Advances in Fingerprint Technology* (2nd edn), CRC Press: London.

Bibliography

Menzel, ER (1980) *Fingerprint Detection by Laser*, Marcel Dekker: New York.

National Policing Improvement Agency (NPIA) (2007) *Footwear Marks Recovery Manual*, London.

—— /National Training Centre for Scientific Support in Crime Investigation (NTCSSCI) (2007) *NPIA CSI course notes*, Co Durham.

Ozin P, Norton, H, and Spivey P (2006) *PACE—A Practical Guide to the Police and Criminal Evidence Act*, Oxford University Press: Oxford.

Police National Legal Database (PNLD) (2007) *Blackstone's Police Operational Handbook* (2nd edn), Oxford University Press, Oxford.

Rinker, RA (2006) *Understanding Firearm Ballistics* (6th edn), Mulberry House Publishing: USA.

Saferstein, R (2004) *Criminalistics* (8th edn), Pearson Education Limited: Essex.

Zander, M (2007) *The Police and Criminal Evidence Act 1984*, Sweet & Maxwell: London.

Appeal Cases

R v Sean Hoey [2007] NICC 49 Ref: WEI7021.

R v Anthony Edward Martin [2001] EWCA Crim 2245.

R v Sion David Charles Jenkins [2004] EWCA Crim 2047, no 2003/02883/B4.

Index

abdomen 155–6
accelerants 47, 55, 57, 61–2
  liquid 47, 55
  suspected 49, 55, 57, 61
acetate sheet, clear 87–8, 249
Acid Black 1 142–3
Acid Violet 17 142–3
Acid Yellow 7 142–3
ACPO (Association of Chief Police Officers) 4, 115
adhesive tapes 34, 52, 54–5, 57, 62, 221, 224
  low tack 78–9, 87–8
  sticky side of 91
adipocere 157
AFOs (authorized firearms officers) 47, 172, 179–80, 185–6
age ranges 166, 211, 213, 215
air drying 50
air weapons 172–3
airways 139, 158, 161–2
algor mortis 151
amino acids 87, 143
ammunition 78, 172–8, 180–1, 183, 185–6, 203
  shotgun *see* shotgun cartridges; shotgun pellets
  types 172–3, 175, 177
amphetamines 230, 235
anagen phase 219
analysis of hair 220, 226
animal hair 220, 226
antimony 176
apparent blood 56, 72
approach paths, common *see* common approach paths (CAP)
arrestees 117, 123–4
arterial spurts 137
asphyxiation 158–9
aspirated blood 139–40
assault scenes 33, 111, 202, 219, 221, 223
assaults 13, 34, 72, 111–12, 134, 218–19, 221
Association of Chief Police Officers *see* ACPO
authorized firearms officers *see* AFOs

backward fragmentation 206
bacteria 14–16, 122, 155
bags
  nylon 55
  tamper evident 53–4, 72, 74, 76–8, 125–6, 221, 223–4
ballistic examinations 172, 178–9
ballistics 172–8
  external 178–9
  internal 177–9
  terminal 178–9
  wound 178–9
ballpoint pens 53, 246
banknotes 238–9
barcodes 108, 110, 123, 125–9
bars, metal 21–2, 24
belief 6, 62, 104, 129–30
biohazards 47, 50, 54–5, 91, 108, 144–5, 184 *see also* health and safety
biological fluids 8, 14 *see also* blood; mucus; saliva; semen
bitmaps 249
blades 56, 58, 135, 196, 239
blanching 154
blood 13–14, 56–7, 70–3, 90–2, 118–20, 134–47, 152–5 *see also* bloodstains; BPA (blood pattern analysis)
  apparent 56, 72
  aspirated 139–40
  DNA 70, 92, 109, 112–13, 119–20, 122–3, 128
  dried 14, 47, 144
  fingerprints in 142
  non-visible 142
  pattern analysis *see* BPA (blood pattern analysis)
  physical properties of 134, 136, 145
  possible *see* bloodstains, possible/potential; possible blood
  wet 14, 50, 138–9, 141, 143, 145
blood borne infections 14–15
blood loss 119, 137, 153
blood pattern analysis *see* BPA
blood vessels 152–3, 158

Index

bloodstains 56, 71, 119, 134–47 *see also* blood; BPA (blood pattern analysis)
  absence 140–1
  arterial spurt 137
  aspirated 139
  cast-off 137–8
  chemical development 142–3
  elongated 136, 145
  impact patterns 138–9
  interpretation of patterning 139–40
  non-visible 120
  passive 135, 139
  possible/potential 71, 98, 112–13, 120, 146
  projected 136–7, 141, 145
  transfer 141–3
body cooling 151, 168
body fluids 13–14, 46–8, 50, 66–8, 77–8, 108–9, 166–7 *see also* blood; mucus; saliva; semen
body temperature 151–2, 157
bone marrow 162
booby traps 234, 239, 241
bottles, broken 111–13
boxes 48, 53–4, 57, 98–100, 180, 194, 209
BPA (blood pattern analysis) 50, 134–47
  see also blood; bloodstains
  preserving items for 143–4
breaking glass 203, 205–7, 214
broken bottles 111–13
broken fingernails 74, 76
broken glass 33, 47, 205
broken windows 21, 45, 202, 209, 214, 221, 224
brothers 109–10
brown paper evidence sacks 48, 52–3, 81, 163
bruising 67, 154
Buccal swab DNA samples 126
bulk samples 238–40
bullet-proof glass 203
bullets *see* ammunition
burglaries 4, 6–7, 29, 45, 67, 80, 89, 102

cadaveric spasm 152
cannabis 16, 230–1, 233–4, 239–42
  plants 231, 233–4, 240–1
  resin 230–1
carbon monoxide 154, 159–60
card folders 194, 252–3
cardboard boxes 49, 92, 252
carpets 142–3, 191, 222, 224
cartridge base markings 175

cartridge cases/casings 172–5, 177, 179–82, 184–5
cartridges, shotgun 176–7
casings *see* cartridge cases/casings
cast-off stains/marks 137–8, 145
casts 22, 24, 137, 195–6
cause of death indicators 158–60
cellular material 119–22, 218
chain of continuity 33, 43, 59–60
characteristics, physical 101, 103, 109, 218–19, 223
chemical asphyxia 158–60
chemical burns 15
chemical development laboratories 3, 8, 16, 92–3, 244, 248–9, 251
chemical development techniques 87, 89, 91–3, 103–4, 142–3, 252
  blood 87, 91–2, 134, 141–3, 145–6
  fingerprints 86–7, 89–94, 104, 142, 146, 244, 252–3
  footwear 89, 142, 191–2, 194, 244, 252
chromosomes, sex 109–10, 120
cigarette butts 111–13, 119, 121
circular stains 134–5, 145
clear acetate sheet 87–8, 249
cling film 238
clinical post-mortems 12
clippers 74–5
clippings, fingernail 66, 75–6
clothing 65–7, 69–71, 79–83, 111–14, 205–8, 212–16, 222–5
  forensic material on 66–71
  lower 77, 207, 215
  protective 14, 31, 114
  recovery 69, 81, 213, 216, 228
  seizure 70–1
  suspects 21, 23–4, 45, 55, 80, 83, 112, 182, 202
  victims 21–3, 34, 112–13, 180, 195, 210, 218
  witnesses 208
club drugs 235
cocaine 230, 235
collation 8, 10, 12
combs 77–8, 80
common approach paths (CAP) 28, 31–3, 38, 190, 197
comparison
  fingerprints 7, 86, 102
  hair 77–8, 83, 221, 223, 226, 228
  signatures 247–8, 253
  tyre marks 195

Index

complex cases 10–11, 13
containers
  non-rigid 54
  rigid 53, 181, 185, 197, 209–10, 212, 214
contamination 4–5, 20–1, 26–8, 33–6, 45–6, 48–9, 61–3
  definition 45
  risk of 114–15
  samples 116, 239
continuity 25–6, 37–9, 42–3, 59–61, 63, 84, 114–15
  chain of 33, 43, 59–60
  definition 26
  records 58
control room 18, 160, 165, 167, 236–7
control samples 55, 57, 163, 205
control swabs 60, 72, 76, 80
cordons 28–33, 35, 37–8, 237
  control of 37
  initial 30–1
Core Investigative Doctrine 25, 34, 39
coroners 11–13, 17–18, 150, 165–7, 169
coroners' officers 12
corroborative evidence 110, 116, 128–9, 219
coughing 121, 126, 128, 139
crime scene coordinators (CSC) 5, 16
crime scene examiners (CSE) 4–5
crime scene investigators (CSI) 2–8, 25–30, 32–7, 81–3, 87–9, 165–8, 194–8
crime scene management 20–40
crime scene managers (CSM) 5, 16, 30
crime scene marks 94, 96–7, 101, 128, 192–3, 198–9 *see also* bloodstains; fingerprints; tool marks; tyre marks
  unidentified 94–5, 103, 123
crime scene preservation 20–39, 164, 167, 194
  purpose 24–5
crime scenes 4–10, 20–1, 23–8, 35–39, 67–8, 193–9, 218–25
  definition 20–1
  roles and responsibilities 1–5, 8–10, 14, 16
  scene logs *see* scene logs
crime stains 111–12, 117–18, 125, 128–9
  see also bloodstains; crime scene marks
cross-contamination 63, 79, 84, 104, 131
cross-transfer 24, 26, 36, 38, 43, 45–6, 59–62
  definition 45
crowbars 196, 198–9, 210, 212

CSC *see* crime scene coordinators
CSI *see* crime scene investigators
CSM *see* crime scene managers
cultivation scenes 231–2, 234–5, 241
cursive handwriting 245–7, 254
custody units 66–9, 71, 80, 191
cuttings 232–3
cyanacrolate fuming 90–1

damp 49–50, 52, 55, 163, 209
dandruff 122
databases 7, 81, 94–5, 97, 111–12, 115–19, 127–9
daylight 231–2
death 11–13, 17, 46, 86, 109, 139, 150–68 *see also* sudden death
  cause of death indicators 158–60
  medical cause of 11–12
  suspicious 150, 164, 167
death certificates 11, 17
decomposition 151, 154–7, 165–6, 168
  gases 156, 161
  stages 156–7, 168
defence teams 12–13, 33, 56, 59, 71, 97, 116
density of ink 246–7
dental impressions 73, 83
dental records 166, 168
Deoxyribonucleic Acid *see* DNA
detained persons/detainees 7, 63, 66, 68, 70–1, 82, 84
DFO (Diazafluoren-9-one) 90
diatom analysis 162–3
Diazafluoren-9-one *see* DFO
diet 220, 225–6
direction of travel 134, 136–7, 145
discoloration 153–4, 159
disguising of handwriting 246–8
DNA 8–9, 21–4, 60, 108–31, 166–8, 218–20
  and chemical fingerprint recovery 92–3
  crime scene samples 216
  definition 109–10
  familial 110, 117–18, 129
  familial searching 110, 117–18, 129
  forensic submission routes 111–12
  low copy number 112, 114, 129
  material, potential *see* potential DNA material
  mitochondrial 110, 129, 218–19, 225
  national database 97, 109, 111, 115, 124, 127, 129
  nuclear 109

261

DNA (*cont.*):
  pendulum list search *see* **PLS (pendulum list search)**
  PLS (pendulum list search) 118–19, 129
  police elimination database (PED) 116–17, 129
  profiles 43, 60, 93, 97, 108–10, 112–20, 128–9
    definition 108
  profiling 8, 122, 128, 142
  recovery and preservation of material 122–3
  samples 109, 123, 130–1, 166
    Buccal swab 126
    legislation 127–8
    from persons 109, 123–7, 130
  sources 119–22
    blood 119–20
    dandruff 122
    faeces 122
    hair 122
    mucus 121
    saliva 121
    semen 120–1
    skin 122
    sweat 121
    urine 122
  volunteer/elimination samples 115–16, 127
document analysis 244
  handwriting 244
  indented writing 244
document examination 8, 89, 244–52
document examiners 247–9, 251, 254
doors 29, 151, 160, 191, 196–7, 199
dried blood 14, 47, 144
dried body fluids
  preservation 54
drowning 161–3
drugs 8, 45–6, 111, 163–4, 220–1, 225–6, 230–42
  bulk analysis 238–9
  packaging 237
dry items 48, 52–3
dry land 155–6
dry locations 180–1
dry swabs 72, 76
dust 190–1, 194, 197, 199

ecstasy 230, 235
electrical systems 234
electrical wiring 240–1

electricity 186, 234, 241
  high voltage 166
electrostatic charges 191, 199, 249
electrostatic document apparatus *see* ESDA
electrostatic lifting apparatus *see* ESLA
elimination 7, 67, 96–7, 102, 108, 116–18, 123
elimination fingerprints 95, 103
elongated bloodstain 136, 145
entomology 156–7
environmental conditions 151, 155, 157
environmental contaminants 211
environmental factors 119, 144, 151, 224
environmental temperature 151, 156–7
ESDA (electrostatic document apparatus) 249–50, 252–3
ESLA (electrostatic lifting apparatus) 191–2, 194, 197, 199
evaporation 55, 91
events
  reconstruction of 58, 134, 140–1, 178–9
  sequence of 10, 134, 144, 185
evidence 3–10, 32–5, 42–55, 65–70, 76–89, 178–87, 221–7
  continuity 26–7, 37–9, 42–3, 59–61, 63, 84, 114–15
  documenting 146
  integrity 26–7, 37–9, 42–3, 51–3, 59–61, 63, 84
  packaging 4, 26, 34, 43, 48–55, 61, 237
  preservation 19–20, 24, 26–7, 32–5, 143–4, 167, 194
  securing of 33–5
evidence sacks
  brown paper 48, 52–3, 81, 163
  paper 49–50, 52–4, 57, 180–1, 183, 209
evidential value 8, 42, 66–7, 103, 118, 215, 222–3
  potential 39, 63, 67, 84, 104, 118, 130
exhalation, passive 140
exhaust fumes 159–60
exhibits 10, 43, 47–9, 56, 59–61, 114, 239–40
  continuity 10, 43, 56, 59–61, 63, 104, 114
  continuity record 58
  definition 43
  details of person recovering 58
  handling 42–64, 71
  integrity 10, 42–3, 59–61, 63, 104, 114, 130
  item descriptions 56

labelling 47, 56–9
location details 58
numbers 56
officers 10, 16, 47, 51, 56, 59–61, 116
time and date 58
explosives 46, 68, 70, 78–9, 236
residues 46, 65, 72, 79, 82
extractors 181, 186
eyes 155

fabric 206, 214, 222
fleecy type 205, 224
imprints 183
facial reconstruction 166, 168
faeces 122–3
familial searching 110, 117–18, 129
family, victim's 10–13, 17, 164
family liaison officers *see* FLO
family members 118, 164
fathers 109, 128
FDR (firearm discharge residue) 79, 182–3, 185–6
feet-in-shoes examinations 193
female plants 231–3
fibre evidence 9, 21, 24, 45, 222–3, 225–6
fibres 8, 21–5, 45, 66–7, 77–8, 218, 222–8
common 224
forensic links 22–3
natural 223
non-visible 222
synthetic 223
fingernail sampling kits 74
fingernails 13, 73–4, 76, 80, 161, 239
broken 74, 76
clippings 66, 74–6
sampling techniques 73–4, 98
swabbing 76
Fingerprint Bureau 7–8
fingerprint evidence 8
fingerprint experts 3, 7, 94
fingerprint identification officers 8, 24, 51, 53, 87, 93–6, 102–3
fingerprinting *see* fingerprints, taking of
fingerprints 6–8, 21–4, 49, 60, 86–105, 142–3, 181, 237–8
in blood 91–2, 142, 146
chemical development 8, 89–93, 103–4, 142, 146, 244
comparison 7, 86, 102
CSI role in recovery 88–9
impressed marks 88
latent 87, 90–2, 105

national database 7, 86–7, 94–5, 97, 101–3
on non-porous items 90–1
physical developer technique 90
on porous items 90
recovery 49, 60, 89–91, 102, 191, 244
taking of 97–101
legislation 101
palm impressions 100
plain impressions 98–9
rolled impressions 98–9
types of evidence 86–8
visual marks 87–8
fingers 7, 77, 80, 86–7, 98, 100–1, 151
gloved 77–8, 221, 223–4
firearm and explosive residues *see also* FDR
kits 78–80
firearms 29, 46–7, 78–9, 82, 152, 172–87
see also pistols; rifles; shotguns
accidental discharge 183
ammunition 78, 172–4, 180, 185–6
definition 173
forensic examination 178–81, 183
impact evidence 182
officers 47, 78, 172, 179, 186
residues *see* FDR
safety 47
Firearms Act 1968 173, 184–6
firing 173–4, 185–6
firing pins 174, 178, 181, 186
first bash-no splash 137
first officers 2, 26–7, 29–30, 32, 37
scenes of sudden death 163–5
FISH (fluorescence in situ hybridization) 120
Five Building Blocks principle 26–8, 30, 32, 34, 36
fleecy type fabrics 205, 214, 224
fleet numbers 28, 202, 214, 218, 225
FLO (Family liaison officers) 10–12, 17, 39
floors 30, 33–4, 36, 141, 152–3, 194, 209
fluids *see* blood; body fluids; mucus; saliva; semen
fluorescence 80–1, 120, 141, 146, 225
in situ hybridization *see* FISH
footwear 21–4, 48–9, 141–3, 190–9, 212–15, 222
handling 68
legislation 68

footwear (*cont.*):
  marks 21–4, 67–8, 141–3, 190–2, 194–5, 197–9, 209
    partial 193
  recovery 69, 191–2
  recovery of evidence 67–70
  reference databases 192, 198
  seizure 69
  sole patterns 49, 68, 191–3, 198
  soles 68, 83, 143–4, 193, 207, 215
  suspect's 66–7, 192–3, 198, 213
  trace evidence 69–70
forensic evidence recovery from persons 66–84
forensic laboratories 8, 68, 70, 114, 234
Forensic Science Service *see* FSS
forensic scientists
  role 9–10
forensic submissions 3, 8–9, 16, 74, 112
  department 8–9
  forms 9
forged handwriting 246–7
FPOs *see* fingerprint identification officers
fracture patterns, glass 203–4
fragments, glass 205–7, 212, 214–15
freezers 50, 52, 72, 76, 78, 126
friction ridges 86, 96
FSS (Forensic Science Service) 4, 18, 63, 80–1, 84, 242

gases, poisonous 158–9
Gentian violet 91
glass 21–5, 66–8, 70, 77–8, 111–13, 202–10, 212–16
  breaking 203, 205–7, 214
  broken 33, 47, 205
  fracture patterns 203–4
  fragments 21, 23–4, 45, 112–13, 205–7, 212, 214–15
  laminated 191, 203, 209–10, 214
  non-toughened 203–4
  packaging 48, 53, 55, 66, 208–9, 212
  recovery of 78, 208
  samples 9, 22, 113, 202, 205, 208–10, 212
    recovering 207–8
Glass Refractive Index Measurement *see* GRIM
gloves 15–16, 23–4, 46, 68, 70, 80, 238–40
  marks 4, 22–4, 208
GRIM (Glass Refractive Index Measurement) 205

hair 73, 77–80, 83, 122–3, 207, 214–15, 218–28
  analysis of 220, 226
  animal 220, 226
  collection kits 77–8, 221, 223, 226
  collection modules 77, 223
  combings 77, 83, 182, 221, 223, 226
  comparison 77–8, 83, 221, 223, 226, 228
  DNA 30, 81, 109, 122–3, 129, 218–20, 225–6
  pubic 73, 218, 220–1, 226
  samples 77–8, 109, 123, 220–1, 226
  shafts 122–3, 129, 225
hallucinogens 236
handbags 59–60
handwriting 48, 50, 94, 101, 127, 244–8, 252–4
  analysis 48, 244–5, 248, 252
  cursive 245–7, 254
  disguising of 246–8
  forged 246–7
  samples 248, 253–4
hanging 158–9, 166, 168
hats 34, 121–2
hazards 14, 30, 39, 46–7, 63, 234, 240–1 *see also* health and safety
head hair 221, 226
health and safety 1, 14–16, 46–9, 62–3, 234
  blood 144–6
  body fluids 14, 46–7, 54–5, 68, 98, 108–9, 144–6
  deceased persons 166–7
  exhibit handling 47–8
  firearms 47, 172, 185, 187
  at scenes 144, 160
hepatitis B 14, 47, 150, 166–7
heroin 163–4, 230, 235, 239
HIV 14, 47, 150, 166–7
HOLMES (Home Office Large Major Enquiry System) 59
Home Office 3, 12–13, 17, 30
Home Office Development Branch *see* HOSDB
Home Office Large Major Enquiry System *see* HOLMES
Home Office Scientific Development Branch *see* HOSDB
homeowners 6, 21, 97
HOSDB (Home Office Scientific Development Branch) 90, 92, 142, 147
  fingerprint development 105

hospitals 11, 17, 28, 33–4
human rights legislation 82
hydrofluoric acid 15
hydroponics 232, 240
hypostasis *see* lividity

Ice 235
Ident 1 7, 87, 94–7, 102–3
identification 7–9, 36, 86, 93–7, 101–3, 165–6, 237–9
  deceased persons 7, 36, 86, 102, 165–6
  DNA 8–9, 93, 97, 108, 110–12, 120–1, 127–8
  fingerprints 7–8, 13, 86, 93–7, 101–5, 165, 237–8
  suspects 37
  victims 36–7
illicit laboratories 236–7
impact stains 139, 145
impressed marks *see* fingerprints, impressed marks
impressions 67–8, 98, 100, 143, 190–2, 194–5, 198–9
  dental 73, 83
  indented 48, 244, 248–9, 252–3
  plain 98–9
indentations 49, 191, 194, 248–9, 253
indented impressions 48, 244, 248–9, 252–3
indoor scenes 29, 151
infected body fluids 14
infections *see also* health and safety
  blood borne 14–15
  risk of 14–16, 47, 144–5, 150, 166–7
in-force laboratories 8, 90, 92
inhalation
  poisonous gases 158–9
  water droplets 15–16
initial cordons 30–1
initial observations 28, 38, 238
injection, intravenous 235
ink 68, 87, 98–100, 246, 251–3
  analysis 251–3
  density 246–7
inoculations, tetanus 14
inquests 12, 17, 164
insect activity 151, 156–7
integrity 25–7, 37–9, 42–3, 48–9, 51–3, 58–61, 63
  definition 26
  maintaining 63, 84
  seized items 71

intelligence information 117–18, 159, 210–11, 219–20, 248, 252
interference 26, 34–5, 38, 44
  unaccountable 26, 42, 60–1
interviewing officers 71, 120, 134
intimate samples 65–6, 72–3, 75, 77, 83, 221, 226
  legislation 221
intravenous injection 235
investigating officers 2, 4–7, 16, 21, 28, 116–17, 233–4

Jenkins, Billie Jo 139–40
Jenkins, Sion 139–40

key roles 2–3, 5, 7, 10–11, 13, 56, 89
knife tubes 54–5
knots 159, 168

labels 4, 43, 52–3, 56–9, 70–1, 80, 252–3
laboratories 3, 89–91, 112, 125–6, 142, 211
  illicit 236–7
  in-force 8, 90, 92
laboratory technicians 8, 89–93, 102–3
lakes 16, 162
laminated glass 191, 203, 209–10, 214
larvae 156–7
larynx 158–9, 161
laser microdissection 120
latent fingerprints 87, 90–2, 105
LCN (Low copy number) 112–14, 118, 120, 122, 129
Legionnaire's disease 15, 234, 241
legitimate access 6–7, 95, 97, 102–3
lever marks 196–7
lids 54, 252–3
life, preservation of 27–8, 32, 143, 167–8, 179, 185, 236
ligature strangulation 158–9, 168
light, ultraviolet 80–1
light sources 88–9, 120, 143, 225
  and fingerprint location 89
linked scenes 21, 29, 190, 196, 230, 239
liquid accelerants 47, 55
Little, Michael 118
liver mortis *see* lividity
livescan 94, 96–7, 100–1
lividity 152–5, 160–1, 168
Low copy number *see* LCN
low tack adhesive tape 78–9, 87–8
LSD 230, 236
Luminol 120, 142–3, 146
Lyme's disease 15

265

Index

maggots 156–7
malicious mail 244, 252–3
manual strangulation 158
marbling pattern 155
marks *see also* crime scene marks
  impressed *see* fingerprints, impressed marks
  lever 196–7
  visual 87–8 *see* fingerprints, visual marks
Martin, Anthony Edward 178–9
materials
  definition 25
medical cause of death 11–12
medical teams 28, 32, 39
medico-legal post-mortems 12
medium impact staining 138, 140
metal bars 21–2, 23
methamphetamine 235
MGFSP 9, 111, 113
microdissection, laser 120
microscopic examination 213, 218–19, 223
mitochondria 109–10
mitochondrial DNA *see* MtDNA
mixed profiles 113, 118–19, 129
mobile phones 59–60, 140–1, 236, 238
morphine 235
mother plants 232–3
mothers 109–10, 128
mouth 15–16, 73, 83, 121, 139, 156, 160–2
MtDNA (mitochondrial DNA) 110, 122–3, 129, 218–19, 225
mucus 119, 121
mud 16, 162, 191, 194–5, 198–9
mummification 157
Murder Investigation Manual 18, 26, 39
muzzle 177–8, 182

NABIS (National Automated Ballistics Intelligence System) 172, 186
NAFIS (National Automated Fingerprint Identification System) 7, 94–5, 103, 165
nail clippings *see* fingernails, clippings
nails *see* fingernails
naked eye 28, 87, 134, 141–2, 145, 191, 218
National Automated Ballistics Intelligence System *see* NABIS
National Automated Fingerprint Identification System *see* NAFIS
National Crime Scene Investigation Manual 4, 18

National DNA Database *see* NDNAD
national fingerprint database *see* Ident 1
National Occupational Standards *see* NOS
National Policing Improvement Agency *see* NPIA
natural variations 213, 245, 247
NDNAD (National DNA Database) 9, 108–10, 112–13, 115–17, 123–5, 127–9, 218–19
neck 80, 151, 158
nervous system 235–6
Ninhydrin 90, 143
non-intimate samples 65–6, 72–3, 75, 77–9, 83, 127–8, 221
  legislation 221
non-porous bags 62
non-porous items 90–1
non-porous surfaces 88, 90, 142–3, 194
  smooth 87, 139
non-rigid containers 54
non-toughened glass 203–4
non-visible blood 120 142
NOS (National Occupational Standards) 18
  BPA (blood pattern analysis) 146
  crime scene preservation 38–39
  DNA 130–1
  document examination 254–5
  drugs 241
  evidence recovery from persons 83
  exhibit handling 62
  fingerprints 104
  firearms 187
  footwear, tyre and tool marks 199
  glass, paint and soils 215–16
  hair and fibres 227–8
  sudden death 169
nose 15–16, 121, 160–2, 235
notebooks, pocket *see* PNB (pocket notebook)
notepaper 31, 71
NPIA (National Policing Improvement Agency) 39, 63, 200
nuclear DNA 109
nylon bags 55, 57, 61–2
  packaging techniques 61

observations, initial 28, 38, 238
officer in charge *see* OIC

officers
  fingerprint *see* fingerprint identification officers
  interviewing 71, 120, 134
  investigating 2, 4–7, 16, 21, 28, 116–17, 233–4
  OIC (officer in charge) 2, 16, 25, 34, 92, 166, 168
Omagh bombing 27, 114–15
open wounds 14, 156
operational risk assessments *see* ORA
ORA (operational risk assessments) 47
organ donation 13
organs 13, 156–7, 161–2
outdoor scenes 29, 34, 144

PACE (Police & Criminal Evidence Act) 44, 61–3, 73, 83–4, 101, 103–5, 127
  kits 123, 125
  samples 117, 123–5, 128
packaging 43, 48–55, 59–61, 91–2, 208–9, 237–8
  accelerants 55, 61
  basic principles 48–50
  clothing 34, 55, 66, 69, 71, 212, 224
  drugs 237
  dry items 48–9, 52–3
  glass 48, 53, 55, 66, 208–9, 212
  materials 34, 50–5, 212, 232
  techniques 50–1, 60–1, 69, 234
  wet or damp items 49–50
padlocks 9, 196
paint 66–7, 82–3, 87–8, 196–8, 202, 204–6, 210–16
  flakes/fragments 29, 66–7, 78, 210–12
  samples 73–4, 83, 111, 198, 202, 209–14, 221
  smears 211–12, 215
  vehicles 210–11, 213, 215
palm impressions 100
palms 7, 86, 100–1, 103
paper, sterile 74, 76
paper evidence sacks 49–50, 52–4, 57, 180–1, 183, 209
paperwork 79, 125–6, 244
partial footwear marks 193
partial tyre mark 23–4
particulate material 29, 45, 66–7, 78, 159, 180, 182
passive bloodstains 135, 139
passive exhalation 140

pathologists 12–13, 17, 29, 150, 153–5, 157, 165–8
patterns 86, 140, 145, 154, 167, 192, 195 *see also* bloodstains; glass
  fracture 203–4
  marbling 155
  web type 204
  zig-zag 137, 145
Payne, Sarah 222
PED (Police elimination database) 96–7, 116–17, 129
pellets, shotgun 176–7, 180–1, 183
pen movements 245–6
pendulum list search *see* PLS (pendulum list search)
pens 181, 246, 248, 251, 254
  ballpoint 53, 246
  permanent marker 54
performance criteria 18, 39–40, 62, 83–4, 104, 130–1, 227–8
permanent marker pens 54
persistency 205, 212
petechiae 158, 160–1
petechiae haemorrhages 158
photographs 6, 8, 68, 87–8, 93–4, 195–6, 234
photography 81, 83, 88, 90, 134, 142, 192
physical characteristics 101, 103, 109, 218–19, 223
physical fits 74, 76, 202, 205, 212, 237, 244
pistols 173–4 *see also* firearms
  definition 173
  self-loading 173–4, 181
plain impressions 98–9
plants 213, 230–4, 240–1
  mother 232–3
plastic bags 48–50, 54, 80, 89–90, 103, 163, 252–3
  self seal 92–3
  unsealed 49–50
PLS (pendulum list search) 118–19, 129
PMI (post-mortem interval) 150–1, 155–7, 167–9
PNB (pocket notebook) 24, 31, 43, 46, 48, 61, 70–1
pocket notebook *see* PNB
pockets 206–7, 214
poisonous gases 158–60
Police & Criminal Evidence Act *see* PACE
Police elimination database *see* PED
police vehicles 24, 45, 55, 202, 218, 226

Index

porous surfaces 89–90, 135, 142–3, 194
possible blood 33–4, 56–7, 71–2, 98,
    112–13, 120, 146
  wet 50
post-mortem
  changes 150–4
  examinations 18
  interval 150 *see* PMI
post-mortems 12–13, 18, 149–51, 153–5,
    160–6, 239
  clinical 12
  medico-legal 12
potential bloodstains *see* possible blood
potential DNA material 49, 70, 89, 93,
    112, 123, 130
potential evidential material 6, 17, 20,
    36, 62, 172, 184
potential evidential value 39, 63, 67, 84,
    104, 118, 130
powder suspensions 91
powders 87–9, 92, 191, 235
preservation
  crime scenes *see* crime scene
      preservation
  dried body fluids 54
  evidence *see* evidence, preservation
  forensic material 45–7
  life 27–8, 32, 143, 167–8, 179, 185, 236
presumptive tests 91, 121, 141–2, 238
  blood 70, 88, 119, 141, 146
primers 174–5, 177–8, 182, 211
printers 244, 249, 253
probes 55, 184, 186
profiles 108–21, 123–5, 127–9
  mixed 113, 118–19, 129
  suitable 115, 117, 129
  suspect 116–17
  unidentified 115–16, 129
prohibited weapons 173, 185
projected bloodstains 136–7, 141, 145
projectiles 172, 178, 181–3, 203
propellants 174–5, 177, 182
protective clothing 14, 31, 114
Protein Specific Antigen *see* PSA
PSA (Protein Specific Antigen) 121
pubic hair 73, 218, 220–1, 226
putrefaction 152, 155–6

racial origin 218, 220, 226
radial fractures 203–5
railways 166–7
receipts 43

reconstruction
  events 58, 134, 140–1, 178–9
  facial 166, 168
recovery
  clothing 69, 81, 213, 216, 228
  DNA material 92, 102, 122
  documents 251
  FDR 182–3
  fibres 223
  fingerprint evidence 88
  footwear 67, 191–2, 199
  footwear marks 191
  glass 78, 208
  hair samples 221
  non-intimate samples 65, 72–3, 75,
      77–9
  paint samples 212
  techniques 67, 77, 87, 141, 197, 244
red blood cells 119, 128, 155
reporting officer *see* RO
residues, firearm discharge *see* FDR
    (firearm discharge residue)
resin, cannabis 230–1
responding officers, first *see* first officers
responsibilities 1–18
revolvers 173–5 *see also* firearms
ricochet 180, 183
ridge detail 89, 91–3, 100, 238
rifled weapons 173–4, 181 *see also*
    firearms
rifles *see also* firearms
  definition 173
rifling 174, 176, 181, 186
rigid containers 53, 181, 185, 197,
    209–10, 212, 214
rigor mortis 151–2, 168
risk of contamination 34, 108, 114–15,
    128
risk of infection 14–16, 47, 144–5, 150,
    166–7 *see also* health and safety
RO (reporting officer), 9
road traffic collisions (RTCs) 150
roles 1–18
roots
  hair 122, 218–20, 225–6
  plants 232–3, 240
RTCs (road traffic collisions) 150
rulers 56, 196–7, 234

safety *see* health and safety
saliva 14, 73, 83, 119, 139, 239
  as DNA source 121

samples
  bulk 238–40
  contamination 116, 239
  control 55, 57, 163, 205
  glass 9, 22, 113, 202, 205, 208–10, 212
  hair 77–8, 109, 123, 220–1, 226
  handwriting 248, 253–4
  intimate 65–6, 72–3, 75, 77, 83, 221, 226
  non-intimate 65–6, 72–3, 75, 77–9, 83, 127–8, 221
  paint 73–4, 83, 111, 198, 202, 209–14, 221
  signature 247–8, 253
  soil 212–13
  trace 238–40
  unrequested 252
  volunteer/elimination 115–16, 127
sampling kits 74, 77–8, 126
sand 191–2
SAP (Seminal Acid Phosphotase) 121
saponification *see* adipocere
satellite scenes 20
scalp 78, 220–1, 226
scanning 94, 192, 198
scars 96, 166, 168
scene logs 26, 31, 37–8, 237
scene preservation *see* crime scene preservation
scientific support departments 2–3, 16
  roles and responsibilities within 1, 4
  structure 3
scissors 74, 76–8
scratch marks *see* striations
seals/sealing 15, 50, 52, 54–5, 57, 126
seams 206–7, 214
seats 24, 202, 214, 218, 225, 227
  vehicles 24, 45, 122, 208, 222, 224
seizure of articles 44
  clothing 70–1
  footwear 69
self seal plastic bags 92–3
self-loading pistols 173–4, 181
semen 14, 67, 73, 78, 81, 89
  as DNA source 120–1
Seminal Acid Phosphotase *see* SAP
senior investigating officer *see* SIO
sequence of events 10, 134, 144, 185
sex chromosomes 109–10, 120
Shoeprint Image Capture and Retrieval *see* SICAR
shoes *see* footwear
shooting incidents 174, 178–9, 185
  see also firearms

shotguns 173, 175–8, 181 *see also* firearms
  cartridges 176–7
  pellets 176–7, 180–1, 183
SICAR (Shoeprint Image Capture and Retrieval) 190–2
signatures 31, 38, 58, 61, 245–7
  comparison 247–8, 253
  samples 247–8, 253
  unrequested 247
SIO (senior investigating officer) 2, 5, 10–11, 13, 16, 18, 40
sketch plans 27
skid marks 195
skin cells 114, 119, 121–3, 126, 159, 172
small particle reagent *see* SPR
Smartwater 80–1
smears, paint 211–12, 215
smooth surfaces 87, 121, 139, 183
smoothbore weapons 173, 176 *see also* firearms; shotguns
soils 14–15, 66–7, 192, 194–5, 197–9, 202, 212–14
  samples 212–13
SOLAP (Student Officer Learning Assessment Portfolio) 18
  BPA (blood pattern analysis) 146
  crime scene preservation 38–9
  DNA 130–1
  document examination 254–5
  drugs 241
  evidence recovery from persons 83
  exhibit handling 62
  fingerprints 104
  firearms 187
  footwear, tyre and tool marks 199
  glass, paint and soils 215–16
  hair and fibres 227–8
  sudden death 169
sole patterns *see* footwear, sole patterns
soles *see* footwear, soles
SOLO (Sexual Offence Liaison Officers) 66
SOTI (Sexual Offence Trained Investigators) 66
spasm, cadaveric 152
speculative searches 73, 94, 101, 113, 127–8
sperm 110, 120–1
'spider legs' 203–4
SPR (small particle reagent) 91

staining 72, 120, 134, 136–7, 144 *see also* bloodstains
  medium impact 138, 140
stains
  blood *see* bloodstains
  circular *see* circular stains
  crime *see* crime stains
  impact *see* impact stains
  projected *see* projected bloodstains
stairs 29, 178–9
sterile paper 74, 76
stiffening 151–2
storage 4, 26, 38, 43, 45–8, 57, 59
strangulation 158–9
  ligature 158–9, 168
  manual 158
striations 174, 178, 180, 185, 196, 246
string 53, 57, 209
Student Officer Learning Assessment Portfolio *see* SOLAP
sub-exhibiting 59
Sudan black 91
sudden death 13, 37, 150–69
  reports 165, 167
suffocation 158, 160–1
suicides 11, 17, 150, 152
superglue 90–1
surfaces
  porous 89–90, 135, 142–3, 194
  smooth 87, 121, 139, 183
  textile 182, 223
suspect profiles 116–17
suspects
  clothing 21, 23–4, 45, 55, 80, 83, 112
  footwear 66–7, 192–3, 198, 213
  identification 37
suspicious deaths 150, 164
swabbing 66, 72–3, 76, 78, 81, 88, 92
  techniques 66, 72–3, 76, 78, 88, 92, 142
swabs
  control 60, 72, 76, 80
  Place 80
'swan necked' sealing 57
sweat 87, 114, 119, 123, 239
  as DNA source 121
synthetic fibres 223

tamper evident bags 53–4, 72, 74, 76–8, 125–6, 221, 223–4
tape *see* adhesive tapes
tasers 173, 184–6
tattoos 165–6, 168

telogen phase 219
temperature 151–2, 156–7, 160
tetanus inoculations 14
textile surfaces 182, 223
THCs (tetrahydrocannabinols) 230
tool marks 29, 190, 192, 194, 196–9
trace evidence 69, 181, 192
trace samples 238–40
transfer bloodstains 141–3
transfer of evidence 20, 27, 36, 46, 63, 68, 84
transferability 225–7, 239
transferred material 69, 181, 198, 205, 213, 224–5, 227
transported persons 202, 214, 218, 225
travel, direction of 134, 136–7, 145
trousers 70, 139
turn-ups 207, 214
tweezers 77–8, 221, 223, 226
tyre marks 21, 23–4, 190, 192, 194–9
  comparison of 195
  partial 23–4
  recovery techniques 197

ultraviolet light 80–1
unaccountable interference 27, 42, 60–1
unidentified crime scene marks 94–5, 103, 123
unidentified profiles 115–16, 129
unrequested samples 252
unrequested signatures 247
unsealed plastic bag 49–50
urine 13, 15, 73, 81, 83, 122–3, 239
vacuum metal deposition *see* VMD
vaginal fluids 14
vapour 55, 61–2
vehicles 20–5, 28–30, 82–3, 195, 202–3, 208–15, 223–5
  exhaust fumes 159–60
  paints 210–11, 213, 215
  police 24, 45, 55, 202, 218, 226
  seats 24, 45, 122, 208, 222, 224
vermiculite 232, 240
victims 10–11, 20–3, 31–3, 36–7, 66–7, 111–13, 223–7
  clothing 21–3, 34, 112–13, 180, 195, 210, 218
  family 10–13, 17, 164
  identification 36–7
video 3, 8, 81, 134, 141
video/photographic department 8
visual marks 87–8

VMD (Vacuum metal deposition) 90
volume crime incidents 2, 4, 16, 26, 143, 244
volunteer/elimination samples 115–16, 127

wadding 177–8, 180
walls 34, 140, 179, 191, 197, 199, 232
water 15, 32, 72, 91, 161–3, 234–5, 241
   droplets 15–16
weapons 30, 134–5, 137–8, 152, 172–5, 177–83, 185–6 *see also* firearms
   prohibited 173, 185
weather 34
Weil's disease 15
wet blood 14, 50, 138–9, 141, 143, 145

white blood cells 119
Whitear, Rachael 163–4
wick effect 143
window frames 22, 34, 196–7, 209–10, 212, 221, 223
windows 21–2, 33–4, 151, 196, 203, 206–10, 214–15
   broken 21, 45, 202, 209, 214, 221, 224
windscreens 209–10, 214
witnesses 20–2, 24, 26, 37, 39, 66, 82
wood fragments 83, 181
wool 206, 214, 223
wounds 14, 119, 156, 179, 183
   open 14, 156
writing *see* handwriting